THEATRE IN ANCIENT GREEK SOCIETY

Frontispiece Tarentine Gnathia calyx-krater with comic actor playing Derkylos.
Tampa (Florida), coll. William Knight Zewadski

THEATRE IN
ANCIENT GREEK
SOCIETY

J. R. Green

London and New York

First published 1994
by Routledge
11 New Fetter Lane, London EC4P 4EE

Simultaneously published in the USA and Canada
by Routledge
29 West 35th Street, New York, NY 10001

First published in paperback 1996

Routledge is an International Thomson Publishing company I(T)P

© 1994 J.R. Green

Typeset in Baskerville by Solidus (Bristol) Ltd
Printed and bound in Great Britain by
Biddles Ltd, Guildford and King's Lynn

British Library Cataloguing in Publication Data
A catalogue record for this book is available from the British Library

Library of Congress Cataloguing in Publication Data
A catalogue record for this book is available from the Library of Congress

ISBN 0–415–14359–4 (pbk)

CONTENTS

FIGURES

PREFACE

I come to Greek theatre as a member of the public. What I know about is the archaeological evidence for theatre. This means to some extent the theatres themselves but also the images of theatre that the public bought, the scenes on pots, the terracotta and bronze figurines of performers that were popular souvenirs, the representations of the masks in clay or marble, mosaic or glass. I am therefore attempting to discover something of the audience's view of the theatre and the reader can, if he or she likes, contrast it with the view of the literary scholar which has the text as its central focus. For scholars approaching ancient drama from that angle, the poet's creativity is the important thing, and although scholars nowadays take some account of the performance aspects of the texts, in the history of scholarship it has traditionally meant study of text and appreciation of its literary value almost regardless of whether it was ever performed. In its more blinkered forms – of which examples can be found even now – this style of scholarship entertained itself with a kind of detailed and subtle analysis that depends on an ability to flit backwards and forwards through the pages of a text, something that was certainly not available to the ancient audience as it sat in the theatre. Indeed if one thinks about it, it is a kind of analysis that depends on the existence of books in a modern form and a modern concept of using them.

This is not, then, a book about the interpretation of Greek drama, or even about the way drama was staged, which is another subject again (to which I hope to turn soon). It is about the role of theatre in ancient society, about the way theatre was received and the influence it had. The justification, if one is needed, is that on any definition theatre cannot exist without an audience. Theatrical performance always involves an interplay with the expectations of an audience, following them through, contra- dicting them, and it is and must always have been the audience, by its interest and reaction, that created the theatre just as much as the players. Thus it is that its theatre can be taken as a measure of the vigour and creative energy of a given society. What we shall be exploring is not the impact of society on drama, but the less direct question of the place given to theatre by ancient society, the place it had in people's lives. Writers and commentators in the ancient world tended not to have very much to say about contemporary attitudes (they took them as understood), and so this is a field where the archaeological material has much more to offer than the literary, and much of the emphasis in this book will be on the interpretation of the archaeological evidence.

We should not of course judge fifth-century theatre by the standards and attitudes which became common later; much less should we automatically assume it operated according to what we know of theatre in the modern world. There are surely aspects of the theatrical experience which are generic to theatre, transcending space and time, but we should not assume that attitudes to it have always been the same, especially in the period when it was first evolving. A new experience can be very different from one repeated, and there can be little doubt that the social context in which Athenian theatre was first created was very different from that in, say, the fourth century BC, when it became massively popular but at the same time much less innovative and much more reliant on the classics of a few generations before (as often happens nowadays with popular tastes in serious music). On the other hand, there can be no doubt that the use to which theatre was put at this period was new. It became an identifier of Greeks as compared with foreigners and a setting in which Greeks emphasised their common identity. Small wonder that Alexander staged a major theatrical event in Tyre in 331 BC, and it must have been an act calculated in these terms. It could hardly have had meaning for the local population. From there, theatre became a reference point throughout the remainder of antiquity.

This book could not have been written without the work of generations of scholars such as Carl Robert, A.K.H. Simon, Margarete Bieber, T.B.L. Webster and, in the area of South Italian vase-painting, A.D. Trendall. They began the work of collecting the material evidence for theatre performance, but it was Webster particularly who saw the need to control that very diverse body of material so that it was classified in archaeological terms *before* it came to be used as evidence. He saw the need to establish the grammar and syntax. After Webster's death in 1974, Eric Handley urged me to continue that task and I have done so with a pleasure that has grown as the potential for the use of the evidence has become more apparent to me. The revised edition of *Monuments Illustrating Old and Middle Comedy* was published in 1978. The preparation of the new version of *Monuments Illustrating New Comedy* has been far more arduous, and it would have been impossible without the major contribution of my colleague and friend Axel Seeberg of Oslo. My debt to him is enormous. The New Comedy lists will contain not far short of 4,000 items, and we know them to be incomplete. They come from all over the ancient world in every sort of material from the whole period of the performance of New Comedy. Nevertheless it is with this sort of base, now more clearly catalogued and systematised, that we can start to say something more reliable about the appearance of New Comedy on the stage in the various periods and places of its existence. We are at last able to give priorities to certain categories of material (as it were Athenian Early Hellenistic over provincial Etruscan second-century) as evidence for the appearance for Menander's comedy in his own day, but in thinking about the material with a view to synthesising the history of theatre production, it none the less seemed important to ask the question *why* theatrical material was reproduced in the various media in the various times and places. The function of the material could, after all, have a strong bearing on its reliability as evidence. This material represents an interaction between the theatre and its public, and this book is a first exploration of that interaction.

One of the things this book does not attempt is to repeat the details of *Monuments Illustrating New Comedy*. Indeed it takes for granted a great deal of the argument there for the history and development of mask types and costumes, and readers wishing to check that kind of evidence are urged to look there first.

I am conscious that I have not yet had the chance to work over the material on tragedy and satyr-play to the extent that I have for comedy. The effect is detectable in this book, but if I were to offer justification for pressing ahead at this point, it would be that comedy was throughout its history more self-referential than tragedy, and that its material evidence was much more plentiful. One could also argue, on the basis of the material evidence, that comedy had a more active relationship with its public than did tragedy.

The reader will also detect that I have tended to take an anti-intellectual stance inasmuch as I have been more interested in finding out how the greater public reacted than in the (rather conservative) views of the small proportion of the audience that read the opinions of the even smaller proportion that wrote. The material evidence covers a huge range of tastes, from elegant table silver to the cheapest pottery (not that money is necessarily an indicator of good taste), and it is a simple observation that fired clay survives when other materials do not. And when Plutarch asks (*Moralia* 854B) why it is worth while for an educated man to go to the theatre, except to enjoy Menander, he is writing in a period when the work of Menander was over 400 years old. I recollect the date of Shakespeare relative to our own, and draw obvious conclusions.

I am grateful to Richard Stoneman for encouraging me to write this book. I have enjoyed the pretext it has given me to read all kinds of writing I might never have had the excuse to read otherwise, whether Jack Goody, Victor Turner, Richard Schechner, or many others who have not even made the footnotes, not to mention the provocative French, and all the material on how to read images. Above all it has been good to go back to the masters, those who wrote those surviving plays which are such a pitifully small fragment of what was performed on the Athenian stage.

Inevitably a number of works have been published recently which I could not take into account as I might have wished. One example is David Wiles, *The Masks of Menander* which I did not see until after my text was largely complete. A pity, because in some respects we seem to have been moving in the same directions. Another is A.H. Sommerstein *et al.*, *Tragedy, Comedy and the Polis* (Bari 1993) which I have still not seen.

The Frontispiece is the scene from the front of a recently discovered Tarentine calyx-krater. It dates to the third quarter of the fourth century BC and is painted in the so-called Gnathia technique. There is much to be said about this comic old man, but this seemed to be a good place to introduce him – or for him to introduce himself as he steps forward onto the stage. He wears a traveller's cap and carries what in later times was called a *pedum*. The shrubs to either side and especially the *boukrania* above make it clear that he is in a sanctuary, a concept which we shall see later in the book is not without its relevance. He is also named: Derkylos. The expression given to the mask and the eyes behind it certainly picks up the idea of the verb *derkomai*, which so often conveys the notion of having a gleam in the eye. One Derkylos is of course a known figure in Aristophanes, *Wasps* line 78, although that passage does not tell us all that much, and one would need to be persuaded that a minor figure who is merely mentioned in a relatively early play of Aristophanes would be receiving this sort of treatment at this date in Taranto. Another Derkylos seems to have been a historical figure in the middle years of the fourth century. I am, however, doubtful if this comic actor can represent an actual person, even if comedy could at times make contemporary reference even as late as this period (see Webster, *Studies in Later Greek Comedy* 43ff.). The other really similar figure, Philopotes (i.e. 'the one who likes a drink') on the Gnathia stemless cup in Berlin, published in *Gymnasium* 82 (1975) 26–32, is clearly a character of the stage, and I take Derkylos here as similar, a figure whose name brings out an aspect of his character, a friendly fellow with a wicked sideways glance. The vase has recently been acquired by William Knight Zewadski of Tampa, Florida, and this is an appropriate place to express my thanks to him for his generosity with photographs and information, his hospitality, and his modest enthusiasm in showing me his collection.

There are many other debts to colleagues, and I hope the others will forgive me if I mention only a few. A.D. Trendall's lively mind and unequalled command of the ceramic material have been a constant challenge, and our work towards a new edition of *Phlyax Vases* has prompted me to re-evaluate many other issues. Niall Slater had made extremely useful and sensitively suggested comments on a draft of this book and has more generally provided the best sort of encouragement while it was being written. Having been upgraded to Business Class by KLM, John Jory and I spent happy hours in the air between Singapore and Amsterdam last January going over Chapter 6. I hope he will forgive me for not having taken the notice of his observations that he might think I should have. My debt to Eric Handley goes back to September 1955 and has increased in a geometric progression over the intervening years. He too read a draft and by his comments demonstrated that he could have written a much better book himself. That I have not always made detailed acknowledgement of their suggestions is not a sign of ingratitude. At the same time the reader should not suppose that my follies are of their devising.

My thanks also go to those scholars and institutions who have allowed me to publish the photographs included here.

I did not ask Axel Seeberg to read a draft of this book. The omission was deliberate and was intended as a kindness inasmuch as he had had to cope with me through the much longer and more gruelling task of compiling MNC^3. It seemed unfair to inflict this on him as well. In retrospect, it was probably a bad decision.

I should also thank the National Humanities Center in North Carolina for giving me the opportunity to escape the toils of academic adminis- tration for nine months and so put most of this book together.

Margaret Clunies Ross has constantly given support and advice, happi- ness and love.

Sydney
Easter 1993

ABBREVIATIONS

AA	*Archäologischer Anzeiger*
ABL	C.H.E. Haspels, *Attic Black-Figured Lekythoi* (Paris 1936)
ABV	J.D. Beazley, *Attic Black-Figure Vase Painters* (Oxford 1956)
Addenda[2]	T.H. Carpenter, *Beazley Addenda: Additional References to ARV, ABV . . .*, 2nd edn (Oxford 1989)
ADelt	*Archaiologikon Deltion*
AE	*Archaiologike Ephemeris*
Agora	*The Athenian Agora. Results of Excavations conducted by the American School of Classical Studies of Athens* (Princeton 1953–)
	vi. C. Grandjouan, *Terracottas and Plastic Lamps of the Roman Period* (Princeton 1961)
	vii. J. Perlzweig, *Lamps of the Roman Period, First to Seventh Century after Christ* (Princeton 1961)
AION	*Annali. Istituto Universitario Orientale (Napoli)*
AIPhO	*Annuaire de l'Institut de Philologie et d'Histoire Orientales et Slaves de l'Université Libre de Bruxelles*
AJA	*American Journal of Archaeology*
AJP	*American Journal of Philology*
AM	*Mitteilungen des Deutschen Archäologischen Instituts, Athenische Abteilung*
Anal/RomInstDan	*Analecta Romana Instituti Danici*
AncW	*Ancient World*
Annali	*Annali dell'Instituto di Corrispondenza Archeologica*
ANRW	*Aufstieg und Niedergang der römischen Welt* (Berlin–New York, 1972–)
AntClass	*L'Antiquité Classique*
AntK	*Antike Kunst*
Aparchai Arias	M.L. Gulandi, L. Massei, and S. Settis (eds), *Aparchai. Nuove ricerche e studi sulla Magna Grecia*

	e la Sicilia in onore di P.E. Arias (Pisa 1982)
ArchClass	*Archeologia Classica*
ArchivRelWiss	*Archiv für Religionswissenschaft*
ArchNews	*Archaeological News*
ARV²	J.D. Beazley, *Attic Red-Figure Vase Painters* (Oxford 1963)
ASAtene	*Annuario della Scuola Archeologica di Atene*
AttiVenezia	*Atti del Istituto veneto di scienze, lettere ed arti*
AuA	*Antike und Abendland*
AWelt	*Antike Welt*
BABesch	*Bulletin van de Vereeniging tot Bevordering der Kennis van de Antieke Beschaving te s'Gravenhage*
BCH	*Bulletin de Correspondance Hellénique*
BdA	*Bollettino d'Arte*
BerlWP	*Winckelmannsprogramm der Archäologischen Gesellschaft in Berlin*
BICS	*Bulletin of the Institute of Classical Studies*
Bieber, *Theater*	*History of the Greek and Roman Theater* (Princeton, ¹1939, ²1961)
'Birds'	J.R. Green, 'A Representation of the *Birds* of Aristophanes', *GVGetty* 2 (1985) 95–118
BJb	*Bonner Jahrbücher*
BSR	*Papers of the British School at Rome*
BullComm	*Bullettino della Commissione archeologica comunale di Roma*
CAH	*Cambridge Ancient History*
CambHistClassLit	P.E. Easterling and B.M.W. Knox, *The Cambridge History of Classical Literature* I.2. *Greek Drama* (Cambridge 1986, 1989)
CJ	*Classical Journal*
ClAnt	*Classical Antiquity*
Corinth	*Corinth, Results of Excavations conducted by the American School of Classical Studies at Athens* (1930–): vii.3. G.R. Edwards, *Corinthian Hellenistic Pottery* (Princeton 1975)
CQ	*Classical Quarterly*
CVA	*Corpus Vasorum Antiquorum*
CW	*Classical World*
DArch	*Dialoghi di Archeologia*
Délos	*Exploration archéologique de Délos faite par l'Ecole Française d'Athènes* (Paris 1909–)
	xiv. J. Chamonard, *Les Mosaïques de la Maison des Masques* (1933)
	xxvii, P. Bruneau *et al.*, *L'Ilôt de la Maison des*

	Comédiens (1970)
	xxix. P. Bruneau, *Les Mosaïques* (1972)
Dioniso	*Dioniso. Rivista di studi sul teatro antico*
DOPapers	*Dumbarton Oaks Papers*
DTC²	A.W. Pickard-Cambridge, *Dithyramb, Tragedy and Comedy* (2nd edn rev. by T.B.L. Webster, Oxford 1962)
EAA	*Enciclopedia dell'Arte Antica Classica e Orientale* (Rome 1958–1966)
EMC/CV	*Echos du Monde Classique/Classical Views*
EntrHardt	*Entretiens sur l'antiquité classique* xvi: *Ménandre* (Vandœuvres–Geneva 1970) xxix: *Sophocle* (Vandœuvres–Geneva 1983)
EpistEpetThess	*Epistemonike Epeterida Theologikes Scholes, Thessalonike*
G&R	*Greece and Rome*
GettyMJ	*The J. Paul Getty Museum Journal*
Ghiron-Bistagne	P. Ghiron-Bistagne, *Recherches sur les acteurs dans la Grèce antique* (Paris 1976)
GRBS	*Greek, Roman and Byzantine Studies*
GTP	T.B.L. Webster, *Greek Theatre Production* (London ¹1956, ²1970)
GVGetty	*Greek Vases in the J. Paul Getty Museum*
Hesperia	*Hesperia. Journal of the American School of Classical Studies at Athens*
HSCP	*Harvard Studies in Classical Philology*
IG	*Inscriptiones Graecae*
IGD	A.D. Trendall and T.B.L. Webster, *Illustrations of Greek Drama* (London 1971)
JdI	*Jahrbuch des Deutschen Archäologischen Instituts*
JEA	*Journal of Egyptian Archaeology*
JHI	*Journal of the History of Ideas*
JhOAI	*Jahreshefte des Oesterreichisches Archäologischen Instituts in Wien*
JHS	*Journal of Hellenic Studies*
JRS	*Journal of Roman Studies*
Kokalos	*Kokalos. Studi pubblicati dell'Istituto di Storia Antica dell'Università di Palermo*
LCM	*Liverpool Classical Monthly*
LCS	A.D. Trendall, *The Red-Figured Vases of Lucania, Campania and Sicily* (Oxford 1967)
LCS Suppl.II	A.D. Trendall, *The Red-Figured Vases of Lucania, Campania and Sicily Supplement II* (*BICS* Suppl.31, London 1973)

LCS Suppl.III	A.D. Trendall, *The Red-Figured Vases of Lucania, Campania and Sicily, Supplement III* (*BICS* Suppl.41, London 1983)
LIMC	*Lexicon Iconographicum Mythologiae Classicae* (Zurich–Munich, i [1981], ii [1984], iii [1986], iv [1988], v [1990])
MAAR	*Memoirs of the American Academy in Rome*
MededRom	*Mededelingen van het Nederlands Hist. Instituut te Rome*
MEFRA	*Mélanges de l'École Française de Rome – Antiquité*
MemAccNapoli	*Memorie della [Reale] accademia di Napoli*
H.J. Mette	*Urkunden dramatischer Aufführungen in Griechenland* (Berlin 1977)
Metzger, *Représentations*	H. Metzger, *Les représentations dans la céramique attique du IVe siècle* (BEFAR fasc.172, Paris 1951)
*MMC*³	T.B.L. Webster, *Monuments Illustrating Old and Middle Comedy*, 3rd edn, rev. and enl. by J.R. Green (*BICS* Suppl.39, London 1978)
*MNC*²	T.B.L. Webster, *Monuments Illustrating New Comedy*, 2nd edn, (*BICS* Suppl.24, London 1969)
*MNC*³	T.B.L. Webster, *Monuments Illustrating New Comedy*, 3rd edn, rev. and enl. by J.R. Green and Axel Seeberg (*BICS* Suppl.50, forthcoming)
MonAnt	*Monumenti antichi pubblicati per cura della Accademia dei Lincei*
*MTS*²	T.B.L. Webster, *Monuments Illustrating Tragedy and Satyr-Play*² (*BICS* Suppl.20, London 1967)
MusHelv	*Museum Helveticum*
Mytilène	S. Charitonides, L. Kahil, R. Ginouvès, *Les mosaïques de la Maison du Ménandre à Mytilène* (*AntK* Beiheft 6, Basle 1970)
NJbb	*Neue Jahrbücher für das Klassische Altertum*
NSc	*Notizie degli Scavi di Antichità*
NumAntCl	*Numismatica ed Antichità Classiche. Quaderni Ticinesi*
*OCD*²	N.G.L. Hammond and H.H. Scullard (eds), *The Oxford Classical Dictionary* (2nd edn, Oxford 1970)
Paral.	J.D. Beazley, *Paralipomena. Additions to Attic Black-Figure Vase-Painters ...* (Oxford 1971)
PCG	R. Kassel and C. Austin (eds), *Poetica Comici Graeci* (Berlin 1983–1991)
PCPS	*Proceedings of the Cambridge Philological Society*
PdP	*La Parola del Passato*

Peintre de Darius	C. Aellen, A. Cambitoglou and J. Chamay, *Le Peintre de Darius et son milieu. Vases grecs d'Italie méridionale* (Hellas et Roma IV, Geneva 1986)
PhV²	A.D. Trendall, *Phylax Vases* (2nd edn, *BICS* Suppl.19, London 1967)
Pickard-Cambridge, *Festivals*	A.W. Pickard-Cambridge, *The Dramatic Festivals of Athens* ([1]Oxford 1953, [2]rev. John Gould and D.M. Lewis, Oxford 1968, reissue with supplement and corrections, Oxford 1988)
Pickard-Cambridge, *ToD*	A.W. Pickard-Cambridge, *The Theatre of Dionysos in Athens* (Oxford 1946)
Polacco, *Teatro*	L. Polacco, *Il teatro di Dioniso Eleutereo ad Atene* (Rome 1990)
POxy	*Oxyrhynchus Papyri*
QUCC	*Quaderni Urbinati di Cultura Classica*
RdA	*Rivista di Archeologia*
REG	*Revue des Études Grecques*
RendNap	*Rendiconti dell'Accademia di Archeologia, Lettere e Belle Arti, Napoli*
RendPontAcc	*Rendiconti della Pontificia Accademia Romana di Archeologia*
RevArch	*Revue Archéologique*
RFIC	*Rivista di Filologia e di Istruzione Classica*
RHR	*Revue de l'Histoire des Religions*
RM	*Mitteilungen des Deutschen Archäologischen Instituts, Römische Abteilung*
Robert	C. Robert, *Die Masken der neueren attischen Komodie* (25. *Hallisches Winckelmannsprogramm*, 1911)
RVAp	A.D. Trendall and A. Cambitoglou, *The Red-Figured Vases of Apulia*: i (Oxford 1978); ii (Oxford 1982)
RVAp Suppl.I	A.D. Trendall and A. Cambitoglou, *The Red-Figured Vases of Apulia, Supplement I* (*BICS* Suppl.42, London 1983)
RVAp Suppl.II	A.D. Trendall and A. Cambitoglou, *The Red-Figured Vases of Apulia, Supplement II* (*BICS* Suppl.60, London 1991)
RVP	A.D. Trendall, *The Red-Figured Vases of Paestum* (London 1987)
RVSIS	A.D. Trendall, *Red Figure Cases of South Italy and Sicily* (London 1989)
SIFC	*Studi Italiani di Filologia Classica*
SoobErmit	*Soobshchenia Gosudarstvennogo Ermitazha*
Studies Webster	J.H. Betts, J.T. Hooker and J.R. Green (eds),

	Studies in Honour of T.B.L. Webster i–ii (Bristol 1986–8)
TAPA	*Transactions and Proceedings of the American Philological Association*
TrGF	*Tragicorum Graecovum Fragmenta* (Göttingen 1971–)
UnivCalifPublClassPhil	*University of California Publications in Classical Philology*
VMG	M.E. Mayo and K. Hamma (eds), *The Art of South Italy. Vases from Magna Graecia* (Richmond, Va., 1982)
WS	*Wiener Studien*
WürzJbAltWiss	*Würzburger Jahrbücher für die Altertumswissenschaft*
YCS	*Yale Classical Studies*
ZPE	*Zeitschrift für Papyrologie und Epigraphik*

1

INTRODUCTION
Early Athenian theatre – setting and context

Condamnés à expliquer le mystère de leur vie, les hommes ont inventés le théâtre

Louis Jouvet, Témoignages sur le théâtre

To our eyes and ears Greek tragedies seem complex in both structure and thought, yet the establishment of the genre happened almost unbelievably quickly. According to tradition, Thespis first distinguished an actor from the choral group which lay at the basis of tragedy some time about 534 BC.[1] Aeschylus, who was born only a decade later, began producing tragedies very early in the fifth century and had his first victory in the dramatic contests in 484 BC. Our earliest surviving tragedy dates to 472 BC, our latest to 405 BC. We have no complete tragedy written after that date and it would seem that scholars of Late Antiquity did not think later pieces worth preserving. Our surviving classical comedies are from an even shorter period. Aristophanes' *Acharnians* was produced in 425 BC, his *Plutus* in 388 BC.

If one asks the question how it is that the development to so sophisticated a style of drama could have happened in so short a period, the answer must surely lie not simply in the genius of the playwrights involved but, since playwrights create for their public, in the importance given to theatre, in its reception, in the role it had in Athenian society of this period.

In attempting to discover this role, it is worth considering at the same time why it may have been that Athenian tragedy of the years after Euripides was not thought worth preserving. The fourth century was not without men of genius, and there is good evidence that theatre remained popular – indeed our evidence strongly suggests that it became more popular. It is clear that comedy, while slower to develop a sophisticated form, changed its style to suit new conditions; but in changing its style it changed its function. It may be that tragedy was not able to change so radically so effectively and that it lost its direction as a major force.[2]

In the course of the well-known debate that Aristophanes concocted between Aeschylus and Euripides in the latter part of his *Frogs* of 405 BC, the two agree (lines 1008–1009) that 'one should admire poets ... for their

1

cleverness and advice, and because we make men in cities better'. A few lines later (1031), the character Aeschylus claims that noble poets are 'beneficial' to society, in part because they represent admirable figures and invite their audience to emulate them. Aeschylus is made to present his own mind as moulded by the 'godly Homer'. 'By Zeus, I didn't create sluts like [Euripides' characters] Phaedra and Stheneboia; in fact, nobody knows of my creating a woman in love at all' (1043–1044). Aeschylus (as re-created by Aristophanes in a comedy) sees a corrupting influence in Euripidean tragedy. At some points in the debate Euripides is presented as the kind of dramatist who selects from the common body of myths stories of people in shameful situations (such as women in the grip of illicit passion) but presents them in a realistic and sympathetic way. It is, then, taken as a given that the theatre has an educative function, but at the same time the case is presented by a figure who represents the old school, and one has the impression that by the later fifth century this attitude with regard to publicly performed poetry is a slightly old-fashioned even if deeply ingrained one.[3]

Plato, who seems to have been becoming involved in philosophy about the time *Frogs* was produced, should to some extent represent the reactions of the new generation. Certainly by the time he wrote his *Republic* (towards 380 BC) he seems to be looking at the figures of epic poetry and tragedy by reference to norms of good and bad character, such as bravery, self-control and their opposites. He is concerned with the long-term effect of poetry on the moral character of the citizen-audience (*Republic* 377–401, 603–608). (One might compare the debate about the effects of watching violence on television, particularly on the young.) All this may well reflect a new consciousness of the role of publicly performed poetry, and, perhaps more importantly, a serious questioning of what was assumed in Aristophanes, that the older poetry (at least from Homer to Aeschylus) was necessarily good and improving in its effect. In the *Hipparchus* (228 B–C), attributed to but surely not by Plato, it is simply stated that Hipparchos, the son of the tyrant Peisistratos, organised the rhapsodes' recital of Homer and brought over Anacreon and Simonides 'in a desire to educate the citizens, so that he might rule over the best possible subjects, since he was so good and noble that he did not think he should grudge anyone wisdom'.

Theatre of the kind we are talking about needs a written text for it to exist at all, but we must recognise that for much of the fifth century the audience was still largely at the point of transition from being an 'oral' society.[4] Most Athenians (or more accurately, perhaps, most Athenian males) were able to read, but it seems likely that before the later years of the fifth century they were not in the habit of reading extensively. Detienne has made the important point that writing had no role in the process of government of a city like Athens at this period.[5] The results of the governing process – laws, treaties and agreements – may be recorded in writing as permanent information that could not be altered in individual memory, but day-to-day affairs and discussion were conducted by word of mouth. Writing still had a role that was restricted to the area in which it was found useful initially: one can compare the early use of computers as high-capacity mathematical calculators, before new activities were developed that were inconceivable before them. The new technology had not yet created its own programme of activity. Similarly, it is worth recalling a passage of Euripides' *Palamedes*:

I invented writing and so made possible overseas letters, wills, and contracts.[6]

The play was produced in 415 BC and even at this date these items are seen as among the more obvious benefits of the technology. They are items that have an important and practical value, aimed at overcoming the tyranny of time and distance.

Written texts of any length were still comparatively new, and one may remember that Herodotus in effect published his *Histories* in Athens in 446 BC by reciting passages of it. His seems to have been the first written history of a discursive and explanatory nature in prose; and it has been pointed out that there is a sense in which his history represents an oral style (at least in its attitudes) put down on paper. Thucydides, by contrast, in the last years of the fifth century, had made the transition and in describing his work as a 'possession for ever' is conscious of the nature of what he is doing. He had literate attitudes in the closely textured, rather terse style of his composition – but he none the less introduced speeches into his narrative whenever he wanted to examine motives for action, in part because he believed in motivation by individuals rather than by larger forces, but in part because even he seems to have thought that the semblance of verbal communication brought more immediacy. It is no accident either that early in the fourth century Plato wrote about philosophy as a series of spoken dialogues.

Pericles is said to have been the first to have delivered a written speech in the courts, whereas all his predecessors had spoken *ex tempore*.[7] Our source for this statement is late and unlikely to be reliable, but at an anecdotal level it still has value: it is a statement that was credible in Antiquity. It implies that some time perhaps around the middle of the fifth century, speeches began to be written. They came to be written because the arguments were becoming more complex and the style of language more highly refined. More sophisticated forms of rhetoric began from about this point, and it is against this background that we should set the visit of the Sicilian rhetorician Gorgias to Athens in 427 BC, a visit which caused an enormous stir because of the new directions in which he took rhetoric and the spoken word. But this was a style of speaking that needed careful preparation on paper.

The whole question of the existence and ownership of books in the fifth century is a very complex and difficult one, beginning with the problem of how one translates the Greek words *biblos* and *biblion*. They seem to mean everything from papyrus as a material to what we tend to mean by 'book', in much the same way that we can use 'paper', from the material, to 'newspaper', to 'a paper' (sc. 'article' or 'pamphlet').[8] But we should always be conscious that because of the mechanical problems of copying 'books' by hand, the number of copies was always limited and there may not have been the same expectation of a replica that we have automatically from printed texts; and while there was probably a sense of ownership of ideas or intellectual property, there was surely no idea of copyright as we understand it.[9] Gian Franco Nieddu has presented good arguments to suggest that in the late fifth century the acquisition of books or pamphlets is something like the acquisition of status symbols, and he thus makes good sense of the line in the *Frogs* where Aristophanes has his chorus say that the members of the audience are not uneducated, because everyone has a *biblion* (line 1114).[10] Similarly, at *Frogs* 1409, where Euripides is invited to get onto the scale-pan together with his books to be weighed against Aeschylus, part of the joke is that Euripides is in any case lightweight, with or without his books, but he has his books with him throughout this scene because they typify what sort of man (and therefore poet) he is. Nieddu has also made the point that at this period books are acquired by people in areas of specialisation, especially in areas of 'science' such as medicine, astrology, architecture, geometry and other aspects of philosophy: that is, most books were technical and rather short. He also quotes the case of the mathematician and astronomer Oinopides of Chios (in the second half of the fifth century) who uses the expression 'not in the (book-) box but in the mind' to admonish a young man who accumulated books so as to appear educated.[11] I am reminded of the analogy of one of my students who, when I asked him if his essay was anywhere near ready yet, said yes, he had photocopied the articles listed in the bibliography. In both cases there is a feeling of possession in having the information stored and at hand.

It is on similar lines that one should interpret the well-known passage in Xenophon (*Anabasis* VII, 5, 12–14): 'they arrived at Salmydessos. Here many of the ships that sail into the Pontus run aground and are wrecked, for there are shoals that extend well out into the sea. And the Thracians of that area have boundary markers set up and each group plunders the ships wrecked in their section ... Here were found many couches, many boxes and many written books, together with all sorts of other things that shipowners carry in wooden chests.' This at the turn of the fifth and fourth centuries. While it is not entirely easy to be sure of Xenophon's point here, one suspects that he remarks on these finds because they represented not only Greek material found in foreign parts, but because things like symposium couches and boxes of books were particularly representative of the Greek as opposed to the foreign way of life. Even if one goes so far as to translate *bibloi* here as pamphlets or short texts (rather than as 'pieces of paper'), this is good evidence that the use of papyrus and writing was common enough for sea-captains to carry, and normal enough to be taken as symptomatic of the Greek lifestyle at this period.

This last third of the fifth century, was, then, a period of rapid change in these respects as in so many others, and it was the change itself that fostered the final flowering of tragedy (before it wilted), and a style of comedy that one suspects became more sophisticated with Aristophanes. It was a period when writers and thinkers were exploiting the advantages of written culture while the advantages of the more traditional 'oral' culture still survived. It was a time when most members of the audience were used to listening intently and acutely and were used at the same time to remembering the spoken word. (We should remember too that they were not subjected, as we are, to radio, television, records and the like, with all those words which in sheer self-protection we only half hear, thus building in a habit of not treating spoken words all that seriously. We have an often naive faith in the printed word, as if written were somehow better.) In the fifth century one is dealing with a society which was still used to a great deal of its information storage being in people's heads, not on paper or in books.

The transmission of one's culture is a fragile thing, and even more so when it has no independent storage, for example on paper. In a pre- or proto-literate society, education (or the transmission of one's culture) did not involve the teaching of abstract 'facts' which were to be absorbed without immediately practical aim. It lay rather in the passing on of experience whether by example and/or practical training (as in social behaviour – where we are more used to such an approach – or hunting, or farming or fighting) or by word of mouth.[12] With the latter, the use of myth and legend seems to have been particularly important in Greek society, and this is apparent in their art as well as in the surviving literature. Thus as a warrior, Achilles can be the paradigm for a young man's behaviour, and when we see an arming scene on a vase, there seems to be a ready transference between an 'everyday' arming and that of a hero, and in pictures of battle scenes it is often difficult to tell the difference between the combats of mortals and those between, say, Achilles and Hector. It is typical of many societies that story-telling (whether by word of mouth or through what we call art) has the effect of binding those societies or communities together. The common experience these stories represent reinforces the communal aspect of their life. It is experience shared, and the expression and arousal of the fears, the pleasures, the sorrows and the laughter involved in the stories strengthen this binding process and give the more straightforward knowledge-aspect some context, and further, and perhaps more importantly, can teach the hearer how the community expects him/her to react in a given situation.[13] One aspect of this communal experience is the history of the community, which, with the Greeks as with many other societies, was often related genealogically to what we would call mythical figures, figures who were therefore integrated into the real life of the story-teller and his audience.

Much of this story-telling was done in verse, because poetry through its rhythm was more readily memorable in the long term than prose and thus more readily transmitted from one generation to another as part of an inherited experience or education. It was in this way that the Homeric legends had such an important place in Greek society. Another vital factor in binding a community together was its shared rituals. These normally had a religious setting, that of honouring or propitiating a divinity, but it has often been observed, particularly among so-called more primitive societies, that the ritual itself is just as important as the object of that ritual: the process of ritual involves shared knowledge of an important routine at important times of the year or critical times of life, and meeting as a community under these terms can develop a sense of group identity and pride.[14] The Greeks combined both these elements – the telling of stories and the ritual occasions – and developed meetings (often festivals) when the telling of stories became vital elements in the proceedings. There has rightly been a good deal of emphasis in recent scholarship on the performance aspect of early poetry, and therefore on the interpretation of that poetry in terms of the circumstances in which it was presented.[15] We need not pursue the details here, but it is worth emphasising that poetry in the earlier periods was not created in the study for the studious, but that, even as it came to be written and slowly became more 'literary' in its approach, the setting for its transmission (or its 'reading') was still that which had been habitual in an oral society. And second, that theatre was not the only kind of poetry to be designed for public performance; rather, theatre developed in a context where a level of 'public' performance was the norm, and where stories were heard rather than read. Third, it evolved in a situation where the role of the poet was to some degree thought of as educational, even if in a very broad sense, a sense that was based on tradition. And finally, theatre was at the same time a product and an aim of community activity.

The fifth-century Athenian was able to see major theatrical performances twice a year, at a festival called the Lenaia in January and at the City Dionysia in late March. Earlier in the winter period, in December, were celebrations of the Rural Dionysia at local theatres around Attica. These were the cooler times of year (indeed December and January are, nowadays at least, the rainy period), but the more important point is that December–January is not a very urgent period in the farmer's year. By late March he could also afford to take time off because the seed should be sown, and indeed coming through the ground. We know comparatively little about the Rural Dionysia except that it seems to have originated as an agricultural festival, and historical evidence of a background in a fertility festival is to be seen in the processions with phallos-poles. Celebrations were organised in each local area or *deme* and the equivalent of the local mayor (or *demarch*) seems to have been responsible for the practicalities. We do not know at what period theatrical performances were first incorporated in the festivities, but there is evidence for the performance of both tragedy and comedy by the middle of the fifth century, and one could speculate that comedy, at least, could well have had an early if informal background in such a context. Inscriptional evidence from the fourth century and later reveals a continuing local pride in successful celebration of the occasion, even if modern scholars tend to suppose that the plays performed were less important pieces or repeats of successes from the City Dionysia.

The Lenaia was celebrated in Athens, and though not reckoned as being as important as the City Dionysia, none the less was a venue for major plays by major playwrights, particularly comedies: five comic poets competed, each with one play, while there were two tragic poets, each with two plays (it seems there was no satyr-play).[16] In this case the formal organisation of contests goes back no earlier than the middle of the fifth century, but this does not mean that there were no performances of any kind earlier.

The City Dionysia (also known as the Great Dionysia, or simply the Dionysia) was the major occasion on which dramatic performances were staged. It was also the major festival in honour of the god Dionysos. Among other celebrations and processions, there were competitions between ten men's choruses performing dithyrambic poetry (each representing one of the ten tribes), as well as between ten boys' choruses, and then the competitions between five comic playwrights (each presenting one play) and three tragic playwrights (each presenting a set of three tragedies and a satyr-play). This seems to have been the basic arrangement for much of the fifth century. In the fourth century and later, different combinations were developed in answer to changing taste, part of which included the revival of old plays.

What is immediately clear from these sorts of arrangements is that, unlike us, the Athenians, in the fifth century at least, were not invited or solicited by playwrights, producers or managers to attend the theatre. The contrary was the case: the Athenians themselves arranged command performances. Their agents, the magistrates, selected from the plays on offer those they wished to have performed at the festival. They, through a kind of honour-enforced code known as liturgies, provided sponsors to finance the performances. They offered inducements by way of prizes to writers and actors as well as what may have been substantial honoraria to the writers.[17] They provided the numerous young men needed to sing and dance in the choruses, and, for many families, this must have been at some cost to the economy of the household given the rehearsal time involved. By the mid-fourth century they also tried to ensure, by way of state subsidy through a fund called *theorikon*, that no citizen was prevented from joining the celebration through extreme economic hardship.

It has become fashionable to emphasise the social function of Greek theatre in the fifth century, and especially that of tragedy and its performance at the festival of the City Dionysia which was clearly an event of great state importance. It is less easy to construct such cases for the Lenaia or the Rural Dionysia where there was less pomp, no representatives of the so-called allied states presenting tribute, no crowning of distinguished citizens or visitors, no parade of war-orphaned military cadets (*ephebes*) in their new armour. These other more exhibitionist events were added, surely, because the occasion was a grand one and because it was an occasion when the community was gathered together.[18] There are plenty of ethnographic parallels for this sort of magnetic attraction if one wants to seek them out. On the other hand one should not minimise the central civic role these festivals and performances had in Athenian life. Nor should one ignore the impact that simple things such as the seating arrangement in the theatre, tribe by tribe, must have had on the way the Athenians looked at themselves and at the occasion. There is also the point that these were religious festivals in honour of Dionysos with all that that implies about the state of heightened tension and heightened awareness for the audience. For people who did not meet as a large group very often, there must have been an excitement in the very fact of meeting in this way, not least for those who had left home and travelled some distance and who may well have slept in the sanctuary overnight in the company of the god. One tends to think of those coming in from the countryside, and we know from the opening of Plato's *Republic* that it was thought reasonable to walk from town down to the Piraeus for a day to participate in a festival. On the other hand I would doubt that all that many people would want to make the trip even from the Piraeus every day for several days in a row for events that probably lasted through most of the daylight hours. Far better to stay in town and enjoy the evening festivities, join in the occasion, and escape from the drudgery and responsibilities of the normal daily round.[19]

The audience was also used to enjoying a level of participation in a range of other events which we would call ritual, and these events often involved something that one could call performance.[20] The celebration of a divinity, whether at a festival or not, was often a group activity in which everyone joined even if the group had its delegated leaders, whether priests or others. In early drama and what one can hypothesise as proto-drama, the chorus acted on behalf of the larger group, the audience, but one might suppose that the distinction between performers and the inactive was somewhat blurred. We should remember too that all this took place in the open air but within the confines of a sanctuary where everyone had assembled for the purpose of honouring and celebrating the god. The growing part given to actors slowly eroded the function of the chorus and in doing so it most probably eroded the participatory sense of the larger group, the audience. Indeed the history of theatre has to some extent been the history of the growing passivity of the audience, particularly once theatre went indoors and the stage was separated from the seating by lighting and darkness. But one can think of many variants along the way.

In so-called primitive societies, the dividing line between audience and participant in ritual performances is quite regularly unclear. Experts in some aspects of the performance such as dance or particular categories of song or music-making or knowledge of procedure may be prominent at one point or another, as may members of the community who have a special role in the context of the particular occasion because of their place in the social network of the community. In ancient Greece the dividing lines were only just being established and there was probably a much greater sense of general involvement than we are used to. Dramatic performances were, as we have seen, put on by and for the community, and although foreigners were allowed to attend the Great Dionysia, they were not involved in the other festivals, and direct participation in any case remained an Athenian prerogative. By the fourth century at least there were legal prohibitions against participation in the performances as members of the choruses by aliens or of course by Athenians who had been disenfranchised. Resident aliens were allowed to participate in the Lenaia but not in the Dionysia. Equally, while participation was a privilege of Athenians, it was also compulsory for those young members of the community selected. This would have involved some sacrifice for a less well-off family if a son's labour was needed, for example in working the land. Yet in addition to these legalities, there is evidence, for example on a gravestone of the turn of the fifth and fourth centuries where a young man is depicted holding a chorus-mask, that participation was regarded as an honour.[21]

The performances belonged to the community, the audience. They were theirs. Once one includes the members of the choruses for all the plays, tragic and comic, there was a substantial number of performers, and they came from a comparatively small community. In the performance of the type of song called dithyramb the choral group was made up of representatives from each of the tribes. Something similar may well have been arranged for more formal drama. Winkler's suggestion that the choruses were made up of *ephebes*, young men who were fulfilling their so-called military service, and that the choruses were therefore representative of the community in a further sense is not unattractive.[22] In either case, the audience could reasonably be supposed to have viewed the chorus as in some way representing themselves, perhaps in very specific fashion of identification with the tribal groups to which they belonged. The numbers involved at any given Dionysia were not small. Each tribe presented a dithyrambic chorus of fifty men and one of fifty boys ($10 \times 2 \times 50 = 1,000$).

9

Each comedy had 24 chorusmen ($5 \times 24 = 120$). Sophoclean and Euripidean tragedies had 15 chorusmen, but the total numbers are less certain: perhaps 3 sets $\times 15 = 45$, but it may be that each tragedy and satyr-play had different chorusmen, i.e. $3 \times 4 \times 15 = 180$.[23] Add to these the various trainers and organisers, costumers and musicians (not to mention the actors and mask-makers involved in formal drama), and a noticeable proportion of the free male population would have been involved.

One tends to watch the people one knows or identifies with in a performance in a special way; doing so increases one's sense of participation in the proceedings and sharpens one's observation of what is done and the way it is done. In this respect, the size of the audience was irrelevant, it was the size of the community that mattered.[24] In Athens the citizen community was small enough for one to stand some chance of knowing most of its prominent members at least on sight (as anyone who has ever lived in a comparatively small country town will remember). It was also a participatory democracy, so that one came to know one's fellow citizens more actively than we are used to. And then if one didn't actually know people personally, one would be able to identify them by hearsay and by their being related within a network of family or kinship groups. This acquaintance would also work between the members of the audience and the other performers, particularly in the fifth century when the writers and key actors were members of prominent families. Pavlovskis and Jouan have also argued persuasively that although the faces of the performers were hidden by masks, one would quickly come to know the voices and mannerisms of the more famous actors.[25] They went on further to suggest that Sophocles, for example, structured his plays to take best advantage of the skills of his actors, and to allow the actors to show their best. So although Athenians did not create the opportunities to see theatrical performances more than a few times a year, when they did see them it was with a keen participatory interest and with a degree of what they regarded as inside knowledge.

To come back to the broader issue of the social setting of drama, a further factor which affected the way Athenian drama was created and received is the very straightforward point that the audience has the experience of external events, and even if the playwright makes no overt reference to them, those events will sharpen reaction to certain sorts of situations created on stage. We are surely unaware of most because they have slipped through the historians' net. Local disasters from warfare to disease, weather or earthquake would alert an audience to any evocation of such kinds of events or parallel disasters in a mythical context, or might prompt a writer to venture into or stay clear of certain themes. There must also have been political *causes célèbres*. We are aware of some of the big events like the Persian Wars which were seen as turning points in history, and in looking at surviving plays we see references to them whether implicit or explicit, just as we can see them in surviving art where the reference is usually made through choice of myth. The pursuit of political references in Greek tragedy and comedy has filled many scholarly pages over the years, not all of them profitably or convincingly, and ultimately one's judgement of the amount and complexity of political reference tragedians inserted into re-creations of myth-history is based on one's own assessment of what is credible. The audience was, after all, listening in the open air, not reading a book quietly in a comfortable armchair. James Redfield, however, has made the excellent point that in tragedy the contemporary material was used to lead the audience into the reality of the legend. The modern example helped illuminate the problems or potential of the historical situation, thereby prompting a more active intellectual participation from members of the audience.[26]

The overriding theme of such tragedies as we have is man's relationship with the gods, and other aspects are incidental to that, whether the question of how that relationship may affect a man's relationship to the state, or the young-hero (*ephebe*) age of a number of key subjects. I suspect that the fascination with man's relationship to the state was historically a temporary question, and it is likely that myths with young heroes (by contrast with, say, Agamemnon or Oedipus) became more popular in tune with the widely growing emphasis on the younger generation during the later years of the fifth century. The choice of subjects of drama was not particularly biased in favour of what else went on at the Dionysia. Louis Jouvet, quoted at the head of this chapter, is much closer to the point.[27] It was this broad and basic exploration of human problems through the medium of people re-enacting the impact of their own often gruesome history which was the exciting thing about early theatre. Because the experience was at second hand, it was comparatively painless, but because it involved the actions of their own ancestors and because the audience was convinced by what it saw on stage in the performance of a tragedy to a greater degree than we are, it was real enough.

While Tragedy took the Greeks in general as its basis, Old Comedy had a strong parochial element which must have served to reinforce the bonds within the community through this sense of sharing the occasion, through sharing laughter at and about people one knew, or through treatment of non-Athenians, even other Greeks, almost as foreigners.[28] It is probable that the traditional choruses of animals, foreigners or particular categories of men (for which we have visual evidence from as early as the middle of the sixth century) were characteristically non-Athenian, and so served to prove to the audience (perhaps through the overturning of the aliens' power) the advantages and pleasures of being Athenian. One thinks of titles such as Birds of various kinds (compare Figure 2.10), Gnats, Fig-Flies, Frogs, Lydians, Titans, Persians or Assyrians, Babylonians, foreign Knights (Figure 2.7), Ostrich-Riders, or people who ride dolphins (Figures 2.11,

2.12). This pattern is becoming lost in the plays of Aristophanes, even though it appears that Pherekrates wrote a play called *Savages* or *Wild-Men* as late as 420 BC. Aristophanes' earlier comedies, however, are still very much Athenian and their humour rests very much in Athenian material. His later work becomes less particular and more generally applicable, as part of the development to what we call Middle Comedy, but we can still find social groups that are abnormal from the dominant male perspective, such as women (celebrating the Thesmophoria festival or taking over the Assembly).

In general it is important to maintain a historical perspective. We should realise that even at any given moment, the social function of theatre had many facets, and that it changed, perhaps quite radically, during the course of the fifth century. Theatre had only just been invented, and like many innovations it probably took some time before the full potential of its role in society was realised. We can also see that its role changed, for example in the fourth century, and it continued to develop later. So much more reason then to suppose that it changed quite rapidly in the earlier years. We should not take the narrow period of the surviving texts as being typical of the whole. Although the Dionysia and the theatrical performance that went with it were closely linked to the democracy of Athens, and they surely served to foster the democracy just as the democracy in its turn served to foster the festival and its theatre, the uses to which theatre was put were never static, and it is not unrewarding to consider the themes pursued by the three tragedians in that light.[29]

Another socio-political dimension of theatre resides in the status of its creators. The public use of myth had for long been in the hands of the upper classes. It is normal in most cultures for myth to be used consciously or unconsciously to support its ideologies, and for that matter for particular groups or individuals to use it in the same way, to support their causes or justify their points of view. In Greece, upper-class families regularly claimed descent from gods or heroes of myth. There is therefore a tendency for the traditional myths to become equated with aristocrats and their attitudes. There was nothing unusual in this; one can suppose that the population at large simply assumed this to be the case. One might compare the common expectation that the oracles pronounced at Delphi were likely to be subject to political manipulation. This observation on the political use of myth is a general one, not particularly related to the theatre, and although the institution and/or growth of theatre at Athens was tied to the institution of democracy, we should remember that the running of the democracy and its programme of events was largely in the hands of members of a small number of well-to-do families until well on in the fifth century.

During the first three-quarters of the fifth century, the emerging genre of formal, written theatre was being developed by a fairly small group. They were necessarily well-to-do. They must have belonged to the privileged families to have had a fully literate education, and to have had the time to devote to play writing and the intensive final stages of play production. The speed at which Classical playwrights wrote has always been a matter for speculation and discussion, but there is some evidence to suggest that tragedians in the later fifth century produced on average a set of four plays every other year whereas comic writers tended to turn out one a year (and that they could run late doing it).[30] The mechanics of actual writing must have meant it was fairly slow – given the nature of the available material, the available pens, the style of script, the handling of rolls of papyrus and the fact that one wrote with the papyrus roll on one's knee.[31] (We do not know if the actors and chorus were each given copies of the text – which would have meant quite a lot of copying – or if they learned orally from a single script. We may also recall that papyrus was expensive.) Late antique sources on the lives of the poets are often inventions or at best unreliable, but there is reasonable evidence to believe that Sophocles was elected a general as well as being state treasurer in 443/2 BC, which means that he was a notable member of the community in addition to being a playwright. Aeschylus' son Euaion, who appeared on stage as an actor, at least in his teens and early twenties, is labelled *kalos* (handsome) on a number of vases of the middle of the fifth century. This is an epithet which vase-painters conventionally restricted to the sons of the well-to-do, and especially when, as in this case, his father's name is given as well. There is some inscriptional evidence that Aristophanes was a member of a fairly privileged circle. There seems to be reasonable evidence of Euripides' good birth. We may add to all this the undoubted fact that at least down to the period of Sophocles and at times quite likely beyond, writers often acted in their own plays: it was part of the carrying-through of the creative process, as with some other forms of poetry. Theatrical involvement also tended to run in families over two and three generations. All three major tragedians as well as Aristophanes had sons who became dramatic poets. We have just mentioned Euaion, son of Aeschylus, whom we know to have acted in at least one play written by his father and two by Sophocles. Melanthios, son of the tragedian Philokles and therefore great-nephew of Aeschylus, also seems to have been an actor, as does Euripides' son Mnesilochos. Crates is said to have been an actor for Cratinus before becoming a comic poet in his own right, and it seems that Carcinus too was both actor and poet. The implication of this kind of pattern is, as has often been stated, that the production of drama through much of the fifth century was to a large degree one of personal involvement on the part of the poet, and that it was the sort of activity in which a son might help his father and follow in his footsteps. The creation of theatrical performances must have been regarded as a fairly specialised activity and one that developed its own special talents. Only more slowly, as the genre became established, did many others feel they could participate in the process.[32]

The new tragedy of Euripides is among other things representative of the new democratic spirit of the fifth century in that through his use of the myths he questions the traditional aristocratic views of the gods and heroes. This is perhaps one reason why he was popular and perhaps one reason why he was linked with sophistic teaching (which also rejected the old values) and perhaps why Aristophanes accused him of being low-born (not that he necessarily was – the accusation is enough). The high period of tragedy (at least in the view expressed in the *Frogs*) is linked with that period in which Athens is developing as a democracy led by aristocrats – people like Kimon and Pericles. And the decline of tragedy matches that when ideals rather like those of the gentleman amateur and the concept of selfless dedication to the state were dying away. It is possible to regard the famous Funeral Speech of Pericles as a last gasp of a dying creed, a protestation on behalf of values that no longer obtained automatically.

It is sometimes argued that the establishment of a prize for acting in or about 449 BC implies that actors were now becoming semi-professional. I am not sure that that is the right view. Prizes were regularly given at athletic contests, but until late in the fifth century the sort of people who won victories were of aristocratic background. They again were the ones who could afford the time to practice and develop their skills, or, in some events like horse-racing, afford the equipment. It seems more likely that the prize is a sign of the growing development of the medium and a recognition, first, of the separation of the contributions of actor and writer, and then of the skills needed in an activity that was becoming increasingly demanding as a tradition of expectation built up, and as the audience for its part became more critical and more expert.[33]

With the benefit of hindsight we can identify a number of factors which facilitated the development of formal drama and then encouraged it to flourish. Essentially they rest in that typically Greek combination of the traditional and the innovative, the primitive and developed. One thinks of factors such as the particular attitude to myth and history, the advent of developing literacy in a society with sophisticated orally-based systems, an emerging democracy which could still call on the sense of responsibility and/or self-advertisement of its upper-class families, the willingness to use existing religious settings for the development of new activities aimed at their political good in the broadest sense, to explore their place in the world. There are two other inter-related factors which we should also bear in mind. One is the existence at this period of something of a surplus of wealth in the community, and the other is the development of a more urbanised society. A relatively large group from which creators, performers and audience could be drawn is a *sine qua non*. It is also a matter of the style and sophistication in social contact that comes with urban society. In this sense the experience of the procedures of that phenomenon called Athenian democracy was important. The celebration of the dramatic festivals in town was also costly, both in direct financial terms and in terms of time off from other duties for the considerable number of performers. And then, despite the time of year chosen, when there was relatively little to be done in the fields, there also had to be enough surplus of people in the family economy to have some stay behind to look after the property or the animals while others took the equivalent of a week at a time to attend the theatre. The Athenians of this period were prepared to put a sizeable part of their income into this kind of activity as well as into the construction of temples on the Acropolis and public buildings in the Agora. In other words the Athenians were prepared to pay for it because they wanted it and enjoyed it.

2

THE EARLY PERIOD AND THE FIFTH CENTURY

The visual evidence

Without becoming involved in the controversies concerning the technicalities of the evolution of tragedy, in functional terms we can reasonably suppose that it evolved from a fairly straightforward story-telling or re-enactment of myth-history, to a more complex one in which the motives of human action came under increasing questioning, and, as part of those same issues, the rôle of the divine powers in determining those motives. This is a process which was beginning already with Homer. The Homeric poems, like so much other Greek poetry, had a level of performance in their recital, very often at public occasions and/or religious festivals. The poems of Stesichorus, which were also performed widely, were about the length of a tragedy.[1] There is some danger, though, of losing sight of the differences, both in fundamentals of approach and in certain practicalities. In epic and lyric poetry the performing poet or the chorus of singers could and usually did address the audience directly, while in tragedy the poet is absent from the performance whether in his own persona or as a mouthpiece of the Muses. The setting and story have to arise from within the action as it evolves in the theatre.[2] The poet effaced himself as performer. (It is interesting to contrast the style of Old Comedy which was much slower to make this transition.)

Two other differences were critical and both of them were attributed in the ancient tradition to that shadowy figure Thespis.[3] The first is the separation of the performer we call an actor from the choral group or groups. It was a development which more readily allowed and pointed up discussion and thus difference of opinion within the presentation, so that playwrights were able to create something we recognise as dramatic tension through the interplay of ideas and viewpoints. At another level, it must also reflect the growing interest in the individual which is typical of Greeks in this period. It is a very clever way of crystallising discussion to specific issues and of moving away from the group-view. Greek drama was always developing and changing, so it is risky to generalise about early theatrical choruses on the basis of the later ones which we know. Later ones tend by and large to emphasise their group identity by contrast with the actor-

Figure 2.1 Attic red-figure column-krater with a chorus of youths raising a figure from a tomb, *c.* 490 BC. Basle, Antikenmuseum und Sammlung Ludwig BS 415

figures, and this could be a development which is itself due to the existence of actors. On the other hand we can trace this contrast between group and individual to a date quite early in the fifth century.

The other vital change involved in the creation of tragedy, setting it apart from anything written by other 'serious' poets, was the adoption for this kind of performance of something which already existed for proto-comedy and the earliest satyr-play, the wearing of masks. This step, which is so easily underestimated, not only allowed but encouraged a more thoroughgoing submergence of the performer's personality into that of the rôle played. It fostered dramatic illusion. The performance became a far more realistic enactment.[4]

There is a good deal of evidence, both literary and pictorial, to suggest that what people perceived as one of the most exciting things about theatre when it was first being invented was the visual spectacle. It was what was found attractive and new by comparison with other forms of poetic performance. There is every reason to believe that the audience found it realistic and highly emotive. In the *Persians,* in the crisis following the battle of Salamis, Aeschylus has the chorus summon up the old king Darius from the grave to provide advice and support for the totally demoralised and leaderless Persians after their defeat by the Greeks. It was a highpoint of the play, coming after a sequence of strange, highly emotive song and dance from the chorus. It was a piece of spectacle. Yet we can demonstrate that this was an almost traditional motif by 472 BC, the year of production. There are no less than four vases which demonstrate there were at least four other plays which contained the raising of a dead hero earlier than the *Persians*, beginning from very early in the century. The clearest example is to be found on a vase in Basle of about 490 BC (Figure 2.1). It has six youths dancing before a figure who rises behind or from a monument.[5] The youths represent a chorus: they have identical dress, they dance with uniform step and uniform gestures, words come from their mouths, and the extension of the chin-line suggests that they are wearing masks as do the open mouths, not a normal feature of drawing at this period. It is clear too that they are not ordinary warriors: they have no greaves, no helmets, but wear diadems. The gesture with the arms reflects the movement in the dance of raising the dead hero. The monument is shown as a tomb by the sprays and sashes that have been placed on it. The hero also has a mask-like face with open mouth. As a piece of staging in a period when there was only one actor, this must have made brilliant theatre, particularly if one imagines the tensions built up in the song and the dance.[6] We have no idea who was the first to introduce it, but we shall see other evidence to suggest that once an idea had been introduced on the stage it was regarded as common property, to be re-used, modified or referred to as the occasion arose. This also provides an interesting sidelight on perceptions and attitudes to the creation of theatre: in this sense too it was seen as a community enterprise to which individuals contributed.

It is possible that this motif of raising a hero from the dead is what was referred to in an ancient comment that the chorus of the *Persians* copied the *Phoinissae* of Phrynichus. Aeschylus himself seems to have used the motif again in his *Psychagogoi*. Sophocles could well have used it in his lost play *Polyxena*.[7] One may speculate that behind the actual staging there lies quite a primitive element in which the heroes or successful leaders of the past are summoned by those in need of leadership and direction in the present. It could well go back earlier than formal tragedy. The theme is found in and perhaps given authority by the Homeric *Nekyia* where Odysseus summons the shade of Teiresias to consult him. We could also speculate that in its fifth-century context, in some broad and not necessarily very clearly expressed sense, it reflects a yearning for days gone by and a yearning for direct leadership when a democratic system of government has taken control and Athenians were faced with arguments rather than command decisions. As evidence in our particular inquiry, however, these vases also demonstrate a particularly brilliant innovation in staging at an early stage of tragedy. Alternating song between the chorus and the single actor has the potential to become boring (and one can readily see why a second actor was introduced). One way to cope must have been to have the actor come on and off stage in a variety of roles; but as a means of increasing tension, to have the chorus in distress and then with particular forms of song prompt the appearance of this figure from the past must have been a staggeringly effective use of what (with hindsight) were limited resources – so effective that later writers could not let the idea disappear after one performance. This, then, is a very clear case in which the experience of theatrical performance had a cumulative effect, was for a while liked by the spectators, and was exploited, doubtless with variations, by a succession of writers. There is even something of a hint of this motif in the *Frogs*, and it would not be alien to Aristophanes' style of invention to turn the game on its head in a sophisticated parody: tragedy after the deaths of Sophocles and Euripides is in crisis. Dionysos and the Athenian public are at a loss and need advice. But instead of bringing the heroes of tragedy up to the world of the living, we have the improbable scheme of a god, in this case Dionysos, going down to the world of the dead to find the heroes of the past. More obviously related to this theme, but in a play which is not preserved (his *Demes*, probably of 412 BC), the comic writer Eupolis had a character bring back as many as four great statesmen from the past – Solon, Aristides, Miltiades and Pericles – to help get Athens back on the right track.

It is interesting that it is primarily during the fifth century, and at that not the latest part, that we hear of or can detect notable extensions of presentation technique. Aeschylean silences were notorious for a while, that is his ploy of having the main character, whom one might naturally

Figure 2.2 Attic red-figure hydria with Andromeda about to be tied to stakes, *c.* 450–440 BC. London, British Museum E 169

19

expect to carry the weight of the dialogue and action, stand or sit silent and unanswering for long periods, especially during the early part of the play.[8] This was a deliberate tantalising of the audience and it was a technique which must have made these characters' utterances when they did eventually speak all the more compelling. In historical terms one might guess that it was evolved in reaction against the increase in the number of actors and so was an overt and deliberately attention-getting rejection of what was seen as a recent advance. Our sources suggest that the audience certainly became conscious of it as a technique, almost to the point at which Aeschylus could be perceived as over-doing it. Our main evidence for these silences is Aristophanes' *Frogs* (905 ff.) of 405 BC. As a milestone in theatrical technique, they were still recalled more than a generation after their use.[9]

A further example of attempts to stun the audience is Sophocles' *Andromeda*. Although nothing but a few scraps of the play are preserved, we for once have a good idea of the staging from a series of some five vases which seem contemporary with the original performance in the 440s (Figures 2.2–2.4).[10] Two aspects are striking and common to most of them. The first is the dress and the pose of Andromeda: she is shown in a costume which the Greeks saw as Eastern, in knee-length tunic and trousers and wearing a typical eastern hat. This is common to all the representations and

Figure 2.3 Attic red-figure pelike with Andromeda tied to stakes, *c.* 450–440 BC. Boston, Museum of Fine Arts 63.2663

Figure 2.4 Attic white-ground calyx-krater with Andromeda tied to stakes, *c.* 450–440 BC. Agrigento AG 7

it must reflect the way Sophocles showed her on the stage. The vase-painters also chose to show her either being tied or already tied to stakes which have been fixed in the ground by Ethiopian servants. She is tied to them with her arms spread. It is important to understand what this signifies in the ancient context where, by the rules of contemporary society, women were modest and normally (at least in the case of upper-class women who provide the norm in tragedy) confined to the home. Ideally, we are told, women of virtue were not even spoken of by men. Andromeda by contrast is both exposed and defenceless. She is set up as if for rape. We know from the myth that her father Kepheus had her placed there as a sacrifice to a sea-monster which was ravaging the country. (Kepheus' queen, Kassiopeia, had offended the sea-nymphs by boasting that she was more beautiful than they; the monster had been sent by Poseidon, god of the sea, in retribution; Kepheus had been forced to this action on learning from an oracle that there was no alternative way to save his country.) Another element in a number of these pictures is that of further servants bringing chests, cloth, perfume vessels and a mirror, an object that to the Greeks connoted a certain eroticism. All these are characteristic offerings at a wedding ceremony. What Sophocles is doing, therefore, is exploiting a duality of view that was in fact inherent in the Greek view of a young woman's death.

21

A woman was always under a man's protection, in her childhood her father's (or if he died, her brother's); in her adult life under her husband's; when she died she went to a new house, that of Hades. The step taken on marriage, from her father's house to her husband's, was a parallel for the step taken on death, and it is for this kind of reason that many of the offerings found in the graves of young women also function as bridal gifts.[11] Sophocles takes these beliefs and exploits them. Kepheus forces his daughter to surrender to the monster for the good of the state (and one might imagine with a good deal of inner turmoil and debate, both with himself and, as some of the vase-paintings make clear, with her). It is a situation which implies marriage but also death, and at the same time the way she is tied up hints at how the monster is going to use her, a use in which she has no choice. Her father, her supposed protector, has forced her into this situation, but the question is whether he had any choice either. The playwright uses visual elements to underline the horror and the dilemma. Five different vase-painters reacted, and they characterised the play by the way Andromeda was exposed.[12]

A performance in Taranto in the early fourth century may be reflected on an early Apulian red-figure vase by the Sisyphus Painter in the J. Paul Getty Museum. The details are not the same as in the Athenian performance, but again the princess is being tied to stakes. Here again the vase-painter has shown her as a bride, suggesting that he (along with his fellow-members of the audience) also found this a preoccupying aspect of the presentation.[13]

If the contemporary vase-paintings are in any sense a reliable guide, this play made a bigger impact than any other of that period, and perhaps than any other in the fifth century, at least in terms of the staging. While Sophocles clearly aimed to shock the audience, his use of stage techniques was, as one might expect, more subtle and sophisticated than in the early fifth century. Another case where, to judge by representations in vase-painting, his staging had a stunning effect was in his satyr-play *Pandora*. In this case satyrs seem to have taken a key part in the creation of the goddess and they revelled in her appearance.[14] He was also extremely clever in using material objects as a focus or symbol of the stage action, as the urn in *Electra*, the sword in *Ajax*, the bow in *Philoctetes*.[15] All these are symptoms of a lively theatre, and one that was eagerly experimenting with and exploiting the possibilities of presentation. We should also remember that this was all done for an audience, and for an audience that must have been expressing interest in and consciousness of these developments.

From later in the fifth century we may have some evidence of the way Euripides staged his version of *Andromeda*, with her wearing long dress rather than a short tunic and trousers, and fixed to a rock rather than stakes (Figure 2.5).[16] But in this case we have to rely on a single vase, so that we have nothing else against which to judge, and it is more than likely that in

Figure 2.5 Attic red-figure calyx-krater with Adromeda tied to a rock, late fifth century BC. Berlin inv.3237

other respects it introduces a strong element of interpretation on the part of the vase-painter. He seems to have introduced more characters than one would have on stage, and to have attempted to give an encapsulation of the play rather than a scene from it. On and around the rock he places various plants, something it is highly unlikely that Euripides put on stage. This serves to introduce us to a basic question about the representation of Athenian tragedy on fifth-century vases.

We have seen that in the sixth and fifth centuries the Greeks were very aurally aware. They must also have been very visually aware. On the one hand they were without that superabundance of visual material which goes so far to dull our own perceptions – books, magazines, newspapers, cinema, video, television, billboards, instructions on roadways, advertisements on buses and trains, wrapping papers and cartons, and then art galleries, reproductions of pictures on walls, photographs – items which we learn from infancy to screen out from our memory. Partly because visual material was comparatively rare, the ancient was used to reading images carefully, whether they were painted, sculpted or live. Pictures were given a much greater force than we give them today.[17] Here again it is relevant that we are dealing with a period of transition from an oral to a literate society. If the extensive use of writing alters modes of thought, it must also alter art, since art reflects modes of thought. In broad terms, from the eighth century to the end of the fifth, we can trace a sequence which begins with depictions that are statements, in which the artist draws what he knows rather than what he sees, and which one might further imagine that the viewer elaborates in words. In a sense they are mnemonics. There is very soon a move towards the depiction of narrative, that is, visual story-telling, which would again be elaborated as the story was read on the object.[18] Nevertheless, even though the vase-painter (or metal-worker or sculptor) constantly 'improves' his depiction by reference to the world around him, much of the mnemonic element remains, and his figures stand as symbols of what he intends. The picture-schemes are shown as a series of conventions which are shared between the artist and his audience. In the fifth century, changes occur more and more rapidly. The depictions themselves become more and more naturalistic. In the high Classical period in the middle years of the fifth century, there seems to be something of a reaction against the simple-mindedness of the narrative element in the attempt to encapsulate in quiet, inactive figures or scenes a much broader sweep of a story (that is understood or read in by the viewer), or with single figures, the notion of capturing the *ethos* of an idealised total character or being. In the late fifth century, there is a further sophistication and a move towards a greater complexity of depiction, both in technical terms and in an attempt to express the *pathos* of a figure more explicitly; it runs closely parallel to what Euripides is doing in his plays, and the best work can achieve an elaborate lyric quality which matches that of his choruses. Even so, the changes are not absolute, and many of the earlier principles still hold. The art of the end of the fifth century is still far from aiming at, let alone achieving, the manner of quasi-photographic illustration, and it is still heavily conventional both in the structures it employs and in its subject-matter. We therefore need to exercise care in reading a picture and in using it for our own purposes. They are certainly not illustrations to be taken at face value, and it is worth remembering that in the fifth century, although we have some pictures that may be thought to be taken from tragedy, we have no pictures of tragic actors acting.

In investigating how and why this is so, it is instructive to look at a particular example, where the rule is almost broken. On a vase in Berlin (Figure 2.6) which dates to about 470 BC we have on each side of the vase a maenad dancing to the music of a piper.[19] The piper is shown in the elaborate costume of a piper for the stage, and to judge from the artistic conventions that apply when showing comedy and satyr-play, the figure here is a conventional symbol whose function is to indicate that what we have here is a performance in the theatre. He provides the context for the figure on the left. The maenad has a sword in the right hand and a half fawn or kid in the left, and is shown as 'real'. Yet since the piper signifies that the figure is a chorusman, the figure should, in the actuality of the stage

Figure 2.6 Attic red-figure pelike with maenad before piper, *c.* 470 BC.
Berlin-Charlottenburg inv.3223

performance, have had footwear and, as a young man (as all chorusmen were), cannot have had a naked female breast. One can then ask oneself if the half fawn or kid is a literal depiction of a piece of stage property, or is an insertion by the vase-painter as something that maenads normally have, thus characterising the maenad, or if it is something that the vase-painter was persuaded to imagine was there by the words of the script. We cannot know for sure, but what we can be certain of is that in the theatre this torn animal did not have blood pouring out of it in the way we see here. At the same time the painter leaned the other way in showing, on one side of the vase, a frontal face. This is something very rare in vase-painting of this period, but it is the way one sees a mask. The face of the similar figure on the other side is shown in profile; it was suggested years ago that the odd treatment of the hair above the forehead may represent the artificial hair of the mask. And then, although one cannot see it in the reproduction, the painter wrote above the figure the word *kalos*: the boy (rather than the girl) is fair. The vase is unique in its rather uncertain handling of the ambiguity between the actuality of the performance as it was put on in the theatre, and the further reality of what the performers were persuading the audience to believe in.

25

This kind of ambiguity between the two realities is unusual, but on the vase in Basle we looked at earlier, with six youths dancing to raise a figure from a monument or tomb (Figure 2.1), we saw some slight hints of players playing (identity of dress and dance, open mouths, mask-like chin-lines). In all other respects the painter has shown the further reality of the characters played. This is the norm. It is a habit which creates enormous difficulties for those who try to use vase-paintings as evidence for the appearance and style of fifth-century tragic theatre. How does one know when a painter is reflecting something he has seen in the theatre and when he is simply showing the straight myth? The answer by and large is that one can't tell unless there are some external checks, such as multiple reproductions of the same thing at the same time by different hands, as we have seen in the case of the *Andromeda*.

For our purposes, however, the point is an important one since it demonstrates the reaction to tragedy. The vase-painter can be taken as an ordinary member of the audience. He was, however skilled, an artisan and does not seem to have had that level of creativity, individuality, inventive- ness, and desire to interpret that we associate with modern creative artists. His function within society was a different one. He was also producing for a market (the notion of the lonely artist starving in his garret and pursuing his Art despite the world about him is in any case a Romantic construct) and he was making painted vases as a commercial proposition: he therefore made his pictures in terms of what his purchasers wanted and/or expected to find. A further point is a self-evident one, but one which constantly seems to need repetition: Athenian vase-paintings are not sketch-books, let alone photographs. The vase-painter was certainly not concerned with recording society and its habits in the sense of a later nineteenth-century painter in Paris, a 'painter of modern life' as Baudelaire put it. When he shows tragic actors as 'real', it reflects the audience's view of the theatre performance.

One may also wonder if this not distinguishing the performance from the myth does not also reflect another attitude of the majority of the audience. We with printed texts at our disposal, set out in pages that we can readily turn backwards as well as forwards, with their numbered lines and careful commentaries, are very conscious of the subtleties of the text and of the differences in the treatment of, say, Andromeda or Electra by Sophocles and Euripides. We have traditionally tended (with our emphasis on authorship) to think of the poet and his contribution first and the story second. The bulk of the audience knew the myths through hearing them in repeated poetry and to some extent through seeing them on stage. Myths had no finite absolute form but were in constant flux according to the needs an audience was perceived to have at a particular time and place. It was therefore Andromeda or Electra as told by Sophocles or by Euripides. The audience appreciated what the playwrights were doing, but I suspect that the recognition of the contribution of the playwright as an individual creator was something which emerged rather slowly in the course of time with the growing experience and sophistication of the audience. So far as tragedy was concerned, it was probably helped by the growing complexity and sophistication of comedy and its ability to comment on the activities of the tragedians. But we should remember that the myths were real, and that they represented the audience's own ancestors and history.

The other reason why scenes from tragedy were shown as the reality intended by the performers is the well-known one of dramatic illusion.[20] For a serious drama to work, it has to be taken seriously. The audience has to be persuaded to forget about the artificiality of the creation and to accept the conventions of the performance.

This response to tragedy is thrown into higher relief by the responses to comedy and to satyr-play. In terms of the conventions of depiction, comedy stands at the opposite pole from tragedy. It is not quite true that there is a total lack of dramatic illusion, but depictions of comedy are of men dressed up being funny, and it is clear from the surviving plays of Aristophanes that the illusion of the dramatic process could be interrupted at almost any moment.[21] Just as he comments on the work of other playwrights, and in particular he will make fun of the very conventions of tragedy that the tragic playwrights themselves took care not to emphasise or expose, so too Aristophanes (and so far as we can tell his contemporaries) enjoyed creating humour through self-referentiality. 'Shall I make those same tired old jokes that the other playwrights make?' says one slave-character to another. 'I shan't try to win approval by throwing nuts and figs into the audience.'[22] And one can point to other jokes about their costume, and especially the *phallos* which all the actors wore and which was left exposed for those playing male roles.[23] One effect of all this was to make the audience even more conscious of the way the comic playwright staged his play. It raised the level of critical consciousness of the stage business. We shall never be able to retrieve much sense of the movement on stage and the physical games played, although we shall get some slight idea of it from the scenes on fourth-century vases discussed in the next chapter. It seems fair to guess, none the less, that there was a fair amount of knock-about humour, whether pushing and shoving, as we see on vases, or beating with a whip or stick as we also see on vases or detect from the script of *Frogs* or *Clouds*.[24] What we can be certain of, however, is that this style of comedy with its very outspoken self-referentiality must reflect a style of theatre in which both poet and audience share and enjoy this mutual exchange about what is going on in the performance itself. The audience must have been keeping a close eye on the way things were done and on such things as the costume developed for a production. Indeed one suspects it was not only a mutual exchange, but a mutual challenge in which the poet played to their sophistication and critical ability on such matters, and they responded by their applause and ultimately by the award of the prize. This is a

Figure 2.7 Attic black-figure amphora from Cerveteri(?), with comic chorus of Knights, *c.* 540–530 BC. Berlin F 1697

suggestion which has strong support from scenes on vases.

Depictions which derive from Old Comedy begin as early as the middle of the sixth century BC and run on through the fifth. As with the rest of Greek art, these depictions are governed by fairly strict conventions in the way things are represented. In the early years (see Figure 2.7) there is a piper (as we saw on the vase in Berlin for tragedy, Figure 2.6) together with a chorus of dancers. The chorus gains its very identity from being a group, and so just as its members dance with a uniform step, so they wear identically styled costume. Acharnians are Acharnians, Frogs are Frogs, Banqueters are Banqueters, not a random collection of assorted individuals.[25] To judge by surviving titles and by surviving scenes on vases, earlier comedies generally had choruses either of animals or of foreigners – that is, they were not of the normal human group, the Athenian community. On the early vases we never see normal Athenians: they wear strange garments or headgear, they ride strange creatures like ostriches or dolphins, or they represent non-human creatures like birds or even rivers (we have literary evidence for Cities and Islands). As another example, the famous Knights of about 540–530 BC in Berlin (Figure 2.7) are not Athenians but foreigners, as is made clear by the strange crests on their helmets, crests which are in fact not unlike those worn by

28

Figure 2.8 Attic black-figure hydria with comic chorus of males on shoulder,
c. 550 BC. New York, private collection

contemporary warriors from the hill country of central South Italy.[26]

Nevertheless, if we remember that comic choruses (unlike groups of dancers and/or singers in more modern musicals and musical comedies) were in front of the audience for the duration of the play, there was some point in having variations of the detail and colour of the costume within the overall pattern. Thus, the dancers on the shoulder of the vessel in Figure 2.8: the first, nearest the piper, has his dress yellow with dark brown stripes above the hem, the second red and black quarters, the third red above, yellow with stripes and a line of white dots below the waist, and a black hem, the fourth all red with a black hem. There are other examples of a similar kind and they provide some indication of the effort the playwright put into production, as well as the audience's observation of them.

It seems clear from what we can gather of the history of Old Comedy that the plots of plays before the middle of the fifth century were fairly simple and episodic in character, and that the key element in the play was the chorus. Early plays seem to have been named after their choruses since the choruses were the unifying element and since they were the way the plays were identified in terms of their presentation in the theatre. In early times, the depiction of the chorus was therefore the obvious and in practice probably the only way to represent the play. As time went on and actors had a larger part in the play, visual identification of the play by its chorus remained as an artistic convention. One example is the depiction of the

Figure 2.9 Attic red-figure calyx-krater with two members of
a bird chorus about a piper (Aristophanes, *Birds*), *c.* 414 BC. Malibu,
The J. Paul Getty Museum 82.AE.83

Birds of 414 BC on a vase in the Getty Museum (Figure 2.9).[27] Others are two
stone victory monuments of the fourth century, which, since they are public
monuments and must have been in tune with public attitudes, make it clear
that this was still an acceptable convention for the identification of a
comedy even in a period when the chorus no longer had a recognisable
part in the action of the play.[28] In these late depictions in marble reliefs, we
no longer see variation in dress, but they still keep the other major
conventions of identity of dance step and the lead by the piper. The other
point about these late depictions is that they show how strong the
convention must have become and what this of itself tells about the
importance given historically to the chorus and its appearance by the
audience.

There is more evidence still about the importance given to the staging of
the chorus by the audience. If we look first at the chorus from a *Birds* play
of about 480 on a jug in the British Museum (Figure 2.10a–b), we see on
the left the piper providing the music in standard fashion.[29] The birdman
immediately to the right is seen from his front whereas the other is seen
from the back: contrast the coarser feathers of the one on the right. The
arms on the one on the left are shown against the wings. He holds a strap
near the end of the wing and another runs round his arm at the elbow to

(a)   (b)

Figure 2.10a–b Attic black-figure oinochoe with bird chorus and piper, *c.* 480 BC.
London, British Museum B 509

help keep that part of the wing in place. Both men have red combs on their heads, large pointed noses and red beards. Both of them also have strokes of red running forward from the knee. These must be the birds' feet. While the men were dancing, the feet were above the ground, the birds were flying; when they came to rest, they must have knelt, so that the birds' feet were on the ground. Some of the details of the drawing of the right birdman are not well preserved, but we see the outside of the wings and surprisingly, through them, the outlines of the man's arms shown in added white. This strongly suggests that the wings were semi-transparent and lightweight, so that the material would have floated rather than flapped stiffly. All this gives us some idea of the care that went into the detail of costume. The care with which the vase-painter has shown it gives us a good indication of the care with which he, as an ordinary member of the audience, observed the detail. And it is detail which he thought his customer would like, even on a vase which is not of particularly high quality.

The British Museum Birds are different from some Birds on a vase in Berlin of about ten years later, and from those of Aristophanes 60–70 years later.[30] Chorus types were repeated over the years, just as elements of the

31

subject-matter could be taken over by one playwright from another, as we know from surviving texts of the later years of the fifth century. In the competitive arena of the Athenian theatre there was some pressure to think up new varieties of standard themes, but the comic playwrights also seem to have enjoyed playing about with themes brought up by others, modifying them, refining them, exposing their crudity or banality.[31] It is a process which also flatters the audience for their memory of the previous occasion, and when done explicitly (as it often is) it establishes a bond between audience and writer as a joke shared. This is also a practice which links very neatly with what we observed earlier in the chapter about the repetition of motifs in early tragedy.

Another good example is the two sets of Dolphin-Riders. On a splendid psykter in New York and painted by Oltos about 510 BC, six warriors ride dolphins (Figure 2.11).[32] From their mouths come the words *epi delphinos* (on a dolphin) and they are in a metre appropriate to the entry song of the chorus when it first comes into the theatre. The costume varies only in the shield devices: three different types of symposium vessel (cup, kantharos and volute-krater) alternating with whirligigs. Sifakis has pointed out a very neat idea in the conjunction of the shape of the vase and the subject-matter.[33] The psykter was designed to rest in a larger bowl or krater of cold

Figure 2.11 Attic red-figure psykter with chorus of dolphin-riders, *c.* 510 BC.
New York, Metropolitan Museum of Art L 1979.17.1

water, to keep its contents chilled. When full, its foot would rest on the bottom of the bowl, but as more of the wine was taken from it, it would float and so the figures on the dolphins would bob about over the surface of the water. The dolphin-riders have helmet, shield and a single spear. From about 20 years later we have another set of dolphin-riders on as many as six different vases.[34] While similar in many respects, the later chorusmen have corselets and helmets but no shields; they also have cloaks (unlike the earlier version) and two spears each rather than one (Figure 2.12a–b).[35] These differences are consistent throughout the series which seems to have been painted at a single date. That is they reflect a single play. The playwrights did the costume differently for the two occasions, but what from our point of view is more remarkable is that all six vases in the second set were decorated by different hands and yet they all got the details the same. It is at the same time good evidence for the painters' powers of observation

(a)   (b)

Figure 2.12a–b Attic black-figure lekythos from the Kerameikos cemetery at Athens, with piper and dolphin-riders, *c.* 480 BC. Athens, Kerameikos Museum 5671

but also for the fact that these details were thought to matter. The staging was reckoned and seen as a vitally important element in the playwright's attempt to win the prize.

Another point that we may note in passing is that although the vase-painters took trouble over the detail, the number of chorusmen they depicted did not matter. It was dictated by the space available on the vase and it cannot be used as evidence for the numbers of chorusmen present in the theatre.

With one possible exception, we do not have depictions of figures of comic actors on vases earlier than about 430 BC.[36] From then on they become increasingly common. The fact of their appearance, despite the continuing existence of the convention of identifying comedies by their choruses, is a sign that the public recognised an important change in the nature of comedy. The part played by actors in the totality of a performance is seen as increasingly crucial and interesting. They are something which the public can now relate to. The implication is that coherent plots were becoming more normal, a point which is in fact confirmed in the ancient literary sources.

In Athens on red-figure vases of the late fifth century we have no actors performing in scenes in the way which develops in other centres. Instead there are individual figures, seen as it were off-stage together with non-theatrical figures, even if some are shown wearing their masks and behaving in ways which suit their roles. We do however have actors acting in scenes on a series of jugs found in the area of the Athenian Agora and datable probably to the last quarter of the century.[37] They are a set of plain everyday earthenware jugs that were given polychrome decoration when they were presumably ordered as a special set for a celebration. They have scenes which, to judge by the appearance of the figures as well as the subject-matter, must derive from comedy: a man rowing a fish, a 'parasite' running to a party, two slaves running with meat on a spit (presumably also to a party), two figures labelled Dionysos and Phor ..., and a fragment of a scene from myth with Peleus and Neleus. These jugs show that the idea of representing comic scenes such as we find very soon afterwards on vases from Corinth, Olympia, Taranto, Metaponto and other centres was already under way. But for some reason which we cannot explain, the idea was never taken up in Athenian red-figure, at least on present evidence.

Other aspects of the depiction of comic figures on red-figure vases still await explanation, such as the heavy preponderance of these figures on jugs, and more particularly on the small choes where they associated with children. Indeed on a number of them, children seem to play at being comic actors.[38]

Another vitally important innovation occurs in the later fifth century in Athens and that is the introduction of terracotta figurines of actors. There are some isolated pieces, but best known is a carefully made series known

Figure 2.13 Terracotta figurines from Athens, comic actors, end of the fifth century BC. New York, Metropolitan Museum of Art, 13.225.13, 18 and 20

as the New York Group (see Figure 2.13).[39] The group is named after a set of fourteen figurines said to have been found in a grave in Athens and now in the Metropolitan Museum of Art. Others are associated with this set on grounds of style and the Group now comprises some twenty or so types.

They are mould-made figurines and most are known in multiple reproductions. They are solid (they come very early in the tradition of figurines made with back and front moulds). The early versions which came from fresh moulds are about 10–12 cm high and are characterised by very sharp and lively detail in the modelling which shows up costume and mask and such things as hair and beard very clearly. Typical are the carefully dotted *chitons* of the males. One might almost think they were taken from metal prototypes (and it is of course possible that they were). In practice some of the fine detail would have been less obvious since they were covered in white slip and then a coloured paint, but the bright colours would have added to their attractiveness: red-brown for the faces and hands of the men and slaves; pink for the women's; black, white or red hair depending on the character; yellow on dresses; blue on cloaks. This is what the characters in Aristophanes' later plays looked like. As is particularly obvious in a profile view, they had heavy padding on their bellies and backsides and contained within a body-suit that terminated at ankles and wrists. On the front was attached a leather *phallos* which on these figurines is normally shown as rolled up but on others and on a number of vase-paintings was left hanging

Figure 2.14 Attic terracotta figurine of young woman, probably earlier part of the fourth century BC but from the same series as Figure 2.13. Paris, Louvre N 4864

loose. This is the basic costume which was worn by all comic actors (whether playing males or females). Roles were then given by the particular mask and by the clothing although one does find characters (especially in vase-paintings) shown as stage naked (i.e. without any additional clothing). At this period male characters almost invariably had very short cloaks and tunics and the *phallos* was left exposed. Female characters wore longer dresses and cloaks which concealed it. The reason for all actors wearing the same basic costume was not simply one of convenience since they would have to take on different roles during the course of the play, but doubtless a more fundamental one of tradition, convention and, ultimately, religious practice. In fact the *phallos* and padding were to remain fundamental to comic costume for another 75 years despite the growing 'realism' of some aspects of theatrical depiction.

For our purposes we need to notice two other aspects of these terracotta figurines. The first is the standardisation of the characters and of the masks. The modest or shy young woman for example (Figure 2.14) is known in at least sixteen replicas which were probably being reproduced until the middle of the fourth century, and these replicas have been found in (and were perhaps produced in) a wide range of centres.[40] One could add to this number quite a few variants. This is therefore not a single character from a single play on a single performance, but a type who achieves popularity through appearances in many plays on many occasions. The same is true of most of the others. Mask types also become standardised (a number are repeated within the New York Group), so that the mask used for a slave or for a mature citizen, for an old father, a wife or a courtesan are instantly recognisable. They are carried from play to play – that is, the comedy is becoming a comedy of types and of characters. In this respect the archaeological evidence is demonstrating something which was less clear from our rather limited literary evidence. Aristophanes was either some-what old-fashioned or we have a very particular selection of his plays from the later years of the century. Others were moving more quickly towards the style of comedy we call Middle.[41]

The new vase-paintings and figurines are evidence that this new style of comedy was becoming enormously popular, and quite quickly. This is a theme we shall take up in the next chapter, but it is worth establishing the point in its chronological context and without the benefit of the hindsight that makes the situation more obvious. This new kind of comedy must have filled a need. In the context of late-fifth-century Athens, there was surely an element of escapism from the realities of the political and economic situation (realities which Aristophanes was in fact trying to get his audience to recognise). At the same time in the environment of the new thinking as represented by the sophists on the one hand and playwrights like Euripides on the other, the audience was being trained to appreciate greater nuances in the study of characters and of personal problems. And then we should remember that comedy was still a fairly self-referential activity and that the theatre audience was becoming ever more sophisticated in its appreciation of performance. Sophocles seems to have written plays for his favourite actors to accomplish roles which could properly be regarded as *tours de force*.[42] This goes hand in hand with what we learn of his abilities as a stage presenter and his skills in handling the audience. We learn from other sources that tragic actors were becoming more emotive in their handling of roles, or, as more conservative critics put it, playing to the gallery. The gallery must have liked it. Theatre was reaching a new level of popularity. It is in this context that we may consider the function of these figurines. We are on uncertain ground since by far the largest part of them have been discovered without any record of their context. It is fair to assume that most have been found in graves, but then in making any assessment we also have to bear in mind the accident of the archaeological record. Excavation of graves has been more popular and more possible than excavation of housing areas. We therefore do not have many figurines from houses, although at Olynthos, destroyed in 348 BC and one of the very few urban sites in Greece at all fully excavated, a good number were found. One might guess that they were acquired as souvenirs of performances, whether as individual pieces reminding one of particular characters, or in whatever combinations suited a particular play. Possessing such figurines would increase one's consciousness and attention the next time one saw that character on the stage. In a way they must have been not unlike the cards that American children acquire of their baseball and football stars. They become fans. The figurines were made for fans and at the same time encouraged people to be fans. In the grave, they must have been included as favourite objects and have symbolised happy times, and of course they must have evoked the world of the god for whom the plays were produced, Dionysos.

The remaining category or genre of classical theatre is satyr-play. It is also the most difficult since we only have one complete play (Euripides' *Cyclops*) and part of another (Sophocles' *Ichneutae*) on which to base any judgement of form and style. There is also some reason to suspect that the genre, perhaps even more than tragedy and comedy, changed quite markedly during the course of the fifth century. Certainly the most famous practitioners were the early playwrights Pratinas and Aeschylus, and it may be that as a dramatic form and as a style of presentation it was more vigorous in the earlier part of the fifth century than later. This is very much the impression one has from representations on vases.[43]

Satyr-plays were presented by tragic playwrights as a fourth play after the set of three tragedies, and the theme might or might not be related to that of the tragedies. While there has been a lot of speculation about their function, in the absence of a complete set one simply cannot know much about the interplay between the various parts of a set, and given that there were so many possibilities in terms of echoes or contrasts of subject-matter, style and presentation, it doubtless varied from playwright to playwright. What does seem fairly clear is that they were semi-comic, likely to parody the commonly accepted versions of myths, and that the playwright had the satyr-characters, through the creation of a rather 'carnival'-like atmosphere, act a sort of 'world upside down', in which the audience, after the seriousness and tension of the tragedies, could perhaps identify with their subversions of the norm. And doubtless, as in other contexts, such temporary and controlled subversions and reversals served the purposes of the established order and in their way underlined the aims of the tragedies.[44]

Satyr-plays therefore straddled the serious and the comic, and it is interesting to see that over the fifth century as a whole the audience reaction as we see it in representations on vases is in parallel with the reactions to tragedy and comedy. The representations divide themselves fairly neatly into what one could call the literal and the interpretive, and so use both the conventions for representing comedy and those for tragedy. We have pictures of satyr-players as chorusmen in action wearing their tights and their masks, seen objectively; but we also have pictures which are interpreted through the conventions, so that we see not men dressed as satyrs, but 'real' satyrs. The latter present the same problems of detection and interpretation as pictures deriving from tragedy, except, perhaps, that the traditional range of satyrs' activities as seen in vase-painting is much more limited than that of humans, and so there is some attraction in the principle put forward by Jahn, Buschor and Simon that scenes which fall outside the normal scope of satyrs' activities are quite likely inspired by the theatre.[45] The principle is the more likely to work because their normal range of activities is so much more restricted than that of humans and/or mythical figures, and Erika Simon has given a number of convincing examples of the period of Aeschylus. A good case which is typical of the vigour of early satyr-play is the well-known cup by the Brygos Painter of about 490–480 BC in the British Museum. Iris has stolen an offering from the altar in the sanctuary of Dionysos and the satyrs are attempting to reclaim it. We see the same theme on two other vases, on a cup in Boston of about 510 BC and on a cup-skyphos in Berlin of about 460 BC.[46] We probably have to assume three different plays which re-use this theme, something which is perhaps hardly surprising given the repetition of motifs we have seen in early tragedy and the recurrence of chorus-types we have evidence for in comedy. It is difficult to reconstruct the context of a scene like this, and it is a problem we often have. The scene chosen by the vase-painter is perhaps a key scene, a scene that made the most impact because of a shocking quality, or a scene that had become a favourite with the audience which could be inserted by the playwright into a play with quite a different story-line. The version in Boston includes a satyr carrying a light shield which the other two do not.

There are many other scenes of satyrs with armour, some of which, because of their costume, are explicit in their theatrical derivation. A popular theme, especially in later years, is that of satyrs stealing the arms of Herakles (his bow, club and lionskin) while he is helpless holding up the world and unable to let go as Atlas goes to fetch the golden apples.[47] Boldness and effrontery where there is no immediate threat is typical of their stage character (as is the converse). In the earlier fifth century their use of armour is perhaps to be linked to the Battle of Gods and Giants where they served as Dionysos' assistants, but we rarely see them in actual battle, partly because they were better at pretence than action, partly of course because one would hardly have the Battle on stage.

Some themes are fairly obvious because they appear to be direct parodies of well-known myths, such as the Medea theme of the restoration of youth through boiling in a magic cauldron which we see on a bell-krater of about 460 BC found at Numana and now in Ancona.[48] On the front of the vase a woman leads a blind and bent old satyr with white hair towards the cauldron to which she gestures with her left hand. On the other side we see presumably the same figure, now a small child-like figure, being played with

Figure 2.15 Attic red-figure hydria with council of elder satyrs before the Sphinx (Aeschylus, *Sphinx*), *c.* 467 BC. Tokyo, coll. Fujita

(a)

(b)

Figure 2.16a–b Attic red-figure cup with young man and satyrs, *c.* 430 BC.
Cambridge, Fitzwilliam Museum GR 2.1977

by a satyr while a maenad stands with arm outstretched as if asking 'what's this?'. This is a clear case where, as in scenes deriving from tragedy, the vase-painter has represented the further reality of what was represented by the performance rather than the stage action. There is also the splendid Fujita hydria (Figure 2.15) which Erika Simon has shown represents Aeschylus' *Sphinx* of 467 BC.[49] Here the derivation from the theatre is clear icono-graphically since the painter has preserved the image of the chorus of old satyrs acting like the council of Theban elders in attempting to work out the riddle of the Sphinx. A tantalising example from the later 430s is a late fifth-century cup by the Codrus Painter in Cambridge (Figure 2.16a–b).[50] On the outside of the vase is a line of cloaked satyrs carrying objects which belong (or have belonged) to the elegant young man near the head of the group. The theme should fall within the category well known from satyr-plays of *kourotrophia* or nurturing of the young. One may speculate that the young man has now grown up (note the sandals which would suit an *ephebe*) and that he is about to leave his foster parents. They appear reluctant to see him go and carry the symbols of his childhood and youth – lyre, oil-bottles, discus, pet bird, writing tablet, strigil, knucklebone bag, mug – and perhaps try to tempt him with them; but he ignores them, doubtless because he now has important tasks to undertake. To judge by his appearance, the young man may well be Theseus, but it is difficult to see the depiction as relating to any known play.[51] A somewhat similar theme involving *kourotrophia* is to be found on the roughly contemporary skyphos in Bari which has on one

Figure 2.17 Attic red-figure hydria with piper and satyr-chorus building throne, *c.* 480–470 BC. Boston, Museum of Fine Arts 03.788

side a cloaked *papposilenos* as *paidagogos* in pursuit of a boy who runs away on the other side, but there are no grounds for supposing derivation from a common source.[52]

The figures on this cup are shown as 'real'. Examples of satyr-players shown literally, in their tights, are also common. One of the best was painted by the Leningrad Painter, about 480–470 BC (Figure 2.17).[53] On the right is the piper in his elaborate costume and behind him a man who may be the producer or the playwright. In front of him five satyrs of the chorus dance vigorously and begin to erect the various parts of a throne to sit on the low platform to the right of the scene. The painter has made the artificiality of the masks evident as well as the typical drawers with a tail attached at the back and a *phallos* at the front.

An interesting case is the calyx-krater in Vienna by the Altamura Painter of about 470–460 BC (Figure 2.18).[54] It has a Return of Hephaistos with the lame god on foot in close company with Dionysos; they look like their real selves, not actors acting, but the satyr who leads them and grandly plays the *kithara* wears the drawers of a satyr-player. It is a nice dilemma: the painter depicts a stage performance and so shows the satyr-player for what he is (as one might just have guessed from his use of the *kithara*, the virtuoso's instrument, rather than the more normal lyre), but the gods are shown as 'real', as they would have been for tragedy. If one thinks about it, the

Figure 2.18 Attic red-figure calyx-krater with satyr playing *kithara* and leading Return of Hephaistos, *c.* 470–460 BC. Vienna, Kunsthistorisches Museum IV 985

painter could hardly have shown them otherwise. In earlier depictions of the myth, Hephaistos, who was lame from birth, returned to Olympos on the back of a mule. It may well be that, as others have suggested, to have Hephaistos return on foot derives from satyr-play – there is a well-known law to the effect that donkeys or mules would be at their most perverse when expected to behave compliantly.[55] This is a case where depictions derived from the practicalities of the theatre may well have come to influence depictions of the myth in general. That is, it is an iconography which was picked up by the artist from the stage and then continued because it creates an attractive composition in artistic terms. This then becomes the way one thinks of the myth. It may also become the way the audience thinks of the myth, independently of the artist, because the stage version is the way *they* have become used to visualising it.

As the fifth century goes on, few if any literally depicted satyrs are shown in the action of the play; they are presented in moments before or after the performance. The situation is, however, complicated by the painters' habit of making a figure who wears his mask take on the character or act the part, regardless of his surroundings (as we have seen above for tragic chorusmen, or like the one on the Pronomos Vase, Figure 2.19). A good example is the set of fragments of a red-figure bell-krater in Bonn (Figure 2.20) where the figures act like satyrs although they are clearly not performing – the piper holds his pipes away from his mouth.[56] They are also useful evidence for the costuming of satyr-play about 425 BC. This growing tendency to depict satyr-play in its intended reality rather than the actuality of performance is an interesting comment on the changing perception of the genre. It seems to suggest that early satyr-play was not only more vigorous than it became later

Figure 2.19 Attic red-figure volute-krater from Ruvo with the piper Pronomos and the cast of a satyr-play in the Sanctuary of Dionysos, late fifth century BC.
Naples 3240

Figure 2.20 Attic red-figure bell-krater fragments from Athens with piper and satyr-players, *c.* 425 BC. Bonn, Akademisches Kunstmuseum 1216.183+

(something which seems abundantly clear from the vase-paintings) but that it was also more patently comic or burlesque. The literary sources too suggest that there was a perception of a major shift: even as late as Pausanias in the second century AD and Diogenes Laertius in the early third, neither of whom was particularly interested in theatre, there is preserved a commonplace observation that Aeschylus was the most popular of all the writers of satyr-play, and although the one would give second place to Aristias and his son Pratinas, and the other to Achaios, all belong in the earlier part of the fifth century.[57] With all this in mind, it is the more interesting that the one case from our admittedly meagre surviving texts of satyr-play where there is indisputable play with the dramatic illusion of the performance is from Aeschylus, from his *Isthmiastae*. The satyrs carry likenesses of themselves. Lines 5–21 of Fr.1 may be translated:

> Look and see whether this image could be more like me, this Daedalic likeness: it only lacks a voice. Look at them. Do you see? Come, yes, come. I bring this offering to the god to decorate his house, this finely painted votive. It would give my mother trouble. If she could see it, she would certainly turn and shriek, thinking it me, the son she brought up. He is so like me.
>   Look, then, upon the house of the Lord of the Sea, the Earth-Shaker, and each of you fasten up the likeness of his handsome form, a messenger, a voiceless herald to keep off travellers ... it will halt strangers on their way by its terrifying look ...[58]

The only objects which fit this description are masks[59] – thus, all they cannot do is speak, they are so like the carriers of the objects that their mothers could not tell the difference (of course, since they are reproductions of the masks the carriers are wearing), they are finely painted, they will

45

be placed about a temple (as is in fact normal at the Temple of Dionysos after a victorious performance in the Theatre), and they will frighten off strangers (a known use for satyr-masks as a kind of bogey motif and one that becomes quite common in later art[60]). The humour of the situation rests in the audience's recognition of all this, in their seeing the chorusmen as players wearing masks, and therefore in their recognition that the dramatic illusion is being stretched to near breaking point. This is probably as far as one could go in satyr-play.

A final piece of evidence that we may use in this section is a recently discovered red-figure vase of the earlier part of the fourth century (Figure 2.21).[61] It was made in Taranto but reflects an Athenian comedy performed there, a play that may have been written in the later years of the fifth century. It has two men labelled as producers or sponsors (*choregoi*) who are presided over by someone dressed, masked and named as a slave (Pyrrhias), who stands on an overturned basket. (His tunic [*exomis*] is, however, very fancily decorated for a slave and should be read as indicating that in this scene he has somehow or other achieved a higher role.) The producer on our left gives instructions to a young man labelled Aigisthos. The first point we may notice is that the Aigisthos figure is shown as 'real', that is he is depicted according to the conventions of tragedy – by contrast with the other three who are shown as actors acting in the convention normal for

Figure 2.21 Tarentine red-figure bell-krater with comic scene showing a slave (Pyrrhias) and two *choregoi* with a figure of Aigisthos, *c.* 380 BC. New York, coll. Fleischman F 93

46

comedy. Their dress is that typical of actors in the theatre of Aristophanes and his contemporaries (compare the terracottas, Figures 2.13, 2.14). The subject-matter of the scene is reminiscent of *Frogs* since here again we seem to be dealing with two generations of theatre: the figure on the right (who appears to be sulking) has dark hair and should be of younger middle-age, but the one on the left is an old man with white hair.[62] It may therefore be significant that he is instructing Aigisthos, the lover of Clytemnestra and conspirator in the murder of Agamemnon. He is concerned with the presentation of something related to the *Oresteia*, a sequence known to us from Aeschylus' plays of 458 BC and a subject that was almost certainly regarded as old-fashioned by the late fifth century. The last decade or so of the fifth century, and especially the latter years of the Peloponnesian War, was a period when there was considerable looking back to earlier days. It is a common theme with Aristophanes. Euripides' *Bacchae* picks up an early theme and deliberately remodels it. Lykourgos themes reappear in contemporary art in contexts which seem to have something to do with the theatre. Archaism now appears for the first time in Greek art. This looking back to the old days must in part have been a response to contemporary hardships and disillusionment, but in part it must have been because people realised that things had changed in a way that meant there was no real going back.

Fifth-century theatre was in a constant state of flux. I have put some emphasis on the growing sophistication of the audience, and the evolution of a range of techniques of staging and performance. The introduction of the second and third actors in tragedy must also have had profound effects on the styles of play and performance. Then there was the steadily emerging importance of the actor as a figure distinct from the playwright and as a performer well worth following in his own right. The critical phases of this development seem to have taken place within a very particular environment of community activity. In one sense and another, the performances were staged by and for the audience, and the evolution of new techniques was carried out by playwrights who at the same time shared and competed with each other with the encouragement of this audience.

Throughout the fifth century the three main genres as categories of play were constantly establishing their styles and territories. There is much to be said for the suggestion that it was only during the third quarter of the century that Comedy developed the form which we know from Aristophanes.[63] One can quite reasonably argue that it was the influence of tragedy that prompted the more careful and extensive use of actors and more fully structured plots. This would certainly accord well with the first appearance of comic actors (as distinct from chorus) in vase-paintings in the 430s and in terracotta figurines somewhat later. It is quite possible that this new territory as defined by the newer playwrights of Comedy included areas previously covered by satyr-play. Satyr-play in its turn may have been becoming more respectable. It is tempting to link the maintenance of dramatic pretence in the only complete satyr-play to survive, the *Cyclops*, with the observation that in the later fifth century literally depicted satyr-players are shown only outside the theatre, not in performance. One might speculate that this is an indication of a shift in the genre and the public perception of it. Compared with the wilder days of Pratinas and the young Aeschylus, satyr-play had lost something of its overtly comic, burlesque edge. And there were occasions now when the public did not miss having a satyr-play at the end of the set of four; one could have a lightweight tragedy instead. Yet it is clear from the archaeological evidence that in the fourth century and even later satyrs and satyr-plays remained popular. Tragedy at the same time was becoming rather less serious, less heavy and less concerned with the issues of state. What was happening was something of a convergence. Historically this phenomenon is understandable given that theatre as a formal performance art had been going through an experimental period and a process of establishment, and that although all three genres had from the beginning shared the idea of having a chorus as a fundamental element, the other factors which made them up had been so very different in both style and intent. It is also our perception. What is clear from the material evidence is that the public not only remained very conscious of the differences but that it gave theatre a growingly important place in its mind and in its life.

3

THE LATE FIFTH AND THE FOURTH CENTURIES

Some twenty-five years ago H.D.F. Kitto laid the groundwork for any surmise on the nature of fourth-century tragedy by attempting to analyse just what it is that Aristotle complains about when he discusses tragedy, and then by comparing that with what we know from extant plays to have been the case in the fifth century.[1] What seems abundantly clear is that the audience in the fourth century demanded a different style of serious play. There was no longer any interest in (or, at least on Aristotle's part, appreciation of) plays which, like those of Aeschylus, Sophocles and earlier Euripides, were concerned with the large questions of man's place in the universe, his relationship to the gods and his responsibilities within the framework of divine and human society. Somehow this was all gone, and there went with it, one would suppose, the notion of the dramatic poet as an educator of society – as Aristophanes was lamenting with the *Frogs* in 404 BC. Aristotle was writing the *Poetics*, our main source for his views, not long after the middle of the fourth century BC. That he no longer recognised those values or ideas is a remarkable comment on the changes in society during the intervening years.

For Aristotle, Euripides' *Iphigeneia in Tauris* was a model for what he approved of and that is a play which in our view comes closest to the sort of thing commonly seen on television, the sort of play that we do not regard as really serious theatre. One reason why Aristotle liked it was because the truth was revealed before Iphigeneia could kill her brother Orestes, as she surely would have done. It also seems to have been the case more generally towards the end of the fifth century that there was growing use of divine intervention as a means to resolve deadlocks just before the end of the play. The most dramatic way for a writer to do this was not simply by having the appropriate god appear on stage but by having the god come down through the air on the device called a crane. The comic writer Antiphanes has some marvellous lines mocking the tragedian's easy life: 'then when they run out of things to say and quite happily give up on the action, they raise the crane like a finger and the audience is satisfied'.[2] Even allowing for comic exaggeration, the point must have been credible, and the implication is that so-called tragedies were relying more and more on complications of the plot rather than larger issues, on coincidence as a mechanism for creating and solving crises, on tension and its release, and on using these kinds of means to play with the emotions. These are also to become techniques employed by Menander for New Comedy. Aristotle also tells us quite explicitly that writers were now more restrictive in their choice of myth. They tended to stick to those which included the right kind of plot.[3] This seems to be completely at one with the emerging picture: the role of myth had changed radically in the interim. Myth now is increasingly at the service of a plot which is dealing with more fully three-dimensional characters (as in later Euripides). Indeed Agathon (whom one could describe as a trendy right-wing writer of the late fifth century) even composed a tragedy of wholly invented characters.[4] The 'political' role of tragedy has largely gone. Aristotle himself makes the point (*Poetics* 50 b 7ff.) that the older writers made their characters speak *politikos* whereas the more modern have them speak *rhetorikos*. The poet and his audience have become interested in the presentation and dramatic action (which is what I think *rhetorikos* ultimately means here) and with the individual and his or her motivation and concerns. This must have been what the audience, the Athenian public, wanted. This kind of theatre itself involved a degree of escapism, both as a religious festival in which a person honoured and joined the god, and as an event in which a person came as a spectator at a performance and then identified with the action on stage. It is presumably the coincidence of factors such as these together with others such as the growing professionalism of actors and the audience's appreciation of that professionalism that made theatre more and more popular.

Our knowledge of tragedy, its performance and impact in the fourth century is patchy at best. As a generality it seems clear that the staging of old tragedies (introduced on a regular basis in 386 BC) was regarded as at least as important as that of new, and that the work of Euripides was generally more popular than that of his two older colleagues Sophocles and Aeschylus.[5] For example there is inscriptional evidence that in 341, 340 and 339 BC a play of Euripides was staged at Athens alongside new productions. The actor Neoptolemos won with *Iphigeneia* and *Orestes* on the first two occasions, and the actor Nikostratos won with a play of which the name is not preserved on the third. We have references in the literary sources to the performances of others. In some respects better evidence is provided by references or allusions in the literary sources and the assumptions they make about knowledge of fifth-century tragedy. Aristotle refers to five plays of Aeschylus, twelve of Sophocles and twenty of Euripides. He may of course have known these plays from written texts, and he was in any case writing for a sophisticated and limited public. The same would be true of Plato. More useful because designed for a broader public are references in the orators. Lycurgus quotes Euripides' *Erechtheus*, Aeschines the *Stheneboia* and

Phoenix, Demosthenes three lines from *Phoenix* and sixteen lines from Sophocles' *Antigone*. This kind of evidence is never straightforward because a speaker may wish to make particular points in particular circumstances, but an orator needed the sympathy of his audience. There would be no point unless the allusion was acceptable to a fairly broad cross-section of the people he was addressing. An orator could hardly assume that all members of his audience would have read these plays: they are far more likely to have known them through performance. *Erechtheus*, *Stheneboia* and *Phoenix* do not survive, and yet we have other hints, for example from scenes on vases, that the first two at least were popular as performances.

From the late fourth or more likely the early third century BC are two recently published inscriptions from Delphi.[6] Both seem to record lines from tragedy, the longer one probably a prologue by Euripides or a fourth-century follower. They were inscribed on what were already fragmentary pieces of marble and seem to have been trial- or test-pieces. They are therefore evidence for the popularity and knowledge of tragedy by an apprentice stonemason at this period, and of what seemed to him appropriate text when practising his letters.

Toward the end of the fourth century, Menander's comedies make frequent reference to (usually Euripidean) tragedy by way of quotation, allusion or echo of situations, exploiting them to add a level of meaning to his own creations. For example, Menander's *Sikyonioi* contained a quotation of the messenger-speech in Euripides' *Orestes*, and the brother–sister theme of *Perikeiromene* seems to have evoked Euripides' *Iphigeneia in Tauris*. That this was picked up at a popular level is demonstrated by the fact that some wall-paintings found fairly recently in Ephesos seem to have paired them by placing a key scene from one next to a key scene from the other.[7] The wall-paintings themselves are of the later second century AD, but they go back to Early Hellenistic originals and other such pairings of tragedies and comedies suggest that these sorts of linkages could originate in that period also.

All this said, however, we almost certainly tend to underestimate the popularity of contemporary tragedy. Carcinus, who is mostly remembered for one bad performance,[8] wrote some 160 plays and is quoted along with Aeschylus and Euripides by the old slave in Menander's *Aspis* (line 417). Astydamas, who won his first victory in 372 BC, is credited with having written some 240 plays and was given the unusual honour of a bronze statue in the theatre (the base is still visible). Chaeremon was also quoted in the passage just mentioned. Another passage from him which happens to be preserved gives something of a glimpse of contemporary style: it is a remarkably voyeuristic description of some girls resting after a Dionysiac dance, their clothing pulled apart.[9]

Another possible source on fourth-century tragedy and its popularity lies in contemporary vase-paintings, but it is a source fraught with difficulty.

With only the occasional exception, the habit of showing the myth rather than the performance continues, and it is very difficult to find any representation that gives a clear idea of the play as it was staged. Indeed in many cases it is difficult to be absolutely sure that a performance lies behind any given representation of a myth.[10] A case in point is *Iphigeneia in Tauris*. We have pictures showing aspects of the story on one Athenian, five Tarentine and three Campanian vases.[11] Two may be excluded from the discussion since they fall outside the pattern of the rest: the Campanian bell-krater in the Louvre shows what should probably be regarded as the opening of the play, and the Campanian neck-amphora in St Petersburg seems to show the end, with Orestes, Pylades and Iphigeneia escaping. It is likely that neither shows a stage performance (although the Louvre vase is often used as if it illustrated a stage building, which it cannot be). The others show the striking moment, the moment before the recognition of Orestes by his sister Iphigeneia. None of these, either, shows any evidence of direct inspiration from stage performance, but simply the historico-mythical event, and the background of the story is usually signified by some hint of the temple in which Iphigeneia was priestess (a role emphasised by the door-key she carries), and she often carries the tablet containing the letter and thus the impetus necessary to the recognition. Yet the popularity of both play and depiction cannot be coincidental, and a likely explanation lies in the scene's suitability as decoration on the vases concerned. As a message of hope and family reunion, against the odds in unpropitious circumstances, it is an obvious and attractive one. The South Italian vases involved were all found in graves and were designed for the grave, and there are other grounds for supposing that in many cases the decoration of funerary vases in South Italy was created with either the celebration of the deceased or his/her happiness in the other world as the prime concern.[12] This usage must therefore qualify their value as an indication of what myths were popular in theatrical performance.

Another case in point is to be found in depictions of Niobe, the iconography of which has been analysed by Trendall.[13] Whether or not they are to be related to the *Niobe* of Aeschylus (a point on which Trendall is rightly hesitant), the impact of the scene is evident. A typical version is that on a Campanian red-figure hydria in Sydney (Figure 3.1).[14] Niobe stands within what has to be her own funerary monument, slowly turning to stone – as the white on the lower part of her body shows. Her aged father Tantalos kneels in supplication before her, his sceptre lying loose against his shoulder. The old man is supported by an attendant. A woman, perhaps the children's nurse, sits in distress on the steps. In the front of the structure are various tomb-offerings. Above, to either side, are the gods immediately responsible, Apollo and Artemis. The hybristic side of Niobe, whose boasting about her fertility led to her children's slaughter by Apollo and Artemis, seems to have been played down here. She is a mother in distress

Figure 3.1 Campanian red-figure hydria with Niobe at her grave being turned to stone, third quarter of the fourth century BC. Sydney, Nicholson Museum 71.01

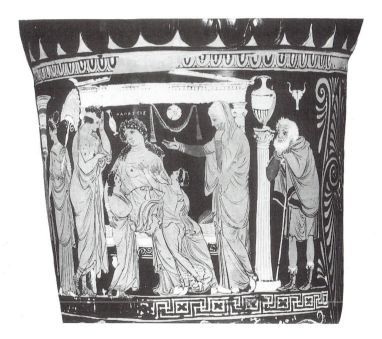

Figure 3.2 Tarentine red-figure loutrophoros with Alcestis on her death-bed, third quarter of the fourth century BC. Basle S 21

at the death of her children. The gods are answering her prayer to be turned to stone. By her death she goes to join her children.[15]

Several other popular scenes fall into this category, such as Alcestis and Electra. Alcestis was a paradigm of the good and loving wife.[16] Her husband Admetos was destined to die but the Fates were persuaded to allow someone else to take his place. Because she loved him, Alcestis accepted this privilege and we have scenes of her on her deathbed, and weeping children about her (Figure 3.2).[17] On the right an anguished family retainer or *paidagogos* watches the scene. He will report on it later. After her death, however, Herakles went and rescued her from the Underworld, and she was reunited with her family. To have this scene on a funerary vase therefore had its point, and Alcestis continues to be used as a funerary motif as late as the second century AD when the theme is referred to on a tombstone from Odessos as well as on a number of Roman sarcophagi.[18]

Electra thinks her brother dead but meets him at their father's tomb.[19] Being reunited at the grave of one's father must, as a scene, have had a compulsive attraction and it is by a long way the most popular of these themes (with over fifty examples). Beyond them, however, there are very many similar scenes where the mythological merge into non-mythological scenes at the grave. This is to be seen in two Campanian red-figure vases by the Libation Painter which Trendall has usefully illustrated side by side.[20] Both have similarly structured scenes at a tomb, the one with a young woman seated on the steps and holding a hydria while a young man with spear and shield approaches on the left. The other has the young woman approaching with wreath and fan (a hydria rests on the step) while a young man without armour stands nearby. Both have an additional young woman nearby (attendant?). The second vase has nothing to link it to the Electra story: the woman does not hold the urn and the young man has no special characteristics. The first vase has elements which seem to be derived from the Electra story since the young woman sits on the tomb with the urn and the young man has armour. As Trendall points out, however, 'Pylades is not present and it may be no more than a generic representation of the kind which appears frequently on the vases in this group.' The depictions of life, myth and theatre merge imperceptibly. So too do the thought-processes which lie behind the popular attitude to the motif. The myth and its representation on stage are adapted for use for this other purpose.[21]

In other cases we catch only a glimpse of stories and plays, the details of which are obscure to us. A good example is one which may be derived from *Melanippe the Wise* of Euripides, which is known to us from one vase (Figure 3.3).[22] In the lower register the key position is taken by the faithful retainer, the herdsman, who holds out to the old king Hellen, the heroine's grandfather, a skin in which lie two infants wrapped in swaddling clothes. They are Melanippe's children, twin sons, by the god Poseidon, and the herdsman must be reporting their discovery, abandoned in the fields where

Figure 3.3 Tarentine red-figure volute-krater with the herdsman producing
the twin sons of Melanippe, third quarter of the fourth century BC.
Geneva, private collection

they had apparently been nurtured by a bull and a cow. Melanippe stands
to the right, obviously in great distress, knowing that she will be found out,
and she is supported by her old nurse. To the left stand her father Aiolos
with his sceptre, and Kretheus, her half-brother, with a horse.[23] All the
figures in the lower register are labelled. Above, as so often in such scenes,
is a gathering of gods, some of whom take an interest in the events below,
others not: from the left, Artemis, Apollo, Athena (in the centre),
Aphrodite with Eros, and Poseidon with his trident, making a gesture of
speech. Above them are stars.

Whether or not the play behind this picture is Euripides', the herdsman
and Hellen seem to reflect a theatrical origin in their costume, with the
under-tunic which covers their arms to the wrist, reddish-purple for the
herdsman, white for Hellen. The former also has very elaborate boots for

55

his station in life, but the style (if not the material) of his cloak is, by the conventions of the theatre, in keeping with his simple rural origin. The painter gives no hint of masks, or even of theatrical costume for the other figures in the lower register.

Among other unusual stories likely to reflect themes of contemporary tragedy, we have two vases by the Darius Painter, datable *c.* 340–330 BC, showing the myth of Anios and his daughters.[24] It is a fairly obscure story and until recently recognised in art only in a marble relief in Delos dating to the second or first century BC.[25] Anios was a son of Apollo and king of Delos. He himself had three daughters, Elais, Spermo and Oino, on whom Dionysos had conferred the power of raising oil, grain and wine respectively.[26] Although there seem to have been several variants in the detail of the story, the main thrust seems to have been that the Greeks needed additional supplies during the siege of Troy and sought them from Anios and his daughters. What we see on the vases is Anios seated on an altar approached by a king who must be Menelaos. Anios would hardly sit on an altar unless he were under severe threat or pressure, and the threat must come from Menelaos and the Greek forces. One would guess that this reflects the dramatic tension of the play. The daughters are characterised by attributes in the form of the commodities they were able to produce. The Darius Painter had a fondness for depicting rare myths and it is reasonable to suppose that his source for this material was the theatre.[27]

What these vases are giving us is not so much evidence for the manner of performance of tragedy in the fourth century (and particularly in Taranto where the majority were manufactured) but an indication of the popular themes in tragedy. The richness and variety of the material shows us that, from the popular point of view at least, tragic theatre was anything but impoverished. They also demonstrate how little we know, even of the classic tragedians, let alone of fourth-century writers. There is other evidence that the Greeks of South Italy, and especially the Tarentines and the Syracusans, were addicted to theatre. Theatre must have been the major source of popular culture, a source of poetry, music, dance and enjoyment as well as an emotional escape that was not restricted to the aristocratic or wealthy segment of the population (as was symposion poetry). The importance of theatre to its audience is underlined by the way that themes of the tragedies, and particularly their great moments, seem to have become points of reference in their lives and so on into their rituals, not least at those key periods of emotional crisis such as the death of a member of the family.

Later Greek literature abounds in anecdotes about the emotional factor in presentation.[28] For example both Aelian (*VH* xiv, 40) and Plutarch (*Moralia* 334A) tell a story of Alexander of Pherai, who had a reputation in antiquity for being the worst sort of tyrant, watching a tragic actor and being moved to pity through enjoyment of the performance. He suddenly jumped up and rushed from the theatre saying it would be a terrible thing if he, who had been responsible for the slaughter of so many citizens, should be seen to weep over the sufferings of Hecuba and Polyxena. The story is attached to Theodoros, the distinguished tragic actor of the earlier half of the fourth century, and the date should be in the second quarter of the century. What matters here is not the truth of the story but the assumption that Theodoros stirred people to tears. Aulus Gellius (*Noctes Atticae* 6.5) reports an anecdote about the great actor Polos whose career covered the later part of the fourth century. His son had died some time earlier and so when he came to give a performance as Electra in Sophocles' play, he took the urn with his son's remains and held them as he played the part of Electra weeping over those of Orestes, giving a totally moving performance through the projection of his genuine emotion.

The attractiveness of the emotional element in tragedy is of course emphasised (from his own point of view) by Aristotle, who was disturbed by it. We have further evidence from the vases of the impact of the stirring moments. Many of the scenes on Tarentine vases which appear to have some reasonably direct connection with tragedy include a figure of a *paidagogos*, an old balding man, normally, who is a messenger in the scene and is or has been a guardian or old retainer to one of the key participants and his/her family. Very often he stands slightly to the side of the action as depicted, and he has his fingers raised in the gesture of speech or clutches

Figure 3.4a–b Tarentine red-figure calyx-krater with the punishment of Dirce, probably after the account in Euripides, *Antiope*, third quarter of the fourth century BC. Melbourne, coll. Geddes, A 5:4

his head in agony and disbelief. It is noticeable too that he is regularly present at scenes of action and violence of a kind that by convention and practicality were not represented on the Greek stage. That is, he gives messenger speeches, reporting on the unseen action of a story, an action which is then envisaged by the vase-painter and depicted on the vase.[29] We have seen him observing the death of Alcestis in Figure 3.2, and he took a key part in the Melanippe scene, Figure 3.3. Another example is found on a vase by the Underworld Painter in a private collection in Melbourne (Figure 3.4a–b).[30] It has an *Antiope* scene, probably inspired by Euripides' lost play. What the vase-painter perceived his customers wanted was not representation of the action of the play as staged, but a visualisation of the terrible punishment of Dirce as reported during the play. She is shown lying dead on the ground, where she was thrown from the back of the bull. One of her companions runs off terrified to the left, while a Fury and a herdsman and his dog lead the frantic bull away. The herdsman is no ordinary figure, but as the snake in his hair shows, a personification of Oistros, raging madness, who provoked the creature. Below, as a reminder, lie the *thyrsos* and tympanon she was carrying as a follower of Dionysos, the activity which prompted her death. In the upper register there is in the centre Lykos (husband of Dirce, who had imprisoned Antiope) sitting in refuge on an altar while Hermes prevents Antiope's twin sons, Amphion and Zethos from attacking him.

The role and function of the *paidagogos* in the art and theatre of the period is a fascinating one. It was a continuing convention of Greek tragedy that violent action was by and large not shown on stage (although there are occasions in later fifth-century drama when there was aggressive, physical handling of individuals).[31] By way of explanation one can point to the practical considerations of performance on an open stage, and the problem of coping with dead bodies and wreckage, or of having raging bulls or crashing chariots in the theatre space. More important is the orality of the theatrical tradition of tragedy in which the spoken word was elaborated by gesture and movement, not the other way around. Yet the audience, like any other, was not without a taste for violence, but it indulged that taste by listening to description of violence – and the description could be far more gruesome and chilling than any actuality it was possible to present on stage. Descriptions were developed in so-called messenger speeches, and we have good evidence from the literary sources of the way that they were delivered as *tours de force* by the top actors.[32] They were delivered by these servants, old retainers, *paidagogoi*, who by their position tended to know both those who had suffered the violence and their families to whom they retailed it, and thus participated directly in the emotion of the occasion. Vase-painting, on the other hand, had traditionally had a function as a starting-point for discussion and description, and had traditionally shown the key moment. In the cases we have been examining, it continues this function by showing not what happened on stage but the crucial action, as recounted by the messenger. Whether the figure raises his fingers in the gesture of speech or clutches his head in agony reflects the way the vase-painter thought of him, as recounting the events we see depicted, or experiencing them. This usage first appears about 360–350 BC in Apulian vase-painting, on the name-vase of the Lycurgus Painter, and is particularly popular in the work of the Darius Painter and his associates in the 330s.

The point is reinforced by a fine calyx-krater which recently appeared on the market.[33] It was made in Taranto in the middle of the fourth century. On one side (which was clearly thought of as the reverse) is an outline drawing of a satyr. On the front (Figure 3.5), drawn very carefully in polychrome technique, is the figure of a *paidagogos*, again with his fingers raised in the gesture of speech. The presence of the satyr on the other side of the vase seems to confirm the point that he stands for tragedy, he is what typifies tragedy in the mind of the audience, he is what the audiences find most attractive.

The messengers of tragedy in some respects have counterparts in the 'running slaves' of New Comedy.[34] They arrive breathless and eager to spill out their news even if they sometimes have difficulty in composing themselves enough to deliver it. One might imagine that the comedy types made deliberate play with the tragic. One element they may have shared is

Figure 3.5 Tarentine Gnathia calyx-krater with messenger (*paidagogos*), mid-fourth century BC. Freiburg, market (1993)

a natural sympathy from the audience, and certainly in the case of tragedy, the greater part of the audience may well have found the humble messenger easier to relate to, more like one of their own kind, than the more remote heroes and heroines of the drama.

Something of an exception to the rule that we never see tragic actors acting is a very fine if fragmentary Sicilian red-figure vase in Syracuse, perhaps to be dated c. 330 BC (Figure 3.6).[35] The use of masks is still not explicit but one has a clear impression of masks from the bearded male and the white-faced female. The children by their feet, however, are maskless, and we know this to have been the rule on stage as well.[36] The columns behind them, and more particularly the platform beneath their feet, remind one of the stages on vases with comic scenes, and it must be the tradition of depicting comic scenes which has inspired this one. The subject is the terrible moment from the *Oedipus Tyrannus* (924–1072) when the herdsman from Corinth (seen on the left) relates the death of Polybos. Oedipus shows his lack of comprehension with right hand to chin, left to hip. The children, Antigone and Ismene, by his feet, through their innocence and incomprehension add to the pathos. Iocasta shows her comprehension of the news and consequent shock with a gesture which is very strong in ancient Greece, the hand to the side of the face. The painter has chosen a moment of great tension, a moment when the spectator is bursting to intervene, and a moment at which, interestingly enough, the messenger figure is involved. Here again he makes his speaking gesture, this time with the left hand.

The emphasis given to *paidagogos* or messenger figures and the visual-isation of the terrible events they recount goes hand in hand with the new standing of actors. These were the treasured parts and were played by the great figures. The development of this kind of histrionic virtuosity was doubtless favoured in contemporary tragedy, but older tragedies may at times have been altered to allow such scenes to have greater impact. There is some evidence that the texts or scripts of old plays were not regarded as sacrosanct but that actors were normally free to cut them about. For example, according to Aristotle (*Politics* 1336b27), Theodoros would not allow any other actor to come on before him. I am not sure how to interpret this, but it could be taken to mean that even classic tragedies (he was famous for his portrayal of Sophocles' *Antigone*) could be altered to suit the occasion. In the later fourth century Lykourgos had to compel actors to keep to the texts of the great poets, but it seems his success was only

Figure 3.6 (Opposite) Sicilian red-figure calyx-krater from Syracuse with the report of the death of Polybos from Sophocles' *Oedipus Tyrannus*, c. 330 BC. Syracuse 66557

temporary. There is evidence too for recitals of famous speeches, certainly at dinner parties (again by Theodoros) and perhaps also in the theatre.[37] Certainly there is everything to suggest that in the performance of tragedy, the presentation was becoming more important than the content.

To oversimplify, theatre in the fourth century moves from re-creation of history and the questioning of major issues of life to a style of presentation with a much higher emotional content which may well have been thought of as realism in its day. The new tragedy and what was often selected of classic tragedy may in our terms be thought of as melodrama. It offered the spectator a high level of involvement in the story. Talent and skill in stirring the emotions were rewarded through the development of a star system for actors. This style of theatre was supported by increased audiences such as we see reflected towards the end of this period, around 330–320 BC, in the huge new theatres such as that at Epidauros or the remodelled Theatre of Dionysos at Athens.[38] The audiences encouraged these developments because they in their turn must have felt a need for escapist pleasures of this kind.

The retreat from the problems of the political world in the face of economic pressures and other crises of confidence in the traditional system is already reflected in the later plays of Aristophanes.[39] Our history of the ancient world is essentially based on ancient writers' perceptions of their past (set, of course, in the light of our own), but Lucilla Burn has recently offered an interesting and provocative summary of contemporary Athenian perceptions of themselves in the late fifth century as one can detect them through both public and private art, and it is interesting to compare them with the literary evidence.[40] Temple sculpture is a public art form not only in its function and setting but also through the fact that its subject matter and arrangement were approved by a public body before the sculpture was executed and set up. Vase-painting was a more private art. It was designed for the use of an individual or small group. On the other hand it was designed by a vase-painter who had to make his living by selling it, and so it was conceived and executed in terms of what would be saleable to the public. It too should therefore reflect public taste but at a private level rather than as official art designed to represent the *polis* before visitors from outside. There are senses in which this sort of material gives a better cross-section of evidence than, say, Aristophanes who tends by and large to take a conservative line and is writing comedy, or Thucydides who also had his own agenda, political and moral. Certainly vase-painting was made for that fairly limited part of the population that could afford painted pottery, but it must have been a large enough part to have the potential to sustain a variety of views. Temple sculpture is official art but at the very least it reflected the views of the majority or the dominant group in the Assembly since the specifications for a temple were submitted for public approval. Burn points out that we do not have straightforward representations of contemporary events in vase-painting (any more, one may add, than we do in tragedy), and that we are not likely to have them in temple sculpture either (despite some claims to the contrary). What we see across the board in the later fifth century is a growing concentration on Athenian myths and Athenian heroes, on youth, the care of youth and the power of youth, and (particularly on pots) on personifications in the form of 'women whose names prove that they embody various forms of happiness, pleasure and good fortune'. One might claim that we knew a lot of this already, but did we really? and did we realise how widely supported these feelings were? The promotion of nationalism, as we know well in the current economic climate, often runs hand in hand with hard times, when one has to look after one's own interests first. We are aware from Aristophanes of the contrast and tension between the young and the old, but he leaned towards the *marathonomachoi* (those who fought against the Persians at Marathon), or rather, the traditions of the Battle of Marathon, and I am not sure that we get the balance right either. Thucydides too in (re-)constructing Pericles' Funeral Speech makes a good deal of the qualities of Athens, but also of duty to Athens rather than to self, and whether we attribute the words to Thucydides or to Pericles as an older man, one could argue that he was trying to stem the tide of change. The pursuit of happiness, pleasure and good fortune, symbolised in so many of the personifications, is an activity we normally associate more with the period after the end of the War, and it is salutary to find the preference for the personal rather than the civic good expressing itself so clearly here already.

It was suggested in the last chapter that Aristophanes was old-fashioned and that his contemporaries were moving more quickly towards the style of comedy that we call Middle. There is great merit too in the suggestion that the plays of his which survive were chosen for their political content. The fact that the so-called New York Group of terracottas seems to originate in the later years of the fifth century is in itself the clearest possible evidence that Middle Comedy was well under way in the last decade of the fifth century. This Athenian series has standardised mask-types and character-types that must have been created for a standardised sort of comedy rather than the more loosely structured comedy of fantasy characteristic of the Old, and their continuing validity is demonstrated by the fact that they remained in popular use, reproduced in direct succession from the originals, until the middle of the fourth century and beyond.

Middle Comedy had at least three features which are important in this discussion.[41] The first is that, since it was situation comedy rather than fantasy, its humour grew from the exploitation of the known and expected. It was therefore easier and more comforting, and the spectator could chuckle in the warmth of the shared knowledge: one knows people like that. The second point, a major one, is related: writers used the new-found structural stability as a setting in which to exploit a growing interest in human relationships, in depiction of the human condition. Here we have to be careful in our assumptions. Realism is comparative. Just because we know that comedy (like painting and sculpture) became even more realistic in the later years of the fourth century does not mean that contemporaries did not see it as lifelike in the later fifth and early fourth centuries. The comparison is with what went before. This change in style (which of course we see in Euripides as well) must have been catering to a new interest. Third, as we have said, this comedy is less patently political in the normally accepted sense. Even though one can find comment on the contemporary scene as late as Menander,[42] by and large the emphasis moves to examination of the universals of life in the *polis*. (It is no objection to this line of argument to point out the popularity of mythological burlesque in Middle Comedy: the genre relied on having gods behave like men.) Comedy begins slowly to take over from tragedy as the popular vehicle for the examination of human relations.

Interest in the theatre also spread very rapidly outside Athens. Reproductions of the New York Group of figurines of comic actors and their very close kin have been found not only in the closer areas such as the towns of Boeotia (where they appear in quantity), or Delphi and Lokris, or Corinth, but through the islands at places such as Paros, Melos, Knossos and Chania in Crete, Astypalaia, Rhodes or up in Thasos, at Olynthos, in Asia Minor at Larisa on the Hermos, the Troad, at Abydos and in some quantity in excellent

Figure 3.7 Tarentine red-figure bell-krater with scene from Aristophanes' *Thesmophoriazousai, c.* 380–370 BC. Würzburg H 5697

versions at a range of sites in South Russia, or then in Cyrenaica, in South Italy at Taranto and Paestum, in Sicily at Syracuse and a range of other sites, in Lipari, or at Ampurias in Spain. This all happened very quickly, and certainly within the first half of the fourth century. Sometimes these are actual Athenian-made figurines; more often they are locally-made copies of Athenian, thereby demonstrating that they are not objects of casual trade which just happened to find their way to these places, but items of serious interest. Less widespread but in some ways more fascinating because they show later fifth- and earlier fourth-century comedy in performance are the so-called phlyax vases of the Greek cities of South Italy and Sicily, Taranto, Metaponto, Paestum and Syracuse. There can be nowadays be no doubt that most of them show Athenian comedy: we even have a scene from *Thesmophoriazousai* as it was performed in Taranto (Figure 3.7).[43]

This vase, decorated by the Schiller Painter, dates to about 380–370 BC.[44] The play was first staged in Athens in 411 BC and this sort of delay may not have been unusual at this period: one has the impression that contacts became closer as the century progressed. (On the other hand the vase need not reflect the play's first performance there.) The scene chosen from the play is a memorable and striking one, and one that draws on a history of stage-practice. At lines 689ff. Mnesilochos snatches a woman's baby and seeks refuge at the altar, sword in hand and using the child as hostage. On being unwrapped, the baby turns out to be a wineskin, complete with Persian slippers. At line 753 Mnesilochos proceeds with the sacrifice of the 'infant' and (at 755, the moment shown here) the woman runs up with a bowl to catch the wine as it squirts out. That done, he finally gives her the empty skin back (which is also a means of getting it off stage). All this by-play takes a mere seven lines of text and is a good instance of the elaboration that takes place in performance.

The scene is a good reminder that the humour of ancient comedy rested in the staging as much as in the words. The anti-hero Mnesilochos is dressed as a male in woman's clothing (the skirt shorter than that of the real woman) and he wears a beardless mask that is grubby about the chin, a remnant of the shaving scene earlier in the play. What was less clear before we had the vase was the business with the woman, who earlier had presumably hidden her face modestly with her veil as she held her 'child', but now lets it loose in her eagerness to get to the wine she had lost and so reveals what a drink-sodden hag she is.[45] The pose of Mnesilochos at the altar is a direct parody of scenes of the Euripidean Telephos with Orestes at the altar. The scene was created by Aristophanes with overt visual references to Euripides' *Telephos* in which the child was used as a hostage at the altar, and that was surely a momentous scene in the play. Yet quite likely Aristophanes and certainly Euripides were also conscious of Aeschylus' earlier use of the motif where the child was apparently not threatened. The older poet had Telephos hold the child Orestes with him on the altar as part

Figure 3.8 Tarentine black-glaze guttus with figure with sword at altar,
c. 330–320 BC. Tampa (Florida), coll. Zewadski

of the supplication process, and this was doubtless striking enough in its day. Euripides had then 'improved' on the motif in a way that must have shocked, so that Aristophanes alluded to it first (among his extant plays) in *Acharnians* (326ff.) in 425 BC, and then again in *Thesmophoriazousai*.[46] The theme may well have been repeated in another (later) comedy since we have three Apulian black-glazed oil vessels of perhaps 330–320 BC (one in a German private collection, one in Naples and the other in Tampa, Florida) which carry small reliefs of the scene (Figure 3.8).[47] This was (or became) a specialised theme within a broader one: we know from contemporary terracotta figurines and slightly later vase-paintings that in comedy a favourite device was the slave seeking refuge on the altar, often with a stolen object such as a purse full of money.[48] Here again we have variations played on a favourite theme, in both tragedy and comedy, the writers in each genre conscious of the other.

Later in the same play, Mnesilochos was tied to a plank, and the scene and the words were played in parody of Euripides' version of *Andromeda* which had perhaps been staged in the previous year.[49] In the original context of the play's performance in Athens, there is no problem in all this and the audience could be expected to appreciate the verbal and visual jokes. We know much less of the situation in Taranto but it is arguable that there would be little point in even bothering to stage *Thesmophoriazousai* if the audience was unlikely to enjoy it. It is a play that relies quite heavily on knowledge of Euripidean tragedy (it also parodied the *Palamedes* among others) and would be a highly unlikely choice if the audience did not understand at least a good part of what was going on. Indeed it is logical to suppose that if Athenian comedy was being staged in Taranto in the early

66

fourth century, so too was tragedy, and this vase is a strong piece of evidence that this was the case.

The vase is also reasonable evidence that Tarentines were prepared to put up with a fair amount of local Athenian content in a comedy. Even if one allows for some re-working of the script to cut out the more particular allusions, the setting and a number of unavoidable points of the action are distinctively Athenian. One might reckon that the Athenian flavour was in itself attractive and remember, for example, that in later years Terence would even use Greek titles for plays put on for a non-Greek audience, but, all in all, it must be true that with the newer style of comedy theatre-goers in, say, Taranto, not to mention the more remote towns of Sicily, must have found it a good deal easier not to have to cope with the particular political satire of Old Comedy. It is not at all impossible that the likes and dislikes of the growing and potentially large audience of Greeks in the West, the North and elsewhere had some feedback in Athens and some influence on the direction comedy took. One could imagine that troupes of actors who were increasingly professional and had a career to make might well exert pressure on writers to produce more universally styled comedy. The idea has some confirmation from Plato's complaint in the *Laws* (659A–B) near the middle of the fourth century:

> The true judge must not learn from the audience, and be thrown off his balance by the noise of the multitude and his own lack of training; nor must he, when he makes his judgement, give a soft and insincere one out of cowardice and unmanliness, lying with those very lips with which he called on the gods when be began giving his judgement! The judge is there, properly speaking, as a teacher of the audience, not as their pupil; he is to oppose those who offer the spectators pleasure wrongly or improperly. Under the old Greek law this was allowable. The present Italian and Sicilian practice of handing over to the mass of spectators and deciding the winner by a show of hands has corrupted the poets, because they regard the vulgar pleasures of their judges as a standard and let the audience be their teachers. It has also corrupted the audience's own pleasures, because, when they ought to put their pleasure on a higher level by hearing things above the level of their own character, they in fact experience the opposite – and by their own action at that.
>
> (trans. D.A. Russell)

Plato does not specify whether the playwrights he means were western or Athenian, but other evidence, not least the archaeological, makes it clear that Athens-based writers predominated. In fact this question was by this period an unreal one. A number of the fourth-century playwrights (especially the comic) one thinks of as Athenian seem to have originated elsewhere but to have gravitated to Athens. One of the greatest comic

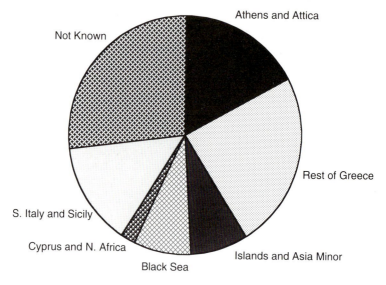

Figure 3.9 Provenances of Middle Comedy material, *c.* 400–375 BC

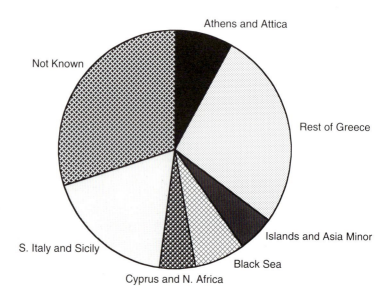

Figure 3.10 Provenances of Middle Comedy material, *c.* 375–350 BC

playwrights of the age, Alexis, came from Thurii in South Italy. Antiphanes came from East Greece, as did Anaxandrides. Philemon may have originated in Syracuse. It is a sign of the importance of Athens in the theatrical

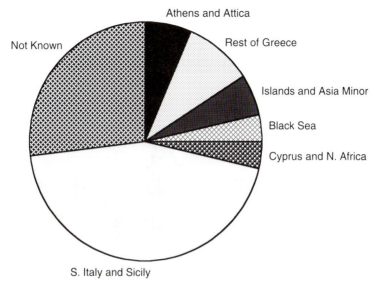

Figure 3.11 Provenances of Middle Comedy material, *c.* 350–325 BC

world and at the same time evidence of the increasingly Greek as opposed to simply Athenian nature of the medium.[50] The provenances of Middle Comedy material confirm the point (see Figures 3.9–3.11).

From early in the fourth century, objects which by their style, masks and costume reflect Athenian practice are found all over the Greek world. The proportions vary, and are in themselves interesting, for example the growing share taken by South Italy. It is one of the tragedies of Classical Archaeology that the best part of a third of all the material should have no record of its findspot. Deductions from present whereabouts would give even more to South Italy, and probably to Greece outside Athens. The bulk of this last category belongs to Boeotia where, in the earlier half of the century, Athenian cultural influence was very strong. In the third quarter of the century, the figures for South Italy and Sicily are distorted by the chance of the massive finds in Lipari, but it would be difficult to judge how much or how little to discount them.

Whatever the case, the cases decorated in the western Greek cities and the more widely distributed terracotta figurines are secure evidence that Athenian comedy was becoming Greek comedy. The movement of people and ideas, for which there is good evidence already in the sixth and fifth centuries (one thinks for example of the philosophers or the story that Aeschylus spent time in Sicily), seems to have grown even stronger in the fourth as communications improved. Art-styles in the West also show how closely producers and purchasers of such items as pottery, sculpture or architecture stayed in touch with developments in the Old Country, and there is more than a hint that in some cases, for example metalwork, the prosperous western cities took the lead. That is, we need little justification for taking iconographic usage on the pottery produced in the Greek cities of Taranto, Metaponto, Syracuse or Paestum as indicative of developments in the Greek world as a whole. And the fact that all follow a similar pattern strengthens the case. This is not the place to discuss the vases decorated with scenes from comedy as evidence for its subject-matter and its style of performance, but it is important to note their very existence and the fact that similar vases were made in Corinth and Olympia, if in smaller quantities (at least on the present evidence).

It is interesting to look at some statistics on the surviving objects that represent Middle Comedy. They fall into two broad categories, vases showing scenes and other material such as terracotta figurines, bronzes and the like, and it is worth keeping them separate since they present different problems methodologically. In terms of the range and types of figures shown, the vases are intrinsically more likely to give a good idea of what happened on stage, although we should bear in mind that there seems to have been a natural tendency for vase-painters to choose striking scenes rather than provide randomly chosen snapshots of plays in progress. To this degree, therefore, they provide evidence of what was popular in Middle Comedy as 'show-stopping' elements. An elitist might claim that we are likely to be given a lowest common denominator in terms of audience reaction. This may well be, but in this case it is useful as a corrective to, say, the tastes of Aristotle, or for that matter Plato who in a well-known passage in the *Laws* of the middle of the fourth century gives his views on the question of the what would please most in an open competition (658C–D). He claims that if the little children were the judges, they would award it to the conjurer; if the bigger boys, it would be the comedian; the educated women, the young men, and perhaps the general multitude would be for the tragedy. (Old men would give it to a good *rhapsode* doing recitations of Homer or Hesiod.) He by implication admits that his is a minority view and it is anyway a rather fruitless exercise for us to attempt to divide the fourth-century audience by the quality of its taste (as it has been with the study of Shakespeare's audiences). A playwright had to play to them all in his attempt to win the prize.[51]

Some 191 vases with comic scenes with groups, single figures, or actor figures incorporated with others are known to me. Of these, five are Lucanian (Metapontine), 107 Tarentine, 42 Paestan, 16 Sicilian, 17 Campanian, one Olympian and three Corinthian. The Lucanian belong to the earlier part of the fourth century, the Tarentine from about 380 BC down to the middle of the century, the fine and carefully drawn Sicilian to the years around the middle of the century, the attractive Paestan to the middle and third quarter of the century; the Campanian examples, which

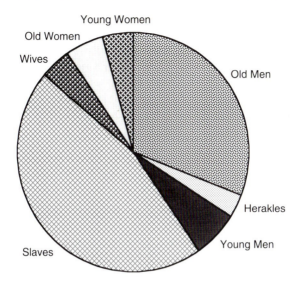

Figure 3.12 Proportions of character-types in comic scenes on vases

soon become poor and unreliable as evidence, are of the third quarter, mostly the later part; the Olympian and Corinthian seem to belong to the earlier part of the century. The weight of the evidence of comic scenes on vases therefore relates to the second quarter and middle of the fourth century (see Figure 3.15). A count of the various mask-types or characters gives results approximately as follows (on the basis of about 300 individuals): Old Men, 31.31 per cent; Young Men, 6.06 per cent; Herakles, 3.37 per cent; Slaves, 44.78 per cent; Wives, 4.71 per cent, Old Women, 6.06 per cent; Young Women, 3.71 per cent. Expressed graphically the proportions are as indicated in Figure 3.12. One of the main factors tending to affect this pattern is the habit in the later part of the Tarentine sequence to have single figures of slaves, for example in their characteristic task of carrying baggage, and another is the practice on the later side of the Paestan sequence of having actor-figures with others who are non-dramatic in contexts that are plainly non-theatrical, for example as companions of the god Dionysos, a subject we shall come back to. Very many of these last are slaves, although they include a few old men. None of them are females and it is interesting to note that here, as elsewhere throughout the history of Greek drama, female characters are never taken to typify or symbolise the comic theatre.

Other kinds of objects present a different picture. They are by and large individual items, mostly terracotta figurines, not groups implying scenes (even if a purchaser could put individual pieces together to make his or her

71

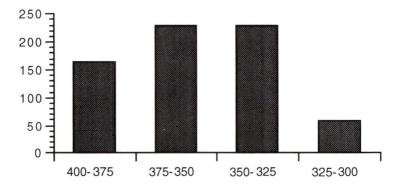

Figure 3.13 Listings of Middle Comedy material other than vases

own set). The choice is therefore directed towards popular character-types, types who in themselves give pleasure and in some way typify the comic stage, types one might buy as souvenirs. A problem in analysis is that the statistical base is not very large – something over 700 items over the period – and the details can easily be skewed by a particular set of finds.[52] For this reason it is best to keep to the broader categories of characters rather than the individual mask-types. First there is the simple point of increase in the quantity of the material through time (see Figure 3.13). These figures in Figure 3.13 are based on the date of introduction of a type, even though the actual date of manufacture may be later. A number of the pieces listed in the first quarter of the century will actually have been made in the second, and so on. The increase in popularity of theatrical souvenirs will therefore have been more marked in the second quarter of the century than appears from this figure, and the number in the third quarter will have been higher. The number of items listed after 325 BC is restricted to Middle Comedy material (excluding New) and so is a useful reminder (a) that Middle Comedy traditions lingered on in some provincial areas after metropolitan centres had taken up New Comedy, and (b) that some Middle Comedy types lasted in the *artistic* tradition simple because they were firmly embedded as popular types of figurines in their own right.[53]

Taking the period as a whole, a count of the mask-types or characters works out approximately as follows: Old Men, 25.47 per cent; Young Men, 7.09 per cent; Herakles, 6.66 per cent; Slaves, 35.46 per cent; Wives, 0.72 per cent; Old Women, 8.25 per cent; Young Women, 16.35 per cent. Wives are generally boring if not unpleasant. If anything were needed to demonstrate that these objects were chosen by the popularity of the characters on stage, this is it, and the figure is in interesting contrast to that of the scenes on vases where the count of wifely characters is noticeably higher at about 4.7 per cent: there they are necessary to the playing out of the scene and are shown as foils to the males (often simply peering out of doorways at what is happening on stage or standing on stage as a reminder of proper behaviour); but overall it looks as if in Middle Comedy the playwrights did not develop attractive roles in this category.

Older women appear more commonly, one suspects for at least two reasons. For one they can be vital to the plot: some of them are the nurses of the foundling babies and can play a pivotal role on that basis. Others can run inns or bawdy-houses and thus be in control of the young women who are the object of attention. They could provide a point of interest or of conflict that the good wife did not, at least in the Greek world of the stage. A comedy wife might complain, raise objections to one's behaviour and more generally be obstructive to the free running of one's life, but it was probably unacceptable to create plots which seriously undermined the male's faith in his dominant role in his own house. Men may be defeated by their sons, even by their slaves, but at the end of the day they cannot be defeated (for example in the sense of cheated on for the advantage of another man) by their wives, nor could the wives be depicted as out-standingly attractive in looks or personality. Indeed they could not be outstanding.

The young women claim a fair share of the purchaser's dollar, and within this category it is interesting to see that they increase their share of the market over time (with 28.26 per cent of the total in the third quarter of the century). The wearer of Mask V, the *pseudokore* or girl who will turn out to be a respectable young girl after all, is popular throughout (she is the only one found in the first quarter of the century) and has a steadily increasing share. She is also the girl described in a passage of Antiphanes:

> The man I'm talking about had a girl living next door to him, a hetaira, and he fell in love with her on sight; she was freeborn, but she had no relatives, no one to look after her – she was a good girl, one with a golden character, a hetaira in the true sense of 'friend', when all the others spoil a good name with their bad ways.[54]

This is a man's ideal girlfriend: attractive, friendly, fun, able to give a man a good time, a free spirit but alone in the world and so protectable, and having behind it all the quality of being Athenian.[55] He also brings out the original sense of *hetaira*, companion or friend, or 'escort' in the terminology of modern telephone directories and newspaper advertisements. Many *hetairai* too had social skills and some of them developed musical accomplishments.

What is more remarkable about this list is the increase in the range of types in the third quarter of the century, the years leading to New Comedy, when we find the introduction of a varied range of *hetairai* or courtesans (Masks W, X, XB and XC), as well as a good if smaller number of *korai* (free-born virgins, Masks S and SS). Their creation must reflect a growing interest in young women in the new theatre and they presumably allowed

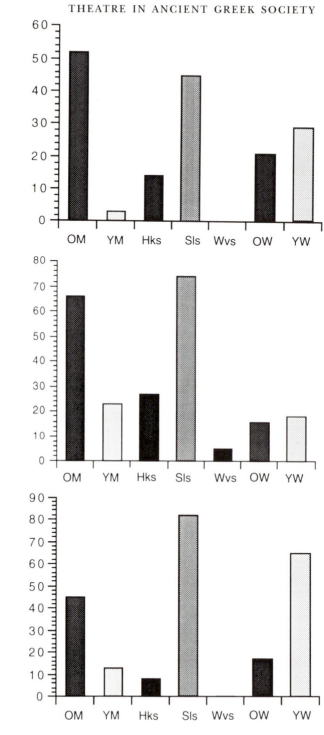

(a)

(b)

(c)

a greater subtlety in plot and/or characterisation.[56]

A breakdown of the categories by the three quarter-centuries yields some interesting results (see Figure 3.14). The emphasis on Old Men and Slaves is expected (overall they make up some 60 per cent of the total) and for the first half of the century it corresponds clearly with the pattern seen on comic vases. The structure of this style of comedy depends on them and their interaction,[57] and it seems likely that they were the ones who provided the broad and often knock-about humour. Looked at in detail, the share given to the Old Men (the fathers, the masters of the household) decreased a little with time: 31.7, 28.82, 19.56 per cent. This too is expected if we consider the place of this generation in New Comedy, where even though at times they are the key players, at others they are simply foils for the activities of the slaves and the younger generation. We should also remember that for Middle Comedy this figure includes Masks G and GA which are normally used for senior gods in mythological burlesques. Among the others, the most popular types are A (with its variant AA), which has comparatively compact hair and beard, and L, which often has white hair and beard of softish curls. These are the predecessors of the two key types of New Comedy, numbers 3 and 4 respectively in Pollux' list, the Leading Old Man and the Leading Wavy-Haired Old Man. The next most popular are Mask C with its peaked hair and raised brows, which is clearly the earlier version of Pollux' no. 7, the Lykomedian, a meddlesome character, and the Mask M who from his depictions on vases seems an equable fellow. The latter first appears in the second quarter of the century and becomes more popular in the third. In the remodelling which seems to have happened with New Comedy, it is possible that this mask was combined with A in the development of Mask 3. In general it is noticeable that just as the Young Women develop greater variety with the approach or appearance of New Comedy, Old Men coalesced into a more limited range. The Lykomedian in fact did not outlast the earliest period of New Comedy.

This sort of pattern is doubtless telling us something about the style of comedy being performed at any given period, but it is worth reiterating that in the Greek theatre especially, creation and reception were an interactive process, that the playwright had strong incentives to give his audience what they wanted, and that terracotta figurines were created in a commercial context and represent what people found most attractive.

Herakles was a popular figure in Middle Comedy and a key character in

Figure 3.14 (Opposite) Popularity of character-types in Middle Comedy, by date
Key: OM = Old Men; YM = Young Men; Hks = Herakles; Sls = Slaves; Wvs = Wives;
OW = Old Women; YW = Young Women
(a) 400–375 BC (b) 375–350 BC (c) 350–325 BC

mythological burlesques. The increase in the second quarter of the century seems to result from the replacement of a version created at the beginning of the sequence by another, and to this extent this series may give a more accurate reflection of the actual state of affairs than the main chart (Figure 3.13) where, as was pointed out above, the first quarter is unduly weighted.

The Young Men played a comparatively small part in Middle Comedy, and it should be noticed that the figures given here include parasites (hangers-on, professional spongers). What is difficult to account for is the small number that show up in the third quarter of the century, when New Comedy is about to appear.

Slaves as a category are the most popular of all. By way of caution, one may note, however, that these figures may well represent the popular appeal of this category rather than their importance in the plot. It is also interesting to see that in the first quarter of the century they are in fact fewer in number than the Old Men but that they steadily increase their share of the total: 400–375, 27.43 per cent; 375–350, 32.31 per cent; 350–325, 35.65 per cent. Their popular appeal is perhaps emphasised by the fact that among the carry-overs into the last quarter of the century, slave types account for approximately 59 per cent of the total. This is surely to be accounted for by the continuation of certain iconographic types that remained popular on the market. Four mask-types (and therefore character sub-types) are involved. First Mask B has shorter hair, usually dark, and the type increases in popularity through time. It is the predecessor of Pollux' no. 22, the Leading Slave of New Comedy. More popular in the middle years of the century in Mask K, with longer hair. The third is Mask N with short often fuzzy hair, which grows increasingly popular but then seems to combine with Mask K into the Wavy-Haired Leading Slave of New Comedy, Pollux' no. 27. One has the impression that he is perhaps more wicked or conniving than B (or 22). The remaining type categorised as Slave is the cook, Mask P for Middle Comedy, Mask 25, with the name Maison in Pollux' list. He is easily recognised with his bald pate, the remaining hair (sometimes white, sometimes red) bunching by the ears and small rather scruffy beard. There are no certain examples among the figurines of the first quarter of the century, but they begin with the second quarter and the number increases with time. The cook becomes a fairly important character in New Comedy.[58]

A further element in the way people thought of comedy is shown up by the use of masks rather than whole figures in the artistic media. The topic is an important one because the use of masks symbolises the way theatre was perceived as well as allowing a far greater range in the manner of representing theatre. The bar-chart (Figure 3.15) shows the number of objects representing masks (whether in terracotta models, carved on marble reliefs, or painted on pots as decorative elements) by quarter century, alongside the numbers of comic scenes or figures painted on pots,

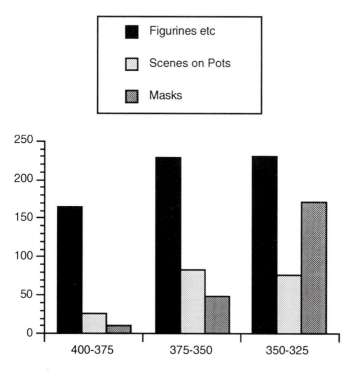

Figure 3.15 Relative quantities of comic representations

and then representations of figures from comedy in other materials, principally terracottas but including bronzes and marble reliefs. The first point the chart makes clear is the overall increase in theatrical material during the course of the fourth century. It is the strongest possible evidence for the popularity of theatre across a very broad cross-section of the population of the Greek world. It also shows how the number of masks increases markedly in the third quarter of the century in both relative and absolute terms. As in all such counts, one is bedevilled by chronological problems, for example in deciding whether a given vase should be dated before or after 325 BC. Similarly many of the vases with depictions of comic actors and comic scenes cluster around the middle of the fourth century, and most of those attributed to the third quarter are to be dated only a little after 350 BC. The figures do not include pieces such as the Pronomos Vase on which the masks are present simply as the equipment of other figures, whether actors or chorusmen.[59]

It is worth attempting to discover what these statistics mean and what is implied by the use of masks as a reference to theatre as distinct from pictures of the participants. We have no written discussion of masks surviving from the fifth century and so attitudes to masks in the early period of theatre can only be guessed at. Analogies in other societies still relatively open to the suggestion of visual media prompt the suspicion that the ancients might well have taken them far more seriously and have regarded them as far more powerful than we do. Certainly, as was pointed out by Gombrich among others, humans are predisposed to give high priority to the face, especially in terms of recognition patterns, even to the extent of seeing faces in the moon, clouds and other inanimate objects, and there is a tendency to attempt to see a face when trying to resolve random patterns.[60] We also learn very early in life to read facial expression in attempting to discern another person's feelings and reactions, so as to properly adjust our own. For the same reasons, humans learn to control facial expression so as not to give away the nature of their reactions, but they rarely learn the same control of body language. Above all, children recognise their mothers from their faces, and humans in general use facial features as the fundamental basis for recognition. Earlier Greek art tends to show faces in profile, which is generally not the direction from which one reads a face.[61] When we find a frontal face, the message is usually a strong one. An obvious case is the *gorgoneion*, where the face is intended as a frightening one (that can turn people to stone), but it is interesting that the next chronologically belong to Dionysos and satyrs (perhaps because of the influence of masks) and then, when one finds humans, it tends to be of people experiencing strong emotion.[62] Masks were normally seen or at least thought of frontally.

Masks not only conceal and change the identity of the wearer, but through their unwavering expression create uncertainty in the mind of the viewer. The viewer has no experience of unchanging expression (the eyes are not clearly visible) and therefore finds the mask difficult to read and relate to, and so to some degree frightening even if its expression is not a particularly terrifying one. Again a face without a body is a worrying thing: it has something of a life of its own.

It is striking that even in the twentieth century many masks created for the modern stage have a studied stylised blankness, devoid of expression, deliberately neutral and remote.[63] I suppose this to be a reaction which, first, reflects an underlying concern about the strength of facial expression and, second, a belief at variance with the practice, that the creation of expression is facial and really does belong to the actor after all. These on the one hand and, on the other, the fantastic masks of Africa, Asia and Melanesia demonstrate how singular the Greeks were in using masks with more or less normal human faces, especially in the more naturalistic phase of Early Hellenistic comic theatre. It is worth remembering therefore that there was a restricted range of facial types with a restricted range of expressive referents. Thus there was a series of codes readily identified by the audience. More on this in the next chapter.

We have seen that it was the habit in the fifth century, and probably later, to dedicate the masks to the god after a performance and to hang them from the architrave of the temple which stood in his sanctuary immediately below the theatre. With time this dedication came to be regarded as part of the celebrations for the winners of the competition, which also included such activities as the dedication of a tripod by the man who had financed the performance. I would suspect, however, that an underlying motive for the dedication of the masks in the earliest days of the theatre was a more serious one, to leave behind with the god in his sanctuary the 'otherness' created in his honour, and not to take it out into normal society. The beings represented by the masks were potentially dangerous and disruptive things.[64]

In later years the mask came to lose this power, but the process was doubtless gradual and came about through growing familiarity – and possibly through such factors as the self-consciousness and self-referentiality of comedy. For reasons one can perhaps guess at, this kind of power was attached to satyr-masks longer than to others. In the passage from Aeschylus' *Isthmiastae* quoted in the last chapter, a mask attached to the temple was described as having the potential to be 'a voiceless herald to keep off travellers ... it will halt strangers on their way with its terrifying look'. Aristophanes also calls a comic mask a *mormolykeion*, a scary, frightening thing, as well as referring to them as hanging in the sanctuary, in the Dionysion.[65] We see a satyr-mask used for this kind of purpose on a

Figure 3.16 Attic red-figure chous from Eleusis with a boy frightening another with a mask, *c.* 420 BC. Eleusis, Museum

Figure 3.17 Fragment of an Attic red-figure volute-krater from Samothrace with celebrations in the Sanctuary of Dionysos and masks hanging about his temple, near the end of the fifth century BC. Samothrace 65.1041

small red-figure jug found in Eleusis and datable to about 420 BC (Figure 3.16) on which a small boy frightens a smaller boy with one.[66] By this period, as we shall see on the fragments from Samothrace of the end of the century (Figure 3.17) where the vase-painter felt relaxed enough about them to show one in rear view, masks were already familiar, but the idea still seems to have been a deeply embedded one which was transferred, as it were, from adults to children. We see it surviving as a pretty conceit well on in Roman times in the form of Erotes using masks to frighten others, and the idea was picked up in the Renaissance.[67]

So far as we can tell, masks for comic actors during much of the fifth century were not particularly stereotyped in appearance and there was a strong tradition of special masks caricaturing individuals – as, for example, Socrates in the *Clouds*. Steadily, however, through force of practice there seems to have developed some systematisation, so that slaves, for example, looked generically similar and were recognisable as slaves through mask as well as costume. Then, shortly before the end of the fifth century, we have the remarkable evidence of the New York Group of terracotta figurines (see Figure 2.13). As we saw, they represent character-types and as such they have standardised masks. It seems to have been a development which belonged to the evolution of Middle Comedy as distinct from the freer, fantasy-based Old. The masks of the characters portrayed in the figurines are and were instantly recognisable, and the same is true of the comic scenes on vases as soon as they appear. The audience knew the moment he appeared on stage whether a performer was playing the role of an adult free citizen, a younger man, a slave, a wife, an old nurse, a courtesan and so on. The identification was of course made clearer by costume and other attributes. Thus Herakles always wears the Herakles mask, but he is also identifiable through his club and his lionskin. An old man normally has white hair and a bent cane whose knobbly, often wobbly form seems to act as a signifier of his shaky hand.[68] Similarly, in art and one supposes on the stage, prostitutes were distinguished from 'proper' women by the way they wore their clothes, by their poses and doubtless by the way they moved, as well as by their masks. Nevertheless these particular visual reinforcements seem to have become less pronounced and less necessary as the theatre public became more and more used to the identification process, and as the style of theatre became progressively more naturalistic in its presentation.

The recognisability of masks seems to have come together in the popular imagination with the practice of leaving them in the god's sanctuary after the performance, where they remained visible. Thus we see them hanging in the sanctuary (Figure 3.17) or examined by the god (Figure 3.18) in company with his satyrs and maenads. Nevertheless it is not until the third quarter of the fourth century that we first find evidence of masks in dedicatory reliefs. Figure 3.19 was, as the inscription tells us, set up by a victorious sponsor (or *choregos*) and shows four out of a probable total set of six masks from satyr-play (above, *papposilenos* and king; below, old woman(?) and satyr). We have two others, one commemorating a tragedy, the other a comedy, also from soon after the middle of the century.[69] This

Figure 3.18 Attic red-figure bell-krater from Spina with Dionysos in his sanctuary, beginning of the fourth century BC. Ferrara T 161C (inv. 20483)

Figure 3.19 Marble votive relief from Ikario, Attica, with masks from satyr-play, perhaps third quarter of the fourth century BC. Athens, National Museum 4531

is a vitally important step in the history of theatrical representation. The fundamental thought-process at this point probably involves little more than a permanent record of the 'equipment', as it was called, that was used in the play, but historically it is a very short step from there to thinking of this collection of masks as the cast-list of the play, the *dramatis personae*, and then from there on to regarding the masks as standing for the various characters portrayed or developed in the play as individuals. The mask steadily comes to stand for the character.

The archaeological evidence seems to point quite clearly to the fact that this last was an idea which caught on and spread very rapidly at this period, after which it became a commonplace of ancient art. One of the best examples is a grave relief from Athens datable to the third quarter of the century. It has been in Lyme Hall, near Stockport, Cheshire, since the nineteenth century (Figure 3.20).[70] A poet (he originally held a papyrus roll in his left hand) contemplates a mask, and another hangs from the wall above. The masks are carefully depicted and are those of a slave and an old man from Comedy. By the style of face and beard they belong to the latest phase of Middle Comedy. The poet looks at the mask and it serves as an

82

Figure 3.20 Marble grave relief of a comic poet from Athens, third quarter of the fourth century BC. Lyme Park, Cheshire

Figure 3.21 Marble relief with Menander holding the mask of a youth with masks of old man and *pseudokore* on the table; perhaps after an Early Hellenistic original. Princeton, Art Museum 51–1 (ex coll. Stroganoff). Ht 49.5 cm

identifier, a tool of trade, but it is surely not pushing the evidence too hard to say that he seeks inspiration from it, in a fashion we see later in the famous Menander reliefs (Figure 3.21).[71] The mask means a character, a person with certain behaviour patterns, and the passer-by looking at the grave relief will recognise all this, and know what these two masks represent, the two most popular character-types in Middle Comedy, as we have seen.

Masks have now come to be familiar objects and can be used with a level of subtlety. Fear versus familiarity is a theme which applies not only to masks in the earlier years but to other aspects of what happens after performance. From the years of earliest tragedy is a remarkable hydria by the Pan Painter in St Petersburg of about 490–480 BC (Figure 3.22).[72] In the centre of the picture Hermes drags two nervous-looking chorusmen of tragedy towards Dionysos. He makes an expressive gesture of greeting and welcome but they are reluctant and their gestures and poses show they are extremely nervous – in fact the figure on the far left tries very hard to hold back. This scene has the air of an unexpected introduction to the divinity, at least so far as the chorusmen are concerned. Indeed the strength of Dionysos' welcome makes it clear that this is not a normal event. He is presumably not used to this mode of impersonation, just as they are on unfamiliar territory, but as a god he is without their fear and he welcomes it. The vase has a number of puzzling aspects, not least the function of the writing tablet carried by Hermes, but it is important evidence of the perception of the place of tragedy in its earliest years: it is an unfamiliar way to honour the god, and the chorusmen are far from used to meeting him.

In this respect comparison with the Pronomos Vase (Figure 2.19) two generations later is instructive.[73] It shows the cast of a satyr-play in the sanctuary after a performance. The painter arranged the figures carefully. Dionysos is in the most important position, at the top centre, reclining on

Figure 3.22 Attic red-figure hydria from Vulci with Hermes introducing chorusmen to Dionysos, *c.* 490–480 BC. St Petersburg B 201 (St. 1538)

a couch with Ariadne. The writer and the musicians are at the bottom, and it is worth noting that it is Pronomos the piper who is directly below the god while the writer is off centre, some way over to the left. We could take this as giving us a clue on the relative importance given to writer and performance. The chorusmen range around the lower level and up at the sides. The actors are shown virtually in the same plane as the god, and one of them, the one who has caused so much trouble for modern interpreters, actually sits on the end of his couch. It is not without significance that the figure has been partially transformed into the part played, a female, and is attended by a small winged figure, a personification of Himeros (Desire).[74] The link between god and actor is explicit. They have met in the god's sanctuary often enough, and they can now mix without hesitation. They are not yet close (we shall see that later), but it is significant that the painter has put them on the same level as the god and immediately next to him.

The thinking which produced the scenes on the Pronomos Vase was the result of a detectable process. In the third quarter of the fifth century we have a number of pieces in which Dionysos is shown in company with personifications of various types of performance, Dithyrambos, Tragoidia, Komoidia, or even, in the later fifth, with a satyr labelled Mimos (mime).[75] On the vases Dithyrambos and Mimos look like satyrs; Tragoidia and Komoidia look like maenads. That is the genres, or more properly, since that may be too abstract a concept, tragedy and comedy as categories of performance are themselves portrayed as companions of the god, as their actors are later. The same idea continues later, for example on the well-known *choregic* monument in Thasos for which Salviat has argued a date in the mid-fourth century.[76] There we find statues of Tragedy, Comedy, Dithyramb and Nykterinos standing in company with the statue of Dionysos.

The scene on the front of the Pronomos Vase is set in the sanctuary of Dionysos after a successful performance. The cast has come to join the god in celebration amidst the victory tripods (which stand at the sides, by the handles). They hold their masks and before leaving they will dedicate them to the god, hanging them around his temple. Some more or less contemporary fragments of a volute-krater in Samothrace (Figure 3.17) show this aspect more clearly: the masks hang from the architrave of the temple above the heads of Dionysos and Ariadne.[77] They also seem to incorporate mask-holding figures and the figure of Dionysos in a *komos* or procession into a single scene, again emphasising that we should not separate back and front of the Pronomos Vase.

We may note in passing that on the largest groups of fragments, a figure holds a mask which is shown from the rear. This is the first such representation I know, and in the history of mask-depictions it is an important step, showing a familiarity with masks as objects that was not in evidence earlier: it has lost something of its frightening potency.

A less well-known vase in Ferrara is a fraction later than the Pronomos Vase and the relationship between the god and his actors is a little more relaxed (Figure 3.18).[78] The sanctuary setting is reflected in the figure of a maenad on the upper right, partially seen behind a rise in the ground, just as one might around the Athenian theatre. As on the Pronomos Vase, an actor taking a female part has been transformed into a female and has a head like the mask in his/her right hand, with ivy through the hair. The actors are not only in the presence of the god, they mingle with his normal companions, satyrs and maenads, and are seemingly in conversation with him as he turns towards them. From one point of view, theatre (here in the form of tragedy) is now familiar to the god, and this may be read as an expression of its familiarity to the audience whose creation the god is. At the same time, the vase expresses a view of the audience's relationship to the god through the medium of the theatre and its practitioners. This is one way that the audience has of reaching the god and the pleasures he brings.

These vases are symptomatic of the developing role of the theatre in the life of its public. We can follow its evolution further in a series of themes which again involve the decoration of what are distinctively symposion vessels. On a magnificent Tarentine bell-krater recently acquired by the Cleveland Museum of Art, we see on the front of the vase the head and shoulders of Dionysos superbly drawn in three-quarter view (Figure 3.23).[79]

Figure 3.23 Tarentine red-figure bell-krater with head of Dionysos and two actors making the discovery of wine, early fourth century BC. Cleveland, Museum of Art 89.73

Coming over his left shoulder is a staff or pole; around it grows the trunk of a vine which then spreads out behind and above his head and is laden with grapes. At the left, by a *thymiaterion* in which incense is burning, an actor dressed as a slave from comedy stands on tip-toe reaching up to and seemingly exclaiming about a bunch of grapes. On the right an actor dressed as *papposilenos* stands on a small platform holding a very large drinking vessel. On the other side of the vase (Figure 3.24), a youth with *thyrsos*, presumably again Dionysos, moves right in procession with a satyr and maenad. They step forward to the music they make as she hits the tympanon and he plays the pipes. Her drapery swings with the movement. His pipe-bag hangs from his left arm. The vase should date fairly early in the fourth century, perhaps about 380 BC.

The scenes on the two sides of the vase are not unrelated. The happy procession of Dionysos and his companions reminds one of the scene on the reverse of the Pronomos Vase (Figure 3.25), and the scene on the obverse of the latter (Figure 2.19) is also helpful in interpreting that on the obverse of the Cleveland krater. It is also relevant for the Cleveland vase that on the Pronomos Vase, Dionysos' *thyrsos* has a vine growing from its stem.

Figure 3.24 Reverse of Figure 3.23, with Dionysiac *thiasos*

Figure 3.25 Attic red-figure volute-krater with Dionysiac *thiasos*, end of the fifth
century BC (reverse of Figure 2.19). Naples 3240

What is important about the Cleveland vase is that it takes the iconography
– and therefore the thought process that lies behind it – a step further. It
develops the notion of the linking of wine and theatre by having not satyrs
picking grapes and remarking on the god's wondrous gift of wine, but
actors.[80] They, like satyrs and maenads, have also become his companions.

4

THEATRE AT THE
TRANSITION TO THE
HELLENISTIC WORLD

In the later part of the last chapter we saw two developments which remain important to our understanding of the place of theatre in Greek society at the beginning of the Hellenistic period: the use of masks and the changing relationship of actors to Dionysos. To take the latter first, there had been an enormous leap from the unfamiliarity symbolised on the Pan Painter's vase of about 490 BC (Figure 3.22) to the sharing of sanctuary and celebration that is evident on the Pronomos Vase and related pieces near the end of the fifth century (Figures 2.19, 3.25). By this period Dionysos and actors were at ease with each other even though there was relatively little interaction between them. The Tarentine red-figure bell-krater in Cleveland of about 380 BC

Figure 4.1 Paestan red-figure bell-krater with Dionysos and Pan, third quarter of the fourth century BC. Richmond 82.15

(Figure 3.23) showed a further significant step in that the actor-figures were taking on a role, the picking of grapes and the making of wine in a version of the 'wonder-of-wine' motif, that had previously belonged to satyrs, the god's closest companions.

By the time we reach the period about 330 BC, we find the motif developing further. This is near the transitional point in the move from Middle to New Comedy (Menander first entered the competitions in 321 BC) and a period of great vitality in Greek theatre, as seen in several ways: the construction of many new large theatre-buildings, the growth of actors' guilds, prolific output by dramatic poets (the figures for comedy are especially striking), as well as an interest in the literary theory of drama as in evidence from Aristotle's *Poetics* (analytic though it is, it is sometimes forgotten that the *Poetics* is in some aspects an answer to other views). Actors were already being depicted in contexts beyond the theatre in vase-painting of a number of other fabrics, but the best examples can be found in the work of the Paestan vase-painter Asteas and his younger colleague Python. Their work shows a strong interest in the theatre and theatrical motifs, some of which can be quite elaborate.[1] It is, however, their later, more mundane work which is of more concern to us, in part simply because it is run-of-the-mill, turned out as a matter of routine and therefore more likely to reflect standard beliefs and attitudes. They (and especially Python) produced quantities of bell-kraters with two-figure compositions, many of them Dionysos with a companion. The standard companions are satyrs,

Figure 4.2 Paestan red-figure bell-krater with Dionysos and comic actor as slave, third quarter of the fourth century BC. Madrid 11028

maenads and Pans, all of them figures we have been used to seeing with the god since the middle of the sixth century (Figure 4.1, by Python[2]); but in addition these artists will quite commonly use an actor in the part of a comic slave or old man or an actor dressed as a *papposilenos*. Thus, with Dionysos on a bell-krater by Asteas in Madrid, we have a comic slave (Figure 4.2).[3] He has an elaborate festive wreath on his head and carries a torch in one.hand and a *situla* (or bucket) of wine in the other. Dionysos moves along behind with *thyrsos* and kantharos. The scheme is just the same as that on a bell-krater by Python in Sydney (Figure 4.3) where an actor as *papposilenos* (note the boots, the body-suit terminating at the wrists) pipes the way and carries the wine for Dionysos again with *thyrsos* and kantharos.[4] There is nothing unusual about these pieces. They are part of a standard repertoire, and it is important to realise that the poses of the actor-figures and the things they do with and for Dionysos are just the same as those of the satyrs and maenads.

One would not, I think, argue that when the painter put together scenes of Dionysos + satyr, Dionysos + maenad, Dionysos + Pan, Dionysos + actor as *papposilenos*, Dionysos + actor as comic slave, Dionysos + actor as comic old man, he saw them all as identical figures – but he clearly saw them as equivalent figures who shared a similar relationship with the god. Python found it reasonable, and the more numerous purchasers of his vases must also have found it reasonable, to regard comic and satyric actors as companions of the god. Like his other companions, these figures serve him by leading him along, lighting his way, providing music and wine, and one could add that the torches and processional compositions indicate that in many cases (but not all) we are seeing the *komos*, the continuation of the partying after the symposion. These scenes are precisely parallel to those we have on the reverses of the Cleveland and Pronomos vases (Figures 3.24, 3.25).

It is worth wondering how literally the Greeks took these scenes. This is not the place for a discussion of religious belief, the unity of religious and secular, and the whole very complex question of epiphanies of gods and hero-figures. There is certainly more than one way to read these images. How much are the actors men dressed up? or have they to some degree become the parts played? is it the characters of comedy who have become the god's companions? The answer to this last question must largely, I think, be no. I suspect the thought-process as it evolved from the end of the fifth century ran rather more like this: on pieces such as Pronomos Vase, the Samothrace fragments and the Ferrara bell-krater (Figures 2.19, 3.17, 3.18), the actors join the god in his sanctuary in a process that was both ritual and practical. The actors have honoured the god through their performance in his festival and I suggested above that in early times they dedicated their masks here as a means of leaving behind the otherness they had created. A number of the comedies of Aristophanes end with the motif

91

Figure 4.3 Paestan red-figure bell-krater with Dionysos and actor as *papposilenos*, third quarter of the fourth century BC. Sydney, Nicholson Museum 47.04

of moving on to the party, a motif which must have been traditional, with origins going back before the creation of formal comedy.[5] There was also a practical purpose since performers in the theatre have a real need after the stress of performance and the shedding of self and taking on of otherness, to release the stress through having a party, or at least a drink, as well as to slowly climb down from the high of being someone else to the ordinary of being oneself again.[6] This happened in the sanctuary where the god was present and the actors joined the god in celebration. They joined his revel or *komos*, a motif we see on those Athenian vases. And it is the *komos* which is the characteristic theme of the Paestan vases, as on the Madrid vase (Figure 4.2), wearing garlands, moving along at night with the torch after the symposion.[7] The link with Dionysos has moved outside the theatre proper, to the drinking party where the participants enjoy happiness and success.

In these depictions, the actuality shown by the vase-painter is not a literal one of the everyday world, and we are reminded yet again that their way of showing things was not ours. In anything to do with theatrical performance it is always difficult to draw lines between the various levels and species of reality, but even if we leave these issues of representation of theatre aside, the divisions that we have formulated for our own society between the mortal world and the divine world simply did not exist for the ancient vase-painter and his 'readers', and we should not expect them to keep to our

Figure 4.4 Paestan red-figure bell-krater with actor as *papposilenos* pulling
Dionysos and Ariadne in procession, third quarter of the fourth century BC.
New York, Metropolitan Museum of Art 1989.11.4

formulations. There was no difficulty in conceiving of Dionysos as being present at a performance and being a part of a performance. Similarly, the performers could participate in his world. And since they shared in the process, so too did members of the audience.

A good instance of this may be found on a splendid vase, again by Python, recently acquired by the Metropolitan Museum of Art (Figure 4.4).[8] Unlike the other pieces of his we have seen so far, this must belong on the earlier side of the painter's career. An actor as *papposilenos* pulls Dionysos and Ariadne along on a cart. Though simple, even rustic in construction, the cart is richly fitted out with draperies and cushions, and wreaths of ivy and vine hang down below. Dionysos has his *thyrsos* and carries a phiale in his left hand. His right hand rests on Ariadne's shoulder. She plays the pipes while a bird rests on her lap, doubtless as a symbol of love. *The papposilenos* figure looks round to them and a maenad keeps them company. This is not a simple ride but a festive occasion – everyone and everything is decked about with wreaths and fillets, and plants and flowers grow along the pathway. The origin of the scene may well rest in an actual procession in which the statue of the god was taken from the sanctuary, translated by the vase-painter into the terms in which the event was envisaged.[9] In any case, the actor is again the god's companion and assistant.

The evidence of pots made in Paestum is complemented by evidence of similar attitudes and similar events in Ptolemaic Alexandria. Athenaios (V. 196ff.) preserves Kallixeinos' account of the Banqueting Pavilion of Ptolemy Philadelphos and his Grand Procession, the staging of which are to be dated no more than fifty years after the last of the vases we have been considering. Both offer useful insights and background on how the developments we have seen on pottery were paralleled in practice.

The Procession has been well treated recently by Rice.[10] The major part of the event of which we have details was put on in honour of Dionysos and comprised a number of set-pieces on floats with attendants and others on foot between. It was an incredibly lavish performance which included a huge number of participants, all manner of exotic materials, animals and people, massive displays of objects in precious metals, cunningly devised automata and so on. But like all such events it was of course largely made up of the familiar and conventional elaborated to an unsurpassed, extraordinary degree, so that in description, whatever it was like in the streets of Alexandria, it almost entered the realm of fantasy. The South Italian vases we looked at earlier are useful in forming an everyday basis from which the imagination can work. For example there were two enormous tripods (13.5 and 18 feet high) and eighty more normal ones. There was an *askos* but it was an *askos* made of exotic leopard skins and so large that it held 3,000 measures (*metretai*) and needed 600 men to pull the 37-foot-long cart it was placed on. It was designed to squirt wine all along the route of the parade.

The key element in this section of Ptolemy's Procession is the Return of Dionysos (Athenaeus 200D), and the emphasis placed on it in the Procession clearly represents a shift of emphasis in his cult. The aim was doubtless to point up the link between Dionysos and Alexander, and there was quite likely a political or ideological programme on the part of Ptolemy or his advisers in the development of the theme of the Return in the Procession.[11] The eastern links, however, were not in themselves new, and it is for this reason that many scenes on vases include panthers (or leopards or lynxes) and occasionally lions. Under this thematic head Ptolemy's Procession included a large range of wild animals, many of them having or perceived as having eastern and especially Indian origins. More important for our present discussion, however, is that the Procession is a further instance of the concept of theatrical performers as companions of the god. There were men dressed as *papposilenoi* in some cases as marshals (197E) and more generally as participants, and then the presence (198C) of 'all the Guild of the Artists of Dionysos'. By this date this is the accepted term for actors and they are there as the companions and servants of the god – they are his artists – and although the account preserved in Athenaeus does not specifically tell us, we surely have grounds for supposing that they were dressed in the costumes of their profession but perhaps carrying masks rather than wearing them. The actors were positioned immediately before the first float, the float which held a statue of Dionysos pouring a libation from what we would call a kantharos. In front of him was a volute-krater and a three-legged table with an incense-burner and two drinking bowls (198D). Over the statue was a canopy decorated with ivy, vine and various fruits, one might guess arranged in swags; attached were wreaths, fillets, *thyrsoi*, tympana and headbands together with masks from comedy, tragedy and satyr-play. By now, this is standard imagery on the vases and Ptolemy's use of it demonstrates that the thought-process is one which is well understood and appreciated.

In parallel with all this we may recall the way that somewhat earlier, in 294 BC, the Athenians had invited the Macedonian general Demetrios Poliorketes as Dionysos to a *theoxenion*, a ritual banquet traditionally put on by worshippers for a god, and so honouring him as if he were the god.[12] For a while, too, they renamed the Dionysia the Demetria. All this reflects not only the growing importance of Dionysos as a god, but his accessibility and the use that was made of him in daily life.

To sum up so far, we can see the coincidence of two major developments in society of the later fourth and early third centuries. One is the privileged position being given to the theatre in life in general as one sees it through the paraphernalia of performance, and the other is a growing emphasis on the cult of Dionysos. In the fifth century in Athens, the City Dionysia became a major festival in state terms, one in which the state put itself on display, and one element of that display was of course dramatic performances. There also seems to have been a strong linking created between Dionysos and popular democracy, to the extent that a century later (by a process with which we are only too familiar) the Dionysos/democracy link can be evoked for political ends, even when or particularly when the democratic or popular element is little more than a sham. None of this would have meant very much, however, if the celebration of Dionysos had not meant something to the individual.

The Pronomos Vase, the Cleveland Vase and the vases by Python are vessels made for the symposion. So too are all the vases with comic scenes, from whichever centre they were made. Scenes and motifs from comedy were thought appropriate for admiration and doubtless for discussion in the symposion: pictures on pots were rarely simply decorative. On the later side of this series, and especially in Taranto, we have many vases decorated just with masks.[13] These are also symposion vessels, mainly wine-jugs of one sort or another. The shorthand of using a mask for a character was, as we have seen, a widespread one and equally at home in terracottas for personal use or in marble reliefs for public display. The increasing use of the mask and the declining interest in whole figures in fact reflects the move towards what we call New Comedy where the emphasis is more on character and plot than on action and farce. Masks have a life of their own which is recognisable. The well-known Princeton (Figure 3.21) and Lateran reliefs,

Figure 4.5 Tarentine skyphos in the Gnathia technique with mask of *hetaira* set within vine, *c.* 325 BC. Once Santa Monica, market

which I suspect go back in some fashion to an Early Hellenistic original, make use of this theme when they have Menander composing a play: he does not write but he contemplates a group of key masks, working out how he will have these characters, these people, interact.[14] The literary version of the motif is preserved in Plutarch's often-quoted story (*Moralia* 347e) of how a close friend pointed out to Menander that the Dionysia was getting close and he suspected the poet had not finished his comedy. But Menander replied 'On the contrary, the plot is all sorted out. All I have to do is attach the dialogue.'

One of the fullest series of masks is to be found on Tarentine vases decorated in the so-called Gnathia technique which used applied colour over the black ground of the vase (as Figure 4.5). They run from very soon after the middle of the fourth century down some way into the first quarter of the third century. They are found on a wide range of shapes, but again restricted to shapes designed for the symposion. The range of masks selected is broad but with changing emphases through time. In the earlier phase, soon after the middle of the fourth century, they are predominantly slaves and old men in keeping with the taste of the time (see Chapter 3) but they move more and more with the passage of time to masks of young women. This must to some extent reflect a changing style of comedy and the way that plots come to revolve around the fate of the heroine, but one might guess that it also reflects the taste of the symposion and perhaps the pleasures provided.

The use of masks on Gnathia vases also differs in another and quite

96

significant respect. In earlier examples the masks are the principal decoration, as they are in the red-figure, but they soon come to be set in what can quite properly be regarded as a symposion context, hanging amid sashes and sprays of ivy and vine, motifs which carry clear Dionysiac connotations. This is the way masks were used in life. Furthermore – as I have attempted to demonstrate in detail elsewhere – masks are employed in parallel with and as equivalent to a range of other motifs which evoke and characterise the symposion, motifs such as pipes, harps and other musical instruments, as well as kraters, cups, tables of food and so on. By the later fourth century masks are regarded as typical furniture of the symposion.[15]

The reason is a fairly straightforward one but one that goes beyond the simple fact that Dionysos was god of both wine and theatre, although that link is of course important. On the bell-krater in Sydney (Figure 4.3), a mask of a comic slave hangs from a stem of ivy above Dionysos and *papposilenos* as they walk along. We can read the mask as an attribute of Dionysos, as symbolising the world of Dionysos and/or as reinforcing the nature of the scene. On the fragments in Samothrace some years earlier (Figure 3.17), masks hang from the architrave of the temple in his sanctuary. This is where one normally expected to see masks outside the theatre season, left as dedications after the performances. What you are doing then if you adorn your symposion room with masks decked out with ivy and/or vine is re-creating the sanctuary of Dionysos. In doing this, you not only join the god with all the blessings of wine and enjoyment that that brings, but you re-create the atmosphere associated with that sanctuary: happiness and success, away from the world, participating in a bonding process strengthened by the god's mystic gift with a group of like-minded colleagues.[16] And it is for the same reason that the motif is used on the walls of a Tarentine tomb (which created a symposion room for eternity).[17]

It is interesting to compare two symposion scenes by Python, both of them datable within the third quarter of the fourth century. The well-known one in the Vatican (Figure 4.6) has three young men enjoying themselves while three comic masks hang above from a festoon of ivy. The new one in Louisville, Kentucky (Figure 4.7) also has comic masks above, but in this case it is almost certainly Dionysos banqueting. He swings a cup in his right hand, aiming to score with the wine lees on the disc at the top of the *kottabos*-stand: he will then be lucky in love.[18] In his left hand he holds a pyramid-cake and he leans against finely woven red and white cushions, a red fillet about his head. At his feet sits a female, perhaps a maenad, perhaps Ariadne, making music on the pipes, her feet swinging above the ground. Above, half-hidden by the rocky ground, are two maenads, the one on the left holding out a wreath with red ribbon attached. On the ground in front of the couch are a kantharos, Dionysos' characteristic drinking vessel, a table and an amphora. From the right approaches an actor dressed as *papposilenos*, bringing wine in a jug. The masks above are those of a comic

Figure 4.6 Paestan red-figure bell-krater with symposion and actor as *papposilenos* asleep on floor and masks of slave, girl and man above, third quarter of the fourth century BC. Vatican AD 1 (inv. 17370)

slave and courtesan. The setting, as the rocky landscape seems to recall, is the sanctuary of Dionysos.[19] In a number of respects this acts as a prototype for the Vatican vase (Figure 4.6) where the three young men are, as it were, transposed to the divine sphere. No maenads (or Ariadne) but a normal girl piper; a young boy brings the wine with a ladle. The actor as old satyr presumably could not stand the pace and dozes on the ground, some pipes in his hand. Here the masks above emphasise the setting, and it may be relevant to observe that they could make up the key characters of a play: slave and master (with red-brown face and white hair), with between them a free-born girl, the love-interest.

Ptolemy's Banqueting Pavilion described by Kallixeinos (Athenaeus 196A–197C) was one of the wonders of its day and he gives a reasonably good impression of what it must have looked like.[20] He first describes the size and the structure of the tent and the draperies that were integrated with it, then the profusion of flowers scattered over the floor and elsewhere (surprising him because it was winter). He then proceeds to describe the decoration of the pavilion, the sculpture and the paintings, the finely adorned military cloaks and the gold and silver shields, and then mentions a series of recesses built into the structure that apparently housed or displayed lavishly arranged set-pieces in the form of symposia of tragic, comic and satyric figures wearing their costume; golden tripods were

Figure 4.7 Paestan red-figure calyx-krater with Dionysos reclining in the presence of an actor as *papposilenos* and maenads; masks of slave and girl above, third quarter of the fourth century BC. Louisville (Kentucky), J.B. Speed Art Museum 90.7

erected between the recesses. Kallixeinos then goes on to describe the seven-metre gold eagles up by the roof, and a range of other lavish fittings. The place of these symposia within the description as a whole, and the physical prominence given to them in the construction and layout of the Pavilion, makes it clear that they were a keynote element in the total decorative scheme. They set the tone or, more properly, provided the context for the activity at the hundred couches on the main floor. The performers were shown celebrating victory amid dedicatory tripods. The performers, and then by implication the guests, were sharing in a celebratory symposion in the sanctuary of Dionysos. This is what more ordinary people, like Python's young men, did on a smaller scale.

The reproduction of masks for use on the walls of the symposion room or on objects associated with the symposion, especially wine bowls, jugs and drinking vessels, presupposes the recognition of character-types and the acceptance of masks as symbolising them. In these reproductions, and particularly in the small terracotta model masks, we can see that the masks associated with New Comedy fell into two largely distinct stylistic series: the so-called Old Style and New Style.[21] As the names imply, Old Style masks are developed out of the traditional types of Middle Comedy (such as those on the Lyme Park relief, Figure 3.20), and though somewhat softer in style than their predecessors and more naturalistic, by contrast with New Style

99

masks they appear fairly strong-featured and conventional. It is noteworthy that they do not have as full a range of young women as New Style. They modify existing types and, not surprisingly perhaps, the types most reproduced within this series are those of the old men and slaves. They are masks full of vigour and character. New Style masks on the other hand are a stylistically close-knit series that gives every appearance of being invented by a single individual. They are characterised by much fuller and softer modelling of face and hair, and in appropriate cases even have bags under the eyes. They are far more naturalistic and sit well with the ancient view that Menander wrote naturalistic comedy.

Some aspects of the treatment of New Style masks reflect the art of Lysippos in sculpture, and the connection serves to remind us that portraiture was being developed about the same time. Again no single factor accounts for its emergence, but from among those that did we must reckon on the further development from the middle of the fourth century of the concept of individuality in personality and appearance, even if within a circumscribed framework dependent on perceived types which served as points of reference for more particular definition and description. (One thinks of Theophrastus' *Characters* and the way he identifies them.[22]) Other factors included the changed social situation, the importance of self-advertisement among generals and other leading figures, or the value cities found in setting up portrait-statues of important people. There was also the

Figure 4.8 Terracotta miniature mask of a wavy-haired youth, later fourth century BC. Copenhagen, National Museum 7367. Ht 6.9 cm

Figure 4.9 Marble portrait-herm from Tivoli (the Azara herm) with portrait of Alexander the Great, Roman copy of an Early Hellenistic original. Paris, Louvre 436. Ht of head *c.* 25 cm

straightforward factor of imitating Alexander.

Another factor which had not a little influence was contemporary interest in physiognomic theory, and this can be shown to apply to both portraits and masks.[23] Wavy hair, for example, which was used for certain masks of young men and for Alexander, was seen as leonine or indicative of an out-going and strong personality. It would be naive to suppose that Alexander's sculptured portraits looked particularly like him in the way that we would expect a portrait. They were intended rather to convey the essence of him. It is useful therefore to compare portraits of him (Figure 4.9)[24] with reproductions of masks with wavy hair, nos 15 and 16 in Pollux' list (one of which (16) is shown in Figure 4.8). They are found in Athenian Early Hellenistic in both Old and New Style versions.[25] The figures who wear these masks are generally characterised as active, vigorous, even aggressive. It is an interesting coincidence that the wearer of Mask 15 often plays the part of a soldier. The face is rather fuller than that generally given to Alexander (which is in fact more like that of Mask 10 (Figure 4.10), the counterpart of 15 with a tight roll of hair, the *panchrestos* or admirable youth[26]), but the handling of the hair is remarkably similar.

We have tended to think of facial expressions and one's reaction to them

(a)

Figure 4.10a, b Terracotta miniature mask of energetic youth (type 10), late fourth century BC, the nose somewhat restored. Brussels A 302. Ht 7.5 cm

as largely culturally determined, but recent work in this area is tending to show that many facial attitudes and responses are common to most primates, including humans.[27] We have normally thought in a rather simple-minded way that raised brows, which we find on a number of male masks (e.g. Figures 4.8 and 4.10), were read as a sign of a somewhat aggressive character. This may be, but inquisitive, interactive may be better descriptions, and it can be shown that this is the sort of expression that looks to elicit a positive response. So we may do better to think of 'warm, out-going, friendly' as well as having the competitive edge admired in Greek culture. What is more germane to our inquiry is the undoubted fact that New Comedy masks (and especially those of New Style) present certain stereotypes that the audience could accept. For example, and as a broad generalisation, we may look at the masks on the Louisville vase (Figure 4.7) and observe that slave and prostitute have snub noses while Dionysos (as an ideal young man) and the maenads have straighter noses. Old men too could develop snub or squat noses (Figures 3.20, 4.6). It is fascinating too that although they show a range of ages, the 'attractive' courtesans are very often young with childlike features, something which men are said generically to find attractive across a range of cultures. More useful work could be done relating these findings to mask-types and comparing with it

(b)

what we know of the characters attributed to them in the theatre.[28]

The facial image created in a mask continues to have a very strong force and individual examples are very particular in their connotations. Masks can be selected to recall performances, even, through careful choice of mask-combinations, specific performances. If, therefore, you place masks in your symposion-room amidst wreaths of ivy or vine, you are not merely decorating your room with theatre tickets, or even, to carry the analogy further, with theatre programmes, you are re-creating the sanctuary of Dionysos and, in doing so, you are re-creating a world of Dionysos. At the same time, in hanging up the masks for the symposion, you become like an actor or even become an actor: you have in some sense dedicated them or can pretend to have dedicated them. You are therefore, like those actors, successful and happy (whatever the worries of the world outside your symposion-room). Actors are also intermediaries between man and god. You are joining Dionysos as his servant and are celebrating with him, enjoying the pleasures of his gift of wine. You join his world through the medium of Comedy.

This was surely the main message in the use of theatrical material at this period, but there is a further dimension which should not be ignored. The masks of Early Hellenistic comedy reflected life and the appearance of reality as the Greeks perceived it.[29] Everything suggests that, given the conventions of the time, they were seen as realistic. The very variety of the masks argues that every likely type of personality was covered. The point is emphasised by the radical change in costume that occurred at the same time that many of these masks were invented or developed out of the earlier tradition. Within a very short space of time, the *phallos*, which had remained integral to theatre costume from the period when actor-figures were first found in the antecedents of comedy proper, was greatly reduced in size and then removed.[30] Costume became decent and in fact assumed a more naturalistic length. The grotesque padding also disappeared, though there are remnants of it in the padded belly standard for slaves and to a lesser extent for old men. Young men and girls were not padded any more. Girls' hair is done is contemporary styles. All this must have been a deliberate rejection of the traditions of the past, a throwing away of past conventions. The comic theatre now depicted life. The fact that it was life in an ideal form, with happy endings inevitable no matter how complex or difficult the obstacles, made it more attractive. It also made it more suitable for the escapist world of the symposion.

We are here at the beginning of a tradition which, while looking back to the uses of poetry in the symposia of the past, leads on to the use of Menander as recalled by Plutarch centuries later: 'one could more readily imagine a symposion without wine as without Menander ...'[31] Plutarch (through the mouth of his Diogenianos) continues in his rather frigid way about the suitability of Menander's poetry for those who leave the symposion to go home to their wives, an idea that might have seemed rather surprising to the poet himself. For those dealing with the problems of life in the Early Hellenistic *polis*, the moral function of Menander is better recalled by Sandbach: 'he quietly inculcates the lesson that understanding, tolerance, and generosity are the keys to happiness in human relationships'.[32]

It is probably no coincidence that at the same time that comic masks and performance became more naturalistic, tragic masks and tragic performance become more exaggerated and stereotyped. This is the period when the boots of tragic actors began to develop platform soles, when masks came to have extended hair above the brow, the *onkos*, and the faces of the masks were given more contorted expressions. This is also the period when we begin to have depictions of tragic actors acting. Tragedy had lost its immediacy and any pretence at depicting life. It was more and more a stylised performance of classic theatre. It could still be (and was) appreciated for its own sake, but the depiction of life now belonged to the comic stage. In the words attributed to Aristophanes of Byzantium, 'Oh Menander, oh Life, which of you imitated the other?'

5

THEATRE IN THE
HELLENISTIC WORLD

The Hellenistic period remains the most complex and probably the least understood of all periods of Greek history, particularly in its social dimensions. The changed political circumstances, the domination of originally independent cities and states by super-powers and at that not the traditional ones, the further-reduced say of the ordinary individual in the larger decisions in the life of his community, the declining economic situation in Old Greece, the necessity for a significant part of the male population to seek income away from home as mercenary soldiers (with the consequent serious disruption of the social system), the loss of the western colonies to the Romans after four or five hundred years of thriving contact and trade, but the massive expansion of Greek control in Asia Minor, Egypt and the East, which at times must have stretched social organisation and resources very thin – all this brought about a breakdown of the traditional way of life within the space of not much more than fifty or sixty years with, say, 300 BC as its mid-point. It is not too difficult for us to understand something of the changes which occurred in Old Greece, and to sympathise with them. What we perceive less readily is the stresses on those in the new territories. Even in the most prosperous of the new centres, Alexandria, there are strong hints that the minority Greek population did not always feel entirely comfortable, surrounded as they were by a subordinate dark-skinned people whose style of life (and crime) was very different and only partially understood. The lands of the new empires had different climatic conditions: the analogy of the European expansion into North America and Australia has shown what problems unfamiliar extremes of climate can cause for the fundamentals of existence, including agriculture, even for those with more sophisticated technologies, no matter how well the natives had hitherto conducted their own lives.[1] The bonding force of religion and cult had traditionally rested in the activity of (by the new standards) small community groups, and so it too was of comparatively little value for those inhabiting the new areas, and given that Greek religion had no creed, no theology, the loss of traditional cult practice must have brought a loss of security and identity. In the face of all this, Greeks had very quickly to realise that security lay in being Greek, not Athenian, Theban, Parian, Cretan or whatever, and that a key factor in their identity was their shared language. Small wonder, therefore, that the Greek language began to change quite rapidly in the course of the third century and to develop away from the old dialects towards a common form.

The other element besides language which remained common to most Greeks was the theatre. Indeed it could be argued that it was this particular conjunction of circumstances that prompted theatre's increasing success. Drama had first developed in the particular vibrancy of the Athenian community in the fifth century. The Athenians had developed a very special role for it in the annual cycle of their affairs and invested its presentation with an elaborate degree of ceremony. The experience of the theatrical occasion, with all the internal comparison that went on from year to year, explicitly with comedy, implicitly with tragedy, was a pleasure shared and a bond created. The success of this Athenian venture seems to have caught on quickly elsewhere, not least in such cities as Syracuse which already had something of a local tradition of drama, but in other places too. The material evidence shows that by 400 BC or soon afterwards, Athenian theatre was spreading through much of the then Greek world. I suggested in an earlier chapter that the popularity of Athenian drama, and particularly comedy, outside Athens in the fourth century could well have been a major factor in its throwing aside local particularity and its move towards universals that would be accepted and appreciated in other communities. This was a process that was begun about the end of fifth century and, in the long view, it is fortunate that it was virtually complete by the death of Alexander in 323 BC (to take an arbitrary date) so that theatre culture could be carried through the ancient world in the process of the Greek expansion. By this point, as we have seen, Athens had become the metropolis from which theatre was diffused and which in its turn attracted the medium's most skilled practitioners. Apart from the straightforward factor of enjoying it, attendance at the theatre had become a social practice which Greeks in general shared. Theatrical performance was a common language. The subject-matter of comedy was everyman. Theatrical motifs were universally understood.

One instance among many is recorded by Plutarch (*Life of Alexander* xxix):

> When he returned to Phoenicia from Egypt [early in 331 BC], he organised sacrifices and processions for the gods, and contests of dithyrambic and tragic choruses which were made brilliant not only by the way they were provided for but by the way they were contested. For the choregoi (sponsors) were the kings of Cyprus (just like those at Athens selected from the tribes), and they competed with each other with amazing rivalry. The competition was particularly intense

between Nikokreon of Salamis and Pasikrates of Soloi. They had been allotted the most famous actors, Pasikrates with Athenodoros and Nikokreon with Thessalos, whom Alexander himself was supporting. He did not of course reveal this support until after Athenodoros had been voted the victor. Then, it seems, he said as he went out that he was pleased with the judges' decision but that he would have gladly given away part of his kingdom not to see Athenodoros lose. And when Athenodoros was fined by the Athenians for not appearing at the Dionysia, he asked the king to write to them on his behalf. Alexander would not do that but sent him the fine from his own pocket. And when Lykon of Skarpheia was giving a good performance in the theatre he inserted a line into his comedy which had in it a request for ten talents. Alexander laughed and gave it to him.[2]

Plutarch is simply concerned to impress us with Alexander's intelligence, statesmanship and generosity, but we for our purposes may note that Alexander found it important to put on this kind of event in Tyre, and that while (on some other occasion) he may have given the actor Lykon, who was a major performer in his day, the princely or royal sum of ten talents, he found it suitable to let this occasion appear 'democratic' with the traditional Greek elements of intense competition led by wealthy sponsors.

We saw in the last chapter that the re-creation of the sanctuary of Dionysos as the setting for one's symposion was not just Athenian either. It was a formula adopted wherever Greeks were found, and the distribution and type of artefacts representing theatre make the point abundantly clear (Figures 5.1 and 5.2). The proportion of objects found in Greece is reduced while the quantity from what might previously have been considered marginal areas, such as Cyprus, Egypt and Campania, becomes more noticeable. The figures for the Early Hellenistic period are of course distorted by the huge quantity of terracotta figurines and masks found in Lipari, although we may also note how the numbers for Apulia include the quite considerable number of Gnathia vases decorated with masks. It will be interesting to compare the quantities of material found in the various Hellenistic kingdoms, but the interest in theatre in Ptolemaic Egypt (and particularly Alexandria) is already becoming clear. At this stage Egyptian finds are mostly made up of imported objects: local manufacture becomes more pronounced in the next period. It is also interesting to compare the popular appreciation of things theatrical in Egypt with that of the other new areas, or even with Macedonia which has yielded remarkably little, despite the professed interests of Alexander or, for that matter, Archelaos in the later fifth century who is said to have had Euripides at his court. If these stories are true (which is not entirely certain) they must have represented aspirations to culture by the ruling classes rather than popular interest in a characteristically Greek activity.

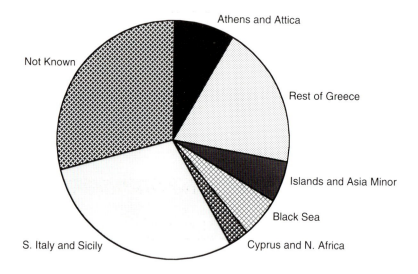

Figure 5.1 Provenances of Middle Comedy material, *c.* 400–325 BC

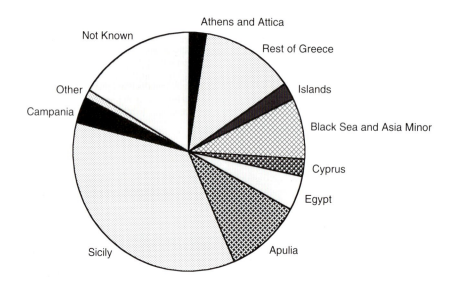

Figure 5.2 Provenances of New Comedy material, *c.* 325–250 BC (note that the categories differ slightly from those of Figure 5.1)

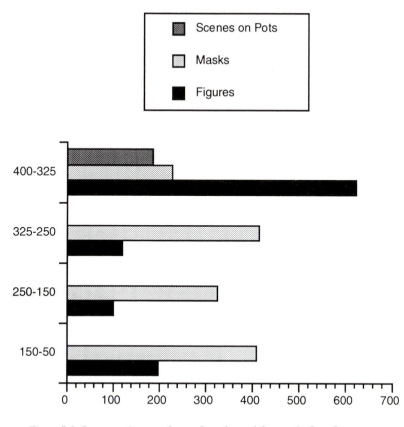

Figure 5.3 Comparative numbers of masks and figures in fourth-century
and Hellenistic comedy

Figure 5.3 confirms what we have already observed happening within the
period of Middle Comedy, that the proportion of masks depicted as
opposed to figures continues to grow. The figure also shows the quantities
of material with theatrical subject-matter for the periods of Middle Comedy
and the three Hellenistic phases of New Comedy. In comparing Middle
Comedy with Early Hellenistic New, the decline in quantity is almost
certainly more apparent than real: the statistics present what survives rather
than what was created and it seems highly probable that a much higher
percentage of theatrical material in this period was manufactured of
materials which for one reason and another have not survived. In
comparing Early Hellenistic with Middle, there are classificatory reasons
why the introductory phase should be heavily loaded, and a number of
items which have been listed there were almost certainly manufactured in
the next. Nevertheless the general pattern seems fairly secure, and there
can be no doubt that the Early Hellenistic period was extremely active in

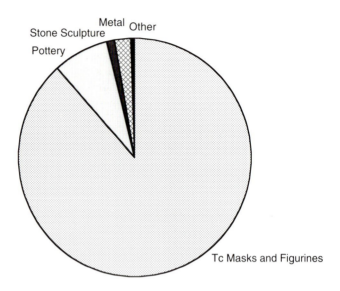

Figure 5.4 The material of surviving objects representing comedy, *c.* 325–250 BC

the devising and production of theatre-related material as well as inventive in the theatre itself. As is demonstrated by Figure 5.4, by far the greater part of the material surviving from this period is of cheap materials, mostly the fired clay of pottery and of terracotta figurines and masks, and the same remains true for much of the remainder of the Hellenistic age (Figures 5.16, 5.20).[3] They are a strong reminder that theatre was loved by those segments of the population that could not afford anything more expensive, and, as we saw in the last chapter, it was used in their lives as a source of consolation and happiness. We should remember, however, that there must have been much in other materials which does not survive, whether because of its inherent physical characteristics (wall-painting, bronze, wood, cloth) or because of its intrinsic value which might prompt it to be re-cycled for other purposes in later periods (bronze, precious metals, marble [for the lime kiln]). We sometimes have hints of their existence. For example there are clay impressions made by gems with engravings of actors which can be shown to date from this period by the context in which they survived, but we have no actual gems of this date with theatrical subject-matter.[4] By the Late Hellenistic and Early Roman periods, however, they become common. We have a little gold jewellery, which has survived because it was placed in graves, but one would expect there to have been much more in this period.[5] Also by way of personal possessions is a superb silver mirror-case of the earlier part of the third century BC found in 1928 in the so-called Tomba degli Ori at Canosa in northern Apulia, a wealthy

110

district at this period.[6] One might guess that it was manufactured in Taranto. It shows a woman (perhaps a Muse) seated and holding the mask of a comic slave in the company of three Erotes. With a somewhat similar motif and of the same period is a bronze mirror-case in the British Museum, from Corinth.[7] For the table or symposion we have a silver-gilt dish decorated with masks, probably from Taranto, and it must be representative of the kind of thing produced in some quantity.[8]

The most important medium of the Early Hellenistic period, however, was generally acknowledged to be painting, and numerous references in literature attest to its quantity, its quality and the outstanding advances being made in technique. None survives, nor do we have any record in literature of paintings with theatrical subject-matter. It is becoming increasingly clear, however, that the well-known mosaics of the late second century BC signed by Dioskourides of Samos and found at Pompeii, which have long been thought on stylistic grounds to reflect originals of the Early Hellenistic period, are but two deriving from what must have been a large series of panel-paintings with scenes from comedy. One of the mosaics, Figure 5.5,

Figure 5.5 Mosaic from Pompeii, 'Villa of Cicero' (found in 1763), with Menander, *Theophoroumene* Act 2, signed by Dioskourides of Samos, late second century BC. Naples 9985. Ht 43.7 cm

111

shows a scene from Act 2 of Menander's *Theophoroumene* or *Girl Possessed by the Goddess.*[9] The young men dance and make music as they move towards the door of the girl's house, visible to the right of the picture. They play what for men are strange instruments, tympanon and castanets, while the girl with them seems to play a particular type of pipes. They are making foreign music in their attempt to make the girl appear: she is possessed by a foreign goddess. Characteristically, the scene depicted is one critical to the dramatic development of the play, and doubtless the one that made the greatest impact on the spectator. It could often therefore be the name scene, and it was certainly the scene by which the play could be recognised. None of the surviving copies of these paintings needed to identify the play by inscription until Late Antiquity, when the traditions were dying and direct knowledge disappearing. Copies of others are found as paintings on the walls of Pompeian houses (the *Theophoroumene* picture, for example, is also found as a painting from the wall of a house at Stabiae) and in a wide range of other material from marble reliefs, to cameos and gems, to bronzes and terracotta figurines.[10]

The originals from which these copies derive must have been readily accessible, presumably in some public place, possibly in the sanctuary of Dionysos. What seems absolutely clear nowadays is that they cannot have been designed as text-illustrations. Illustrated manuscripts containing pictures of this quality, if they existed at all at this period, would have been rare and expensive. The one illustrated papyrus of Menander that we do have simply has a quick ink sketch of a single figure, and though interesting for its own sake, it is a drawing with no artistic pretensions.[11] The wide accessibility of the originals of these pictures and their reproduction in such a wide range of media argues for their quasi-public standing. They also show very good and careful detail in the treatment of the masks, for example, something again unlikely if they were being magnified from small pictures in a papyrus roll. And then (most importantly of all perhaps) they exhibit qualities of composition and painterly technique which belong to a larger scale and a full palette, qualities which accord well with our admittedly fragmentary knowledge of the developments and achievements of this great period of painting.

So far as we can tell, the idea of having paintings of key scenes from comedies was an innovation of the earliest days of New Comedy, although one might imagine that the groundwork had been laid by the comic scenes on vases made in Taranto and elsewhere in the preceding years. Scholars of the later part of last century and the earlier part of this often thought of plaques or paintings dedicated in the sanctuary in celebration of a play, and such an idea might provide a suitable occasion for the creation of paintings such as these. On the other hand we have no hard evidence for such an activity, and so far as we can tell from the surviving evidence, these paintings seem to have been created only in this very limited period, not as part of an on-going tradition of votive representations. The tradition of erecting marble monuments to commemorate successful productions was a longer one, and we have examples going back to near the middle of the fourth century. There are fragments of two more from the early years of New Comedy, one from somewhere in the region of the later Stoa of Attalos in the Athenian Agora, the other from the other side of the Acropolis, near the Theatre.[12] Here again is evidence that a lot of money was invested in the staging of New Comedy, and that such an investment must have been thought likely to be worth the reward that a successful production might bring to one's reputation. Here again we should note that plays were represented by reproductions of the masks they employed.

Parallel in concept but for private use is a small (10 cm square) plaque found at Amphipolis in North Greece and now in the Kavalla Museum (Figure 5.6).[13] It may well be of the Athenian manufacture. The masks are set against a blue ground and all have blue eyes and red lips. Here again there are six (as there probably were on the relief in Figure 3.19 or the lamp Figure 5.7) and it seems possible to work out their identity. Along the top row we have on the left a mature man (the father, master of the household), and on the right a slave; between them is a girl with brown hair and a face which is pale but for a little pink on the cheeks. She is the *Pseudokore* or False Maiden. In Webster's words, a *pseudokore* 'is a maiden because her

Figure 5.6 Terracotta plaque with the masks of the key characters from a comedy, Early Hellenistic. Kavalla 240 (E 489). 10 × 10 cm

113

parents will be discovered before the end of the play, but she is a false-maiden because she has already lived with the man whom she will marry'.[14] She will have provided the love-interest for the plot and one supposes that she has somehow become involved with the young man shown on the bottom left. At the bottom right is the mask of an old woman with orange-brown skin. This mask can be used for the procuress and it is quite possible, indeed likely, that she somehow had charge of the girl here. Her skin-colour as well as her coarse features indicate that she is not a lady. The mask in the centre at the bottom, though, has pale skin, a quite young though not girlish face, a fairly straight nose and close curly hair. It is the sort of mask often used for a wife (one should remember that Greek wives were normally much younger than their husbands). A further factor in the pattern of recognition is the hairstyle of the males: it is worn in an identical roll by all three and this seems to have served as a conventional indicator on the stage that they all belonged to one family, father, son and family slave. The slave would typically have taken the son's side in intrigue against the father (on the basis of an attachment developed in his younger days while the father was out of the house about his business). What we don't know is whether the 'wife' is the mother of the young man and therefore wife of the father, or, perhaps more likely, the mother of the girl at top centre: one could suppose that when the girl was a baby she had had to give her away and therefore lost track of her until the moment of recognition in the play. By her mask she is clearly Athenian, which would be necessary if the girl were to marry the young man. One would hardly buy the plaque unless one understood all this, and it could well have been a memento of a particular play.

Personal mementos of this kind were not common although some come close, for example necklaces with groups of masks which seem to have been selected as having at least the potential to be a cast list, or even the

Figure 5.7 Egyptian terracotta lamp with masks of (1) old woman, (2) young man, (3) cook, (4) girl, (5) procurer (*pornoboskos*), and (6) slave, Late Hellenistic. Paris, Louvre S 1724. Length 23 cm

114

Figure 5.8 Gold ear-rings with Erotes carrying masks of slaves or old men,
Early Hellenistic. Paphos 1931. Length of each, *c.* 5 cm

occasional lamp such as that probably of the first century BC discussed on
p. 141 (Figure 5.7). We also find groupings of masks in the borders of floor
mosaics of the Middle and Late Hellenistic periods, but this kind of thing
is for display when entertaining one's friends and so is not personal in the
same sense. Far more common in personal ownership are representations
of single masks, especially when they are a component of some larger
composition. A good case in point is to be found in ear-rings where they are
often depicted held by Eros (Figure 5.8).[15] Here the mask is used less for
the sake of the particular character depicted but as a generic reference to
theatre. For this reason they are normally slave masks, somewhat less often
old men. The question then arises, what is an Eros doing with a mask? The
motif is one which becomes even more common in Middle Hellenistic
when the two are commonly associated, for example on mould-made relief
bowls. Erotes throughout the Hellenistic period often busy themselves with
minor tasks, not infrequently playing with Dionysiac equipment. On Early
Hellenistic vases they will drive panther-chariots (like Dionysos), or carry
symposion material like amphorae or *situlae*, wreaths or dishes, pipes or
other musical instruments.[16] It looks as if masks in this sort of usage have

become parallel to other paraphernalia of the symposion.

The idea seems to be confirmed by the way masks are used as a motif to decorate the Gnathia vases made in Taranto in the later part of the fourth and the early part of the third century (see Figure 4.5). In this case the masks are used as decoration on symposion vessels. They are almost invariably depicted as set within and hanging from wreaths or festoons of vine or ivy, of the kind that were placed around the walls of the symposion room. One might compare the way that Christmas cards often pick up the themes of decoration found in the house, such as trees, holly or wreaths. Third, masks are not the only elements depicted in this way: there are also other items which seem to characterise the symposion, such as wine-vessels of various kinds or the musical instruments typically played there such as harps or pipes. That is to say, masks, although very popular, come to be but one of a series of motifs evoking the symposion, all of which are treated in a parallel way. Although the meanings of each are not necessarily precisely the same, the motifs are treated as equivalent and are put in the same settings. This is particularly clear on occasions when we have a set of three or four vases, say from a single tomb, which on grounds of style were clearly bought as a set from the same shop and were most likely manufactured as part of a series.[17] There is a sense, therefore, in which the force of the mask as an individual item with individual meaning is becoming down-graded to a level or changed to a level where it has no more force than a drinking cup or a pair of pipes. It recalls party and celebration, occasions of happiness, and so becomes simply a symbol of happiness. We have enough parallel instances in our own society, particularly if we think of the sorts of motifs found on greetings cards, particularly those for Christmas, Easter, weddings or birthdays, how conventionalised they are and how they use the motifs. Another contemporary example from the Greek world is the use of the Herakles-knot, a knot proverbially impossible to undo and so used, particularly in jewellery, as a symbol of indissoluble love.[18] In the later fourth century, and on into the early third, it is used commonly for the handles of wine-vessels designed for use at the symposion as well as for small containers of perfumed oil, doubtless for women's use. Here too the strength of meaning must be weakened (one could hardly think of the original meaning every time one saw such a handle), and the significance must rather be one loosely associated with good friendship and good fortune.

If masks could become an accepted symbol of happiness, one can see how they came to be used as motifs for jewellery such as necklaces, but it does not fully explain the association with Eros such as we have on ear-rings (Figure 5.8). Here we enter a very complex and at times difficult topic. Put briefly, and simply, a number of factors interconnect at this period. First the growing 'cult' of Eros in the sense that we find a growing number of representations of him in the course of the fourth century and later. This

Figure 5.9 Tarentine red-figure calyx-krater with Dionysos and Ariadne in the sanctuary, mask of a *papposilenos* below, soon after the middle of the fourth century BC. Basle BS 468

is in parallel with the pursuit of such deities as Health, Wealth, Good Fortune and so on, and it fits in as part of a general pattern seen in the increasing search for personal happiness, contentment and security. Fourth-century vase-painting also demonstrates a growing link between Eros and the world of Dionysos.[19] As a single example Figure 5.9 shows the embrace of Dionysos and Ariadne blessed by Eros. It is not without interest that a mask (in this case a *papposilenos*) is shown on the ground just below them.[20] The motif of Dionysos and Ariadne, which one sees depicted in a more proper or restrained way on such pieces as the Pronomos Vase (Figure 2.19), itself becomes growingly popular during this period, and there must be a sense in which it is taken to be an aim which one can oneself achieve in the happy world sought through and brought by Dionysos. If the world of Dionysos and the happiness he brings can be symbolised by a mask, the linking of the pleasures brought by Eros is symbolised iconographically by having Eros carry a mask. He carries it as he might carry other items concerned with parties and good times. On a pair of women's ear-rings the sense must be generalised and the message be that happiness is brought by Eros.

117

Figure 5.10 Paestan red-figure bell-krater with Dionysos and comic actor as slave at lady's window after the party, third quarter of the fourth century BC. Würzburg, Martin-von-Wagner Museum H 5771

In the context of the male-dominated symposion, however, the presence of Eros has another more practical connotation: the pleasures of women, whether during or after the party. It is for this reason, one imagines, that masks of *hetairai* from comedy come to outnumber all others on the Gnathia vases mentioned above. This too is the reason for the phenomenon on Paestan red-figure vases of the third quarter of the fourth century where a scene of Dionysos and a comic actor at a girl's window (Figure 5.10)[21] is substituted for the more straightforward one of a stage performance of men at a girl's window (Figure 5.11).[22] On the latter a slave or old man climbs a ladder to the window, a sash or fillet in his hand, while a friend stands watching, a *situla* of wine in his right hand and in his left a torch held high to light the way. This is after the party. On the former, Dionysos has the part taken by the senior figure in the other scene. He leans on a staff and has a phiale and fillet or sash in his left hand while he holds up two eggs with his right. His companion, the actor in the role of comic slave, carries a *kottabos*-stand tied with a red fillet in his left hand and holds up a torch with his right. The equipment makes it clear that here again we see an aftermath of the symposion. They both look up to the woman in the window. The god in real life does not need a ladder. Being a god, he would of course be successful in such an enterprise (as he was with Ariadne). What is happening in the iconography is that there is a building of equivalences

118

Figure 5.11 Paestan red-figure bell-krater with two actors as slaves approaching woman at window, soon after the middle of the fourth century BC. London, British Museum F 150

between the world of the stage (where this seems to have been a standard motif), the world of Dionysos where the actor acts as an assistant to the god, and the world of one's wishes or even experience where one looks for success with a girl, a success perhaps achieved with one's inhibitions removed and self-confidence promoted by the gift of the god. The purchaser of the vase might be supposed either to be hopeful enough to equate himself with the god and thereby wish himself success in his own amatory adventures under the inspiration of wine, or in a looser sense to associate himself with the happy band of Dionysos and his associates for whom the same fortunate results might be expected to follow.

Motifs such as these and Eros carrying a mask are symptomatic of the changing function of theatrical material and the way that the significance of an individual item can be simple or complex, depending in part on its context and on the clues the context may give of its original function. More difficult because we have no clear idea about their meaning are the so-called Tanagra figurines of boys or girls standing or sitting carrying masks (Figure 5.12).[23] There are not many girls and at this period they do not seem to be Muses (for one thing they look too young). The boys can wear wreaths or fillets about their heads, which makes one think of festive occasions and possibly of their involvement in the production process as assistants and thus in the celebration afterwards, but somehow they do not

Figure 5.12 Terracotta figurine from Tanagra of a youth holding a slave mask,
Early Hellenistic. Athens 4664. Ht 12 cm

have that air – they look too idealised. Others of them wear broad-brimmed
hats (*petasoi*) which again seem out of place in the theatre. Temple- and
therefore Sanctuary-attendants is a possibility and it would tie in well with
what we have seen of the use of theatrical material, but on present evidence
it can be no more than just a possibility.

In assessing the increasingly broad range in the use of the theatrical
material, it is important to bear in mind that throughout the third and
second centuries, depictions of masks made in the main Greek centres
seem to remain by and large accurate reflections of types as worn on
stage.[24] Occasionally a potter or coroplast will continue to manufacture
pieces from old moulds, but in general purchasers seem to have expected
depictions of masks and figures to be true to the contemporary stage. They
went to the theatre often enough and took it seriously enough to expect a
good standard of accuracy.

The patterns of distribution in Middle Hellenistic (say from the mid-
third to the mid-second century BC) to some extent become more even
than they were in Early Hellenistic (Figure 5.13). The markedly increased
number for Athens and Attica is due almost entirely to the habit of putting
representations of masks as an element in the decoration of relief bowls, to
be discussed in a moment. Asia Minor has increased numbers, particularly
towards the end of the period, and the trend continues in Late Hellenistic.
Egypt (together with a few pieces from Cyrenaica) also steadily increased its

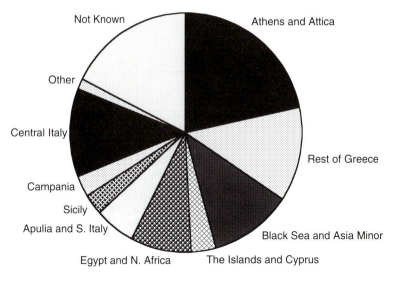

Figure 5.13 Provenances of New Comedy material, *c.* 250–150 BC

share but the proportion found in South Italy drops markedly after the Roman invasion, as of course does that of Sicily and the Lipari Islands. The role of Campania is a difficult one to assess. The quantity of material is not very great but for various reasons, as we shall see, one has a sense that its position was important. In the earlier part of this period, it seems to have been provincial, at least in style and taste if not in wealth, and the area seems to have been pivotal in the transmission of material and the ideas to Etruria. The chart makes clear the increase in the quantity of material found in Central Italy and a lot of it seems very strange and provincial by mainstream Greek standards, some by being at second remove, as it were, by way of Campania, but some with a distinctive character that must be due to the way that the Etruscans used this material, both as art and, one suspects, in performance. It is idiosyncratic and has very strong links with mime.

In the Greek world, the attitudes towards theatre that were evolved in the fourth century and the Early Hellenistic period continued in this, but so far as we can tell no radically new ideas or uses were developed. Masks, for example, continued to increase their share of the market (see Figure 5.3). In the same way we see extensions of existing ideas across (if anything) a broader range of materials. On any statistical count, the most important contribution still came from Athens, and that was the idea just mentioned of incorporating masks into the decorative schemes of clay relief bowls.[25] It has been argued that they were introduced as less expensive counterparts to metal bowls at the time of the visit of Ptolemy III Euergetes to Athens in

Figure 5.14 Mould-made relief bowl from the Athenian Agora with Erotes carrying slave masks and goats about kraters, Middle Hellenistic. Athens, Agora P 590

224/3 BC. Figure 5.14 is a fairly typical example.[26] The masks are included along with such motifs as Erotes, goats, wine vessels, dolphins, birds and similar motifs. They are included in their role as symbols of festivity and happiness. Sometimes the combinations of masks reflect conventional situations of the comic theatre, as old man and slave, old man and girl, but other combinations are with satyrs or *papposilenoi* where the reference to theatre is patently generic. More often, however, the bowls have repetitions of single masks, usually those of slave or old man. Other centres such as Delphi and Corinth soon came to imitate the Athenian bowls and incorporated masks as part of the general imitation.[27] On the other hand Delos, which became an increasingly active trading centre during this period and increasingly wealthy, took over the idea but was more original in its handling of motifs, at times incorporating figures from comedy as well as masks. In this case the figures seem to have been inspired by representations in other media, for example wall-painting.[28]

These clay bowls with relief decoration (often referred to by the conventional name of Megarian bowls) are part of a more general trend towards increased production of inexpensive counterparts to more costly metalware, a trend which was already beginning in the later part of the fifth century but which became more pronounced in the Hellenistic period. The sheer quantity of these bowls suggests that the metal versions were not uncommon. They reflect the increased use of precious and semi-precious

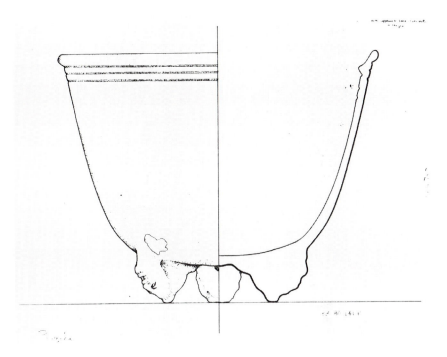

Figure 5.15 Bowl with mask feet from Pizzica (Metaponto), Middle Hellenistic.
Metaponto 141P (PZ 80)

metals as the material looted or acquired during the Greek expansion in the eastern Mediterranean flowed back into Old Greece. Also deriving ultimately from metal but with a much longer and fuller tradition in clay are masks used as appliqués at the handle-attachments of drinking vessels, particularly of the shape known as the kantharos, which itself seems to have become popular because of its associations with Herakles and Dionysos. In this case too the idea seems to have originated in Athens and to have spread widely. Another type of appliqué seems to have been of non-Athenian origin and that is the use of masks as feet (usually three in number) for bowls made to drink wine from or, in larger versions, simply to contain wine.[29] In this case Corinth, a famous centre for metalwork, may have been the point of origin, and we have clay versions from there and other parts of southern Greece as well as from Asia Minor, Sicily and especially South Italy (where Corinthian influence in pottery and metalwork was demonstrably strong). Figure 5.15 is such a bowl from the *chora* of Metaponto.[30] In section the bowl describes a parabolic curve and examples typically have thin walls (doubtless an aspect of the imitation of metal). It has three feet at the bottom to give it greater stability, and in this case they are in the form

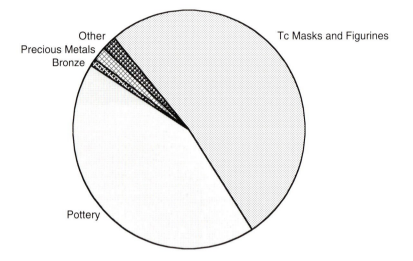

Figure 5.16 The material of surviving objects representing comedy, *c.* 250–150 BC

of masks of a comic youth. The vessel has the capacity of a drinking cup. A pair of silver bowls with gilded details acquired not many years ago by the Metropolitan Museum of Art in New York are larger, with a height of about 19 cm, and they must have served as wine containers.[31] They are part of a hoard of silver-ware including other bowls and drinking vessels, a casket with relief decoration, a wine ladle and a small portable altar, all of which seem to have been designed for the symposion. It is likely that they were found in South Italy. The two bowls have the masks of young men and slaves attached to form the feet. Both types wear wool fillets wound about with ribbons and with ivy-fruit attached: they are festive. The hair, the wreaths and the beards of the slaves were gilded.

Figure 5.16 demonstrates the impact of these pottery vessels, and I have also included in that category a series of braziers ornamented with masks on their sides that makes its appearance some time shortly before the middle of the second century. The more common versions have a lively reproduction of a comic slave mask (Figure 5.17).[32] About fifty of them are known.[33] There is also a female equivalent, a *hetaira* with snub nose and hair arranged in melon waves.[34] These are less common but equally widespread. Recorded findspots for the series range from Heraclea Minoa in Sicily, to Rome, Naples, Bari and Taranto, to Athens and Corinth, Benghazi, Carthage and Cyprus, together with an impressive number from Egypt. In many cases the clay of which they are made suggests they were manufactured locally, but they always remained close to the pattern and in this respect are a strong argument not only for the unity of the Greek world at this period, but more particularly for the unity of its theatre practice. The

Figure 5.17 Brazier from Corinth with slave mask, *c.* 150 BC. Corinth C-48-126.
Preserved ht *c.* 25.5 cm

masks themselves often exhibit a very lively character and this of itself argues for direct inspiration from the theatre rather than studio copies of copies. These were ordinary inexpensive charcoal burners which served as heaters or on occasion grills or broilers. They emphasise once more that direct appreciation and knowledge of the theatre was common to all levels of society.

A more up-market version of the same sort of thing is to be seen in a splendid brazier-foot found in Delos (Fig. 5.18a–c).[35] It probably dates to the Late Hellenistic period. It is only 16 cm high and is composed of three relief masks, (a) a young man, (b) a girl with rather forlorn expression who is probably a *pseudokore*, and (c) an older woman. The young man is a rustic (like Gorgias in Menander's *Dyskolos*), the old woman a procuress. In some senses they evoke a standard comedy situation, but the use of a rustic's mask is unusual and the set may have recalled a particular comedy. The quality of manufacture is outstanding, with clear, sharp features and careful detail; the way the hair ends in twisted corkscrew curls is typical of this period and is a feature that becomes more prominent on later examples.

The Late Hellenistic period (from roughly the middle of the second century to about the middle of the first) is one which is slowly coming to be better understood, due in no small part to work on the Italian side. Important as a factor in any assessment is the political and military

(a)

(b)

(c)

Figure 5.18 Foot of brazier from Delos decorated with the masks of
(a) a young man, (b) a girl, and (c) an older woman, Late Hellenistic.
Delos B 3718. Ht *c.* 16 cm

expansion of Rome which brought with it the phenomenon of the looting
of Greek material and the enormous impact it had back in Rome.[36] More
significant perhaps for our purposes here (because it concerns objects that
survive and we can assess) is the growing importance of Italian traders, and
especially Campanians, in the Aegean world. This is a connection which
seems to have been building up through much of the earlier part of the
second century. There is good evidence for Campanian black-glaze pottery
in Delos, and it must have belonged to traders who had established
themselves in this very wealthy and active port.[37] There is also said to be
similar pottery in Alexandria and in Corinth, although for the moment it
remains unpublished. It begins to look as if the cities of the Bay of Naples
(including those to be destroyed by Vesuvius) played a major part in the
transmission of Greek culture and material at a more mundane level. Some
of the key material from Pompeii was preserved until the time of the
destruction in AD 79, presumably as recognised antiques. The role the
Campanians played in this period is a development of the one they had
played in earlier times with material and ideas from the Greek cities of
South Italy and Sicily.

127

We have already looked at the mosaics made by Dioskourides and set into a floor in Pompeii probably in the later part of the second century (Figure 5.5). It is noteworthy that he identified himself as coming from Samos.[38] We may also recall two well-known terracotta statuettes which were found by the garden door of a house near the Theatre of Pompeii in the early excavations in 1762.[39] They are each something over a metre high. By the time of the town's destruction they were old and they may have been put out in the garden because they no longer deserved a place in the house. One of them represents one of the leading young men of New Comedy, the other a *pseudokore*, the heroine, in a mask with drooping brows and earnest expression, her brown hair parted and brushed smoothly back, and then tied elaborately with a thin ribbon. She wears a blue dress and a mauve mantle. The best and virtually only known counterpart to terracottas of this kind is a head from a statuette of approximately the same large size found years ago on the island of Paros in the Cyclades and now lost.[40]

Stylistically related (and close, too, to the Delos brazier shown in Figure 5.18) is the so-called Vollmer Group, a series of masks quite probably of Campanian origin but found (in originals and copies) in other parts of South Italy, Sicily, Etruria, and then in Egypt and the eastern Aegean.[41] It is good evidence that Campania was becoming an active participant in the Hellenistic world and not simply a recipient; her theatrical products were acceptable to more long-standing members of that world. In their modelling and style the masks exhibit an immediacy which suggests first-hand acquaintance with contemporary developments in staging and performance. In this case the strongest links seem to have been with the eastern Aegean and coastal Asia Minor, and one thinks of the policy of cooperation with Rome maintained by the Pergamene kings Eumenes II and Attalos II, culminating in Eumenes III bequeathing his kingdom to the Romans in 133 BC.

Finds from the Islands and Asia Minor (together with a little from the Black Sea) make up about half the total represented in the distribution chart, Figure 5.19. That the share of Athens and Greece proper is now so small is an indication of their comparative lack of wealth. The quantity from Central Italy declines a little with the final decline of the Etruscans (and in part, one suspects, because we happen to have very little by way of direct discoveries of small finds of this period from Rome itself). The Egypt of the Ptolemies continues to demonstrate its interest in theatre. What is evident in such a chart but has never been explained is the fact that while the kingdom of Pergamon and that of the Ptolemies possessed and manufactured a great deal of theatrical material, there is hardly anything from any point in the Hellenistic period from the territory of the Seleucids in the eastern Mediterranean. Indeed much of the little we do have seems to be coincidental, as the decoration of an object imported for its own sake.

Another set of objects which emphasises the links between Campania and

128

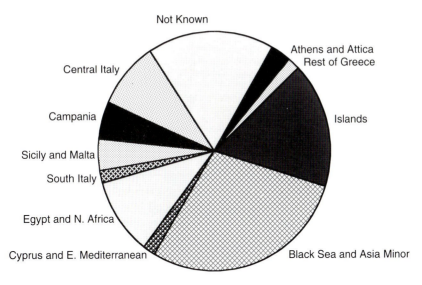

Figure 5.19 Provenances of New Comedy material, *c.* 150–50 BC

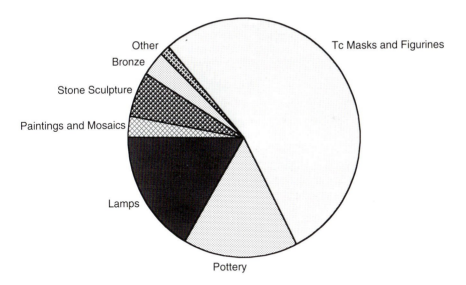

Figure 5.20 The material of surviving objects representing comedy, *c.* 150–50 BC

the Aegean world is a series of reproductions of masks and figurines of actors modelled in the form of small oil vessels and perfume pots. They were manufactured through much of the Middle and Late Hellenistic periods and one can even find late secondary versions under the Empire.[42]

129

The favourite masks represent the young heroes and heroines and the slaves of New Comedy. The figurines often seem to derive, directly or indirectly, from more major art but at the same time are chosen as figures representing typical popular situations.[43] Thus the character found most often is one popular since the late fifth century, the slave sitting on an altar, in refuge from punishment for the mischief he has been up to. Similar in its function is a figurine from this series now in Canberra but originally found in Cyprus (Figure 5.21).[44] The subject is a slave from comedy drunk and happy (as the gesture with the right arm shows), lying against a wine amphora, a festive wreath about his head. He is the wavy-haired comic slave (Mask 27 in the list by Pollux), a character often associated with party-going and the good times, and it is for this reason that he usually wears the wreath. He is found too in the company of flute-girls or bringing his young master home after an all-night party. His intrigues to achieve a good time or to justify such escapades clearly made him a popular character in the theatre and the sort of character one liked to have as a souvenir.

One has the impression, admittedly subjective, that these charming little vessels are original inventions, not copies from metal. They come in a fairly wide range of varieties and a number have counterparts in the form of non-dramatic figures such as blacks and other genre-types. They are usually covered with a lustrous black glaze, often with details picked up with red and white paint, and are pleasant and comfortable to handle. Known

Figure 5.21 Terracotta figurine from Cyprus of slave reclining with wine amphora, Late Hellenistic. Canberra, Australian National University 79.05. Ht 11.1 cm

findspots include Campania, Etruria, Egypt, North Africa, Cyprus, Sicily, and cities of the Black Sea coast. Like the braziers mentioned above, they serve to demonstrate the shared culture of these parts of the world at this period.

A glance back to Figure 5.3 will show that the quantity of material preserved from this period is somewhat greater than that from Early Hellenistic.[45] The statistics are partly a reflection of the repetitious nature of some of the material (although that was true of Middle Hellenistic also), but it is evident that despite the declining economy of Old Greece, other parts of the Greek and Italian worlds were prospering. What is perhaps more surprising is the increased proportion of representations of figures from comedy as compared with masks. The reason for this arises out of a new phenomenon which seems to have developed with the period.

The so-called House of the Comedians at Delos had in its main reception room a painted frieze about 25 cm high and originally 11–12 m long. It was decorated with a series of scenes from tragedy and comedy.[46] Only a little over 5 m of it survives, and most of that is in poor condition, but there is enough to make out the character of a few of the scenes. One has a slave seated on an altar supporting himself with his left hand; facing him is a standing figure, probably male, wearing a white cloak which comes to his knees; also present is an old slave with white peaked hair and wearing a grey *chiton* and mantle.[47] The scene seems to have been a famous one, referring to a well-known play (some have thought of Menander's *Perinthia*). It is known in a number of copies and in numerous excerpts, especially the slave on the altar, who, as we have already seen, appears in terracottas as well as in bronze figurines, marble statuettes and on gems. Other pictures from the frieze have the same character, with scenes possibly from *Perikeiromene* and *Aspis*.[48] They are copies of famous scenes from comedy collected together into a continuous frieze, mixed with scenes from tragedy.

It is reasonable to ask what the function of this use of copies of famous masterpieces might have been, even if any answer can be no more than hypothesis. This is a period when copies and adaptations of earlier motifs became extremely popular in general. The Greeks had become much more conscious of their past and looked back to the fifth and fourth centuries as something of a golden age. Copies and imitations of earlier styles became popular in most arts, and in sculpture one finds a range of material that refers back in a rather post-modernist way to earlier work in constructing new and so in imbuing it with meaning. This is a fashion which argues for a fairly sophisticated audience.

It is possible to argue that something of this can be seen rather earlier in the comedies of Plautus which exhibit a consciousness of the artificiality of New Comedy and at times make deliberate play with it, developing the medium on the basis of the audience's knowledge of traditional routines.[49] Terence, by contrast, in the years just before the beginning of this period, attempted to maintain, or more likely, rather, revive something of the purity of the original, and it is tempting therefore to compare him with the neo-classical wing of contemporary art, and especially sculpture. One should not, however, make too much of all this, particularly so far as Plautus is concerned. Comedy had always been to some degree self-conscious and self-referential, and reference to comedy routines is explicit already in Aristophanes, and one supposes implicit also. In this respect Terence is perhaps the more interesting case. Despite all the scholarly effort, one still wishes there was more evidence to clarify the principles involved in his handling of earlier material. The seasoned and well-read member of the audience must have been conscious of what he was borrowing and from where, and Terence must have been consciously adding levels of meaning in the combinations and the way he carried them through.

The other important point to remember in this context is what must have been the curious and artificial appearance of comedy by this date. Menander had already been dead for two centuries and his comedies were classics rather than contemporary in their relevance. His plots related to an Athens that no longer existed, and to a social and economic world that had long passed away. His language must at times have appeared old-fashioned. The costumes too were certainly less and less like those of life outside the theatre. Masks were becoming more conventionalised. The hairstyles of the female masks were largely frozen in the fashion of the Early Hellenistic period, or, better, were contemporary interpretations of Early Hellenistic fashion. The beards of the old men were formed into quite artificial arrangements of vertical corkscrew curls. Most male masks were given side-hair in the form of ringlets by the ears (see for example, Figure 5.18). At this period this side-hair was short, but it was to become longer and more obvious under the Empire. Its function had nothing to do with life: it was included as decoration for the mask itself, framing the face. The artificiality of the mask was given explicit expression. Comedy had become a conventionalised performance and was presented in those terms.

Among theatrical material there is another interesting body of evidence for copying and adaptation and that is the series of terracotta figurines from Myrina in Asia Minor. It can be shown that several members of the group are translations into three dimensions of figures taken from Early Hellenistic paintings of scenes from comedy.[50] Figure 5.22, for example, is a cymbal player from the key scene of Menander's *Theophoroumene* which we have seen reproduced in mosaic by Dioskourides (Figure 5.5).[51] If further proof were needed, the angle at which the figure was meant to be seen is demonstrated by the fact that the vent-hole was cut in the figure's left hip, the side away from the intended viewing point. We also have terracotta versions of the tambourine player from the same picture.[52] Another example of this same process is that of a seated slave (Figure 5.23).[53] His pose only makes sense when he is arranged with his arm over the shoulder of a flute-girl, as we see in mirror-

Figure 5.22 Terracotta figurine from Myrina (Asia Minor) of the cymbal player
from the scene in Figure 5.5, perhaps later second century BC. Athens,
National Museum 5060. Ht 19 cm

image in the scene reproduced in Figure 5.24, a painting from Herculaneum,
one of a pair of such copies of Early Hellenistic archetypes.[54] We cannot
identify the play from which it comes with any certainty, and it is tantalising
that we cannot be sure what the object is that lies by the slave's feet: it surely did
something to particularise the scene. One might guess that the older figure
leaning on his stick on the left is chastising the slave for his carelessness and
drunkenness, but the latter is too happy and preoccupied with his musical
companion to take any notice. (We may note in passing that this is the same
slave type as in Figure 5.21, the leading slave with wavy hair, the one so often
associated with party-going.)

In the figurine of the seated slave the actor's lips are shown. Many of the
figurines from this remarkable series exhibit a considerable objectivity in
depiction, for example in showing the edge of the tights at ankle or wrist,
and more particularly in showing the mask as a mask, its back edge
distinguished, the actor's head with its short-cropped hair and, as here, the
actor's mouth sometimes visible inside; the features of the mask are often
modelled in dry, clear detail. In this respect they doubtless added to the

Figure 5.23 Terracotta figurine from Myrina (Asia Minor) of seated slave from the scene in Figure 5.24 (in mirror-image), perhaps later second century BC. Athens 5029. Ht *c.* 18 cm

detail present in the paintings from which they were drawn.

The tombs at Myrina in which these figures were found seem not to have contained any complete sets of figures which would have made up one of these scenes. These particular examples must have been sold separately as favourite figures. At the same time it is hard to imagine that a provincial site such as Myrina would have been the point of origin for such a series. It is probably reasonable to think of Pergamon as their centre of manufacture and to place them in the broader context of the Pergamene, and particularly Attalid, interest in the 'classical' past as seen in other copies of earlier work set up in Pergamon, or the interest in Athens demonstrated in the Attalid dedications on the Athenian Acropolis or the Stoa in the Athenian Agora. In any case they demonstrate something of the enterprise of artists of this period and the patterns that this enterprise took. They are also a further example of one of the ways in which major art was utilised for the ordinary citizen. They also explain something of the resurgence in the numbers of whole figures in theatrical material of this period (as compared with masks) and of what prompted it.

Figure 5.24 Wall-painting from Herculaneum with scene of girl piper and seated slave, perhaps third quarter of the first century AD. Naples 9035. 39 × 40 cm

Figure 5.25 Marble relief from Pompeii with a set of masks, perhaps Early Imperial. Naples 6633. Ht 29.5 cm

So far in this section we have looked at some examples of the copying process and the way it was conducted, and at adaptations such as the translation from a two-dimensional medium into a three-dimensional. Another important feature of the art of the period is so-called Neo-Classicism. It is a style which, as we have it, belongs to sculpture and it is to be seen in a variety of subjects. The most important for us is the series of still-lifes composed of masks. The idea seems to have come from Athens and it is a good and fairly early example of the way that the city came to trade on its past as a seat of tradition and old learning. This is a pattern which continued on through the first century AD and into the second. Figure 5.25 is typical.[55] It is a rectangular relief, apparently of Pentelic marble, with what were originally four masks. They seem to represent father (upper right), son and family slave (lower left). From other versions we know that the missing mask on the lower right was probably that of a *kolax* or professional flatterer or sponger. It is likely that the original concept was inspired by the cast of a play. The subsidiary elements, the temple here, the altar on other examples, give the setting as a sanctuary. The idea evoked is the dedication of masks after a successful performance. The order of the temple here is Ionic, the order of the Temple in the Sanctuary of Dionysos at Athens. The masks depicted echo Early Hellenistic types (even if from our perspective we may judge them not to be quite correct archaeo-logically), and so the purchaser could have supposed them to depict, reflect or more distantly recall the theatre of the classic age of Menander. One could use such a relief as a decorative souvenir, but those set in the wall of the peristyle of the Casa degli Amorini Dorati at Pompeii, or those erected on small pedestals in the central garden area suggest that a key function was to help re-create the sanctuary itself in one's garden.

The neo-classical reliefs with Dionysos visiting a comic poet (the so-called Ikarios reliefs) may also be mentioned here even if a number of them were actually manufactured at a somewhat later date.[56] The theme is a typical creation of this period. The figure of the drunken Dionysos supported by a satyr is one with a long history, going back to the fifth century, and in this particular version it appears in a number of reliefs all of which are presumably taken from a famous original (some think by Praxiteles) and incorporated into some suitable scheme. On these he enters the courtyard of the house (or sanctuary?) of a comic poet who reclines on a couch to the left of the scene and turns round to express surprise and greeting at the appearance of the god and his retinue. On a number of the examples, the poet is characterised by a group of masks. The theme is the poet inspired and sharing the world of the god. It is a development of the motif we saw on fourth-century vases and is handled in a way typical of this period. This same idea is also seen in two well-known plaster casts from metalware.[57] The first, in Oxford, was found in Egypt and its scene would appear to be set in Egypt;[58] it has a male with right arm raised in the company of a female at a symposion which includes dancers and has a row of masks in the background. The plaster from Begram has a poet seated under a tree before a woman, perhaps a Muse, who holds a mask. The Menander reliefs mentioned above also fall into the same category.

In the Late Hellenistic period, then, theatrical material was often used within terms of contemporary fashion. The art of the past was used as a vehicle through which to approach theatre and the dionysiac. In an uncertain world it provided a link with tradition and the past that was in itself valuable. This process can also be viewed as an attempt by individuals to take into their own domain works of a type and character that had hitherto been public, the property of a sanctuary. This is an important phenomenon in the history of the relationship between the individual and his community, between the individual and the state. We may remind ourselves that in antiquity this was not the easy process that it is for us in an age of comparatively simple copying techniques, especially through photographic means. It was not inexpensive and demanded skill and often ingenuity on the part of the artists – as we have seen for example with the Myrina terracottas. It was not without its creative side. It must have been driven in part by an acquisitive instinct on the part of the purchaser. More important, though (since these objects do not always belong to the houses of the particularly wealthy, but rather the prosperous), is the way that this material represents a retreat from the public world and enjoyment of what had been the benefits of communal activity at a private level, in a smaller social circle.

One can see elements of the same attitudes in a number of other important works of the period. One is the border of the so-called Tiger Rider mosaic from the House of the Faun at Pompeii.[59] It was found in the triclinium, the equivalent of the Greek symposion room, and was an integral part of its decoration. The central motif of the young Dionysos riding a tiger is surrounded by a thick garland wound with ribbon, and about it eight comic masks, six male and two female (two old men, an old slave and a younger slave, two youths and two females). The 'Dove Mosaic', though of poorer quality and less well preserved, seems likely to derive from the same original.[60] Fragments of yet another, published not long ago by Janine Lancha, seem to follow the same pattern.[61] It too seems likely to be from one of the Vesuvian cities, if of slightly later date: it is likely to be early Augustan. The style of the masks, and particularly of those of the Old Men, quite clearly echoes Early Hellenistic. One may also note them as another instance of the way the Campanian work is linked to that of the Aegean. They are precisely parallel to two mosaic floors in Delos.[62]

More distinctly personal possessions are engraved gems. As mentioned above, there is good evidence from some surviving impressions that gems with theatrical subject-matter were already being manufactured in the Early Hellenistic period, and there is a fine example with a Muse holding

Figure 5.26 Cast of a sardonyx cameo with scene from comedy of angry father and drunken young man, late second or early first century BC. Geneva 1974/21133. 3.95 × 5.7 cm

Figure 5.27 Marble relief possibly from Rome with same scene as Figure 5.26, perhaps late first century AD. Naples 6687. 45 × 53 cm

a mask from a grave datable to about 200 BC. M.-F. Boussac has recently published a gem impression from Delos, from a house that was destroyed in 69 BC.[63] It was made by a stone bearing the frontal mask of an Old Man or Slave of typically Early Hellenistic style, implying long survival of a single gem, or copying of Early Hellenistic types at this date. Either is possible. Such cases as this apart, however, the dating of gems is slowly becoming clear despite all the problems posed by the longevity of individual pieces and what seems to have been a common habit of close copying of earlier motifs. Many pieces (particularly copies in glass paste) are now plausibly placed in the first century BC, and this appears to be the period with the fullest range of types. One of the finest and most interesting theatrical gems to survive is a cameo in Geneva, datable to the years about 100 BC (Figure 5.26).[64] It is after the same archetype as the well-known marble relief in Naples with a scene from Comedy (Figure 5.27), and again both should derive from an original of the Early Hellenistic period.[65] The gem is a typical Late Hellenistic creation both in this respect and in the transference of public art to personal possession. Comic scenes on gems are rare, although extracts from scenes are fairly common. These take the form of individual figures, such as the slave seated on an altar, which in the earlier stages seem to have been recognised as extracts from and therefore representatives of fuller scenes. With the passage of time, however, their particularity seems to have faded and they became simply favourite figures. Even their identity could change, as with the fairly common type of an old man standing frontal, a crook in his hand and very often his other hand to his beard.[66] Sometimes he seems to be understood as a leading Old Man, but at other times he is certainly characterised as a *pornoboskos*, complete with the elaborate clothing of fine material that is said to have belonged to the part. The date range seems to run from early in the first century BC until well on in the Imperial period.

Gems decorated with masks were a popular item. The most popular are those of the *pornoboskos*, the cook, and of course the Leading Slave, which by far outnumbers all others and probably outlasts them, evidence yet again that the mask of the slave typified the comic theatre for a large number of people. Gems in antiquity often had a talismanic significance, and we should probably not be far wrong in seeing here a development of the Early Hellenistic idea of figures such as Erotes holding masks as symbols of good fortune and happiness. Certainly it becomes more and more obvious, once one reaches the late first century BC and beyond, that gems were largely created within their own iconographic tradition rather than as snapshots from contemporary theatre. The styles of mask were modified through time against current fashion, but the same mask types tended to continue and in the same combinations. But this takes us beyond the present period.

The less well off maintained an interest in theatrical motifs in the Late

Hellenistic period in much the same manner as they had before. Bowls with relief decoration including theatrical motifs continued, though in diminished numbers, notably in the more provincial areas.[67] Pergamene pottery of this period was at times decorated with applied reliefs which included theatrical motifs such as masks or the popular *papposilenos* carrying a basket.[68] Important numerically are the so-called Knidian and Ephesian lamps which used relief masks as a regular element in their decoration.[69] The mask-types used include some Old Men, more are *Pornoboskoi*, but most are Slaves. They can be interpreted as reflecting the popular view of what was interesting in comedy, or what comedy was about. Old men had typified comedy for a long time, and these are the masks often held by a Muse or an Eros. The Old Man's part was essential to the plot, if only as a foil to the action, the conservative element. Among the Slaves, the one with wavy hair (Mask 27) is again the most popular, and presumably for the same sorts of reasons we have just seen in other material, because he typifies ingenuity in bucking the system and engineering a good time. The interest in the *pornoboskos* is paralleled in gems and is not easy to explain in either case. It may well be that he was given a new importance in contemporary comedy (we do not have the evidence to say). His prominence could be a reflection of a growing importance of the profession in contemporary society, as part of a more organised arrangement of the sex trade; or it could reflect an equation of theatre and symposion, and what was reflected as a result of the symposion.[70] Whatever the explanation, it is an interesting social phenomenon. Indeed the series in general reflects what some elements of contemporary society saw in the comic theatre. The interest has become generic, less technically interested in the detail of plot and variation in character. This impression is strengthened by the handling of the motifs on these lamps. The production is repetitious, the moulds for the masks are often worn and it becomes difficult to distinguish them from the equally popular masks of satyrs and *papposilenoi*. This was mass production without any close relationship to theatre practice. The theatre is used as a popular image that carries with it the idea of festivity.

The Ephesian and Knidian lamps represent one end of a range of theatrical material. A series of clay lamp-lids whose origin seems to lie in the region of Smyrna has a different character.[71] It includes a greater number of mask-types. The masks are in high relief and, in the earlier part of the series, carefully made with sharp detail, providing seemingly accurate representations of contemporary masks. They almost certainly copied bronze prototypes and the metal versions must have been more expensive. Even these little clay ones must have been a little more expensive than the routine Knidian and Ephesian, but not so as to be out of range for a wide public: they are good evidence for a widespread and discerning interest in the theatre in this region.

Also having links to bronze is one of the finest and most interesting lamps of this period (see Figure 5.7).[72] It is a box-shaped lamp of Egyptian manufacture with seven spouts for the wicks. On the upper face are six masks in relief. They are slightly overcrowded into the available space and it seems unlikely that they were made for this use in the first instance. The details are sharp and carefully modelled, and the masks were quite possibly copied by making moulds from a metal original of some kind. They are, from the left, an old woman, a young man, a cook, a girl (probably a *pseudokore*), a procurer (*pornoboskos*, with typical bald head, raised brows and flowing beard), and a slave. There is no old man but the selection could otherwise represent the case of a play, and it may have done so in the original, where there may, of course, have been more than the six masks included here.[73] The lamp-maker may have borrowed them with no such direct intention; we cannot know. It remains a unique piece.

These various varieties of simple clay objects show that it would be running ahead of the evidence to suppose that there was a simple equation between the more wealthy members of society and more sophisticated interest in theatre. This is something which will emerge later, as popular theatre developed in different directions, and traditional comedy and tragedy became the province of a more educated elite, but it has not happened yet. The difference lies, rather, in the material product itself and the labour costs involved in its manufacture.

6

CONVENTIONS AND THE CLASSICS

Greek theatre in the Roman world

As we know very well nowadays, the problem with classics is one of survival. They survive as long as they have meaning for a society. Once they lose their relevance, which is normally as some sort of reference point, they disappear into an academic twilight, possibly to be lost altogether. The debt of the Romans to Greek culture was a complex one, and it had in fact been accumulating since as early as the eighth century BC when we first find imported Greek pottery at the site of Rome. Nevertheless the level of awareness of Greek literary and material culture rose sharply with the expansion of Rome's political and military power in the early part of the third century BC. Thus the Roman theatre-buildings of Latium and Campania are constructed in a direct tradition from such buildings as the late-fourth century theatre at the Greek colony of Metaponto in South Italy.[1] Plautus in the late third and early second century, Terence, Ennius and Pacuvius in the first half of the second, and Accius in the later second century are the best evidence one could have for the development of a Roman counterpart to Greek drama (even if we know frustratingly little about its appearance on stage). Plautus and Terence are the best preserved and it is clear that they not only preserved Greek settings and names from the originals that they exploited as the basis of their comedies but that Plautus in particular would exaggerate the 'greekness' for comic effect.[2] Audiences must have enjoyed the exotic flavour, and have had some measure of respect for that foreign culture.

By the later years of Republic this fashion seems largely to have passed. Material of the same style and/or quality was no longer being produced, although in the late Republic the great actors like Roscius and Aesopus played them as classics. One finds echoes and reminiscences of them, of course, and some passages are given an extended life as points of reference, like the lover's despair from the beginning of Terence's *Eunuchus* which was picked up by Horace and Persius.[3] This is parallel to the copying with up-dating that one finds in art. Contemporary theatre was a different matter and theatre audiences were turning to a variety of other enter-tainments, including mime and pantomime which were to become more and more important. In the prologue to his *Hecyra* Terence already provides good evidence for the variety of entertainment presented in Roman theatres in the course of a single programme. The playwright complains about having to compete for attention with tight-rope walkers, boxers and gladiatorial combats. The period in question is the years immediately preceding 160 BC, but it was a pattern which continued. In the time of Augustus, Horace (*Ep.* 2.1.180–207) makes an eloquent statement along the same lines, and one might think that the greater public preferred anything to the traditional genres of tragedy and comedy.

Given all this, that theatre of the kind we have been discussing was a foreign implant and that its importance in Roman culture was limited, it is fascinating that the Theatre of Pompey, Rome's first permanent theatre building constructed in 55 BC, was said to claim ancestry from the theatre of Mytilene in Lesbos,[4] and then that the so-called Theatre of Marcellus, built by Augustus in the period between 20 and 10 BC, should have the keystones of the first two levels of the exterior arches decorated with large marble masks of characters from tragedy, comedy and satyr-play.[5] They were each approximately 70 cm high. These masks were not, however, of contemporary appearance. In a typically Augustan classicising way, they imitated the appearance of Early Hellenistic masks and so formed an explicit link with traditional theatre. One purpose of the decoration was presumably to give the building a legitimacy, and even conservatism, in an environment that had a reputation for being volatile. The scheme falls neatly within the broader Augustan policy of piety in the visible attitude to the past. One thinks of the emphasis in the emperor's *Res Gestae* on the restoration of temples, or of his restoration of the Erechtheion on the Athenian Acropolis and then the use of motifs from it, such as the Caryatids in the Forum Augusti in Rome or the copying of the detailing from the door of the North Porch for his Temple of Mars Ultor in the same complex. In quoting past monuments for present purposes, the Princeps was following a tradition discussed in the previous chapter.[6] What was different here was the importance these quotations acquired as a result of the scale of the enterprise and the standing of their patron. As a consequence they developed a life of their own.

The masks which decorated the Theatre of Marcellus seem to have been carved from a variety of marbles, including Pentelic, and it is not unlikely that Athenian sculptors were imported to carry out the work. Having done the job, it looks as if they moved on to other similar work. It is hard to be sure if some closely comparable masks in Athens such as one in the Kerameikos, perhaps from the Council House of the Actors' Guild, came before or after.[7] The key piece preserved is a large marble representation of a slave mask of Augustan style but looking back to Early Hellenistic in some aspects of its appearance. A rather battered pair of comic masks on a double herm in the Museo Barracco in Rome and doubtless from Central

Italy, seems to be of Pentelic marble, and the fact that they represent the unusual combination of a Flatterer (*kolax*) and an Old Woman suggests some particular origin or informed choice by the patron rather than run-of-the-mill copy-work from a shop producing garden sculpture.[8] More certainly in a tradition following the Augustan series are masks from Pompeii and environs (including a superb set at present on the New York market), and pieces such as these seem to have inspired others in their turn. In other words, a distinctively Augustan style emerged and it had as its basis Early Hellenistic. But it was an art style and had little to do with contemporary theatre practice. Similarly, the masks decorating the outside of the Theatre of Marcellus should not be taken as evidence for the sort of performance that was presented inside.

The Theatre of Marcellus was in many respects a prototype for a long series of theatre-buildings constructed under the early Empire. The Augustan theatre at Verona seems to have followed it closely enough to have also had masks on the exterior.[9] Other such buildings may not have been quite so elaborate, but it is worth noting how many of them were built at this period in northern Italy and the western provinces. They were an integral feature of the urban development projects encouraged by the central government and they had a role that was both symbolic and functional – as meeting places for the population of their cities and the surrounding areas.[10] It is for this sort of reason that the huge and elaborate façades of the stage-buildings (the *scaenae frontes*) came to be adorned with images of Augustus and the Imperial family. It is significant that in Vergil's *Aeneid* (1.427–9), when Aeneas has a view of the building works of Dido's Carthage, they include just such a theatre, with vast columns for the *scaenae frons*.

These theatres were a vital part of the Augustan programme of urbanis-ation. What happened on their stages is a much more difficult question.[11] The Romans had a tradition which associated their own early performances with those of the Etruscans,[12] yet if we try to assess the style of performance in Etruria even in the Late Hellenistic period, it seems noticeably provincial by the standards of other parts of the Hellenistic world. Some of the terracotta figurines are well-known and attractive, but they are now demonstrated to have only marginal relevance to the tradition of Greek theatre practice.[13] It helps that large numbers of terracottas were produced in Etruria at this period and local styles are steadily becoming recognisable. The material from the Museum at Tarquinia, for example, has recently been published by Stefani and allows other unprovenanced material now scattered round the world's museums to be attached to the same work-shops. The most popular of the Tarquinian masks are versions of that favourite figure of New Comedy, the cook, but there is an interesting number of masks of old women – in a higher proportion than is found in other centres. One suspects that their grotesque, caricatured appearance had something to do with their popularity, not least because the features of some of the cook and slave masks are also exaggerated to the point of being grotesques. One has the impression that they were adapting imported Greek types for their own purposes. A very fine set of Tarquinian terracotta masks and figurines is now in the Virginia Museum of Fine Arts in Richmond (it must have been a tomb group). It combines masks which would pass muster within the Greek tradition with re-interpreted copies from the Greek, and then grotesques and what seem likely to be mimes. The group is an excellent case of the blending of the two traditions and it may be evidence of the way that mime developed at least in part as a response to or reaction against their local and rather distant view of Greek theatre. There is room for more work along these lines.

The written evidence for performance of what we may call traditional theatre in Late Republican and Early Imperial Rome is extremely difficult and ambiguous.[14] There is little firm evidence for the performance even of so central an author as Menander. One of the problems is that it is difficult to distinguish in the sources between knowledge of an author based on performance and one based on literary knowledge. Even when the evidence for knowledge through performance seems reasonably certain, it is difficult to distinguish between public performances and private, and then between performances of complete plays and recitations of famous passages or highlights. The latter was a practice which had become increasingly common, although it has recently been argued that the performance of complete comedies at dinner-parties was not as rare as is sometimes thought.[15] Statius, for example (*Silvae* 2.i.114), describes a young slave reciting Menander, in a passage where the poet is admired for his language and the boy for his beauty and a skill which would being him a victory-crown of roses.

The problems are not dissimilar when one tries to assess knowledge acquired by literary means. Does a quotation in itself provide evidence of a love of and deep acquaintance with dramatic literature? or is it based on knowledge of a popular passage, perhaps learned painfully at school, or simply a famous tag, known without context, as many know particular lines or phrases of Shakespeare, a commonplace of one's culture? There is no doubt that Menander, like Terence, had a key role in education, particularly for the sons of the upper classes who tended to undertake rhetorical training and were expected to practise declaiming key speeches.[16]

The material remains also suggest that performance of traditional theatre was hardly popular with the greater public. The cheaper objects made in Central Italy at this period, such as lamps, relief bowls or terracotta figurines, include very little that is theatrical, and even what there is seems only partly understood. Arretine pottery has surprisingly few proper masks. The majority have closed mouths and generalised features. They belong to that iconographic tradition in which such bowls are decorated with masks

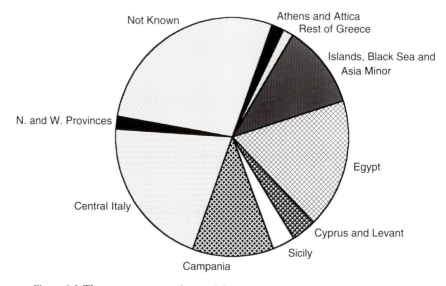

Figure 6.1 The provenances of material representing comedy, *c.* 50 BC–AD 50
(gems not included)

as symbols of festivity, but in using them to decorate the bowls there has
been no reference back to the theatre itself. Possibly something of an
exception is the comparatively large number of terracotta antefixes
decorated with masks which add so many to the count of terracottas for this
period (Figure 6.2). There are two major series: those with representations
of slave-masks at the heart of a triangular-shaped palmette, and then a large
series of panels with slave-masks in arched frames.[17] Both must have lasted
for a long time: there is noticeable re-working of the moulds within the
series. Their primary function should have been decorative, but we know
very little of the structures to which they were attached and so it is difficult
to deduce much of their function. On the face of it, it seems rather an odd
use for theatrical material.

Figure 6.1 is interesting evidence of the shift in the balance of power. Old
Greece now has a very minor share as Athens, for example, only slowly
recovers from the Sullan sack and Corinth is only recently re-established.
The Islands and Asia Minor have also lost their wealth and economic
activity: note the enormous shrinkage compared with Figure 5.19. Sicily and
South Italy are also impoverished, especially the latter. Campania's figures,
on the other hand, now include the earlier material from Pompeii. The
development of the nearer parts of the northern and western provinces
under the Early Empire begins to be reflected in material of this kind too.
The proportion of material of uncertain centre of manufacture is now
large, as it is too in Figure 6.3, but in both cases a good part of that section
comprises material such as bronze figurines and other minor objects, easily

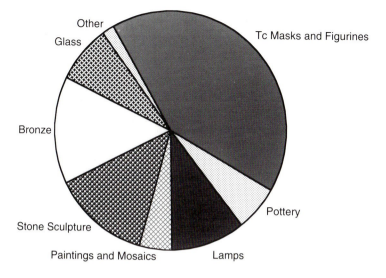

Figure 6.2 The material of surviving objects representing comedy,
c. 50 BC–AD 50 (gems not included)

transportable, that were made for Roman patrons. If gems had been included, the section would have been considerably larger.

Somewhat unexpected in Figure 6.1, perhaps, is Egypt's share. To some degree this must reflect her continued wealth at this period, but it must be admitted that we continue to underestimate her importance in the continuation of the Hellenistic tradition, and the way in which Egypt acted as a channel for Hellenistic ideas. The effect of Alexandrian scholarship and learning tends to be taken for granted. Her influence in other areas is often ignored, despite the fad at that period for Nilotic mosaics, the importance of Egyptian-manufactured glass and semi-precious materials such as carved gemstones and cameos, or vessels made of the same materials, or most obviously the schemes of the enormously popular Second Style of Pompeian wall-painting which derive directly from Alexandrian architecture.[18]

The number of objects reflecting theatre declined markedly after the middle of the first century AD, and again we have to be careful in assessing those that were produced as good evidence for theatre. Many could be regarded as secondary: one thinks of the popular masks on grave monuments where the intent, so far as we can discern it, seems to have been to evoke the happiness of the Bacchic afterlife. Many of them have a generalised, non-specific character, even to the extent that it can be difficult to distinguish between comic and tragic. They became very common on garland sarcophagi of the second century where they are combined with satyr and maenad masks and a range of other bacchic

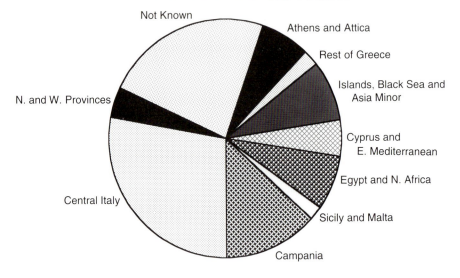

Figure 6.3 The provenances of objects representing comedy, *c.* AD 50–180

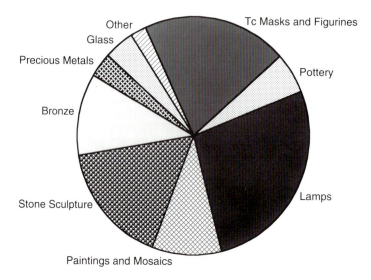

Figure 6.4 The material of surviving objects representing comedy, *c.* AD 50–180

motifs.[19] There is also a good number of bronze masks used as attachments on furniture, vessels of one kind or another, and on lamps and other household items. Their quality and their relationship to contemporary stage practice vary widely. They are used in what is now a normal function as indicating festivity and happiness.

Lamps with masks on the disc were common in the second century and have been popular with modern collectors. Most of them were made in Central and Northern Italy, and somewhat later in Gaul and North Africa. They were sold all over the Empire. Although there are one or two notable exceptions,[20] the great majority of these masks have a traditional character without direct reference to the contemporary stage. Again some designs were used over a number of generations without being remodelled or brought up to date. Most are slave masks, a few old men, and a good number Dionysos/Bacchus, and as before they must have been selected for their symbolic value, representing theatre, happiness and festivity. An interesting counterpart to the masks on lamps are those found in relief as decorative attachments on glass vessels.[21] They seem to have begun in Egypt where they were reasonably true to life, but the motif spread with the manufacturers and by the early second century were being reproduced in Gaul and Germany where they steadily lost their faithfulness to the theatre.

Figures 6.2 and 6.4 reflect the increased use of more expensive materials as media for theatrical motifs and this is a trend that was to continue into Late Antiquity. We noted in the last chapter that gems were extremely popular and that they carried theatre figures and masks in some number.

Figure 6.5 Bronze incense-burner in the form of a slave seated on altar, perhaps early to mid-first century AD. Malibu, J. Paul Getty Museum 87.AB.143. Ht 23.2 cm

Small bronze figurines also appear in quantity. They fall into a number of categories, some of which can reasonably be taken as personal possessions, and they raise the question of their owners' interest in the theatre. Some are demonstrably related to major works of art, from which they are often extracts; others are at least related to work in other media and so possibly have a similar derivation. One can therefore ask if the purchaser bought them as art objects or as souvenirs of the theatre – not that the alternatives are mutually exclusive. It is a question which occurs with gems as well. Other bronze figurines are of fine quality and rank as ornaments for the table and so involve an element of public display in which the owner might pretend to theatrical interest for the sake of appearances. An example of well-above-average quality is a bronze in the J. Paul Getty Museum (Figure 6.5).[22] It stands a little over 23 cm high and is in the form of a slave seated on an altar, his legs crossed; he supports himself with his right hand. His eyes are inlaid with silver. The type is a well-known one which occurs in a number of other small bronzes, terracotta figurines, marble statuettes, gems, moulded vase-figurines, as well as in a painting, a mosaic and a terracotta plaque with a scene from comedy, some twenty-four or so items in all. That is, he is an extract from a famous scene (just possibly from Menander's *Perinthia*).[23] It is not always possible to see the detail, but on a marble statuette in the Vatican, which, incidentally, was drawn by Rubens,[24] he can be seen to be holding a ring in the hand in his lap. The ring is an object of importance in the play and the slave hangs onto it as precious evidence as he seeks asylum on the altar. As often, these extracts become popular figures in their own right and not infrequently they lose their reference to the particularity of the scene from which they came. There are reasons for seeing something of that process here. In terms of simple mechanics, one can see that the maker of the piece took the figure-type from elsewhere: the right hand only barely rests on the altar whereas the fingers should normally be at the edge. Again, with his short *chiton* coming to above the knee, the figure draws on tradition rather than contemporary practice. And then the figure and his altar are in fact an incense burner. The figure is attached to the top of the altar which is hinged to swing up as a lid so as to expose the hollow drum of the altar which held the incense. The bottom of the altar is pierced with holes to allow the air to rise through, and the smoke of the incense escaped through the actor's mouth. It is an elaborate table-piece and was in fact matched by another figure in the form of another kind of performer, perhaps a mime, also seated on an altar and holding a *sistrum*.[25] It too was a incense burner. They were a matched pair, the one representing comedy, the other a more popular form of performance. There is a sense, therefore, in which the figure stands for comedy in general. The knowledgeable will appreciate the point of reference (and it was surely designed as an amusing conversation-piece), but the type was common enough for the less well versed to recognise it simply as comic theatre, as a counterpart to the other figure.

What is emerging is something of a difference between cheap and more expensive materials and it is a difference that in this case seems to reflect the status of the owners. The interest in theatre of the Greek tradition seems to belong to the upper strata of Roman society. Here again, however, it is not easy to distinguish between a real, well-based interest and a superficial one.

Expensive by any standards was a sardonyx kantharos, one of the finest pieces of the Saint-Denis treasure, now in the Cabinet des Médailles in Paris (Figure 6.6).[26] It has probably spent its entire life above ground although mention of it in written records occurs no earlier than the medieval period. It is one of the very finest cameo vases known from Antiquity and has often been connected with the workshops of Alexandria. It is probably to be dated to the first century AD. The piece is almost as difficult to describe as to photograph given that the scenes on each side, when viewed, effectively merge into a single three-dimensional unity given the translucency of the thinner parts. The decorative elements on each side are framed by trees from which hangs an awning. The centres of the scenes are taken up with tables with sacrificial equipment. Six masks are scattered in seemingly random but prominent fashion among statuettes of Priapus and Demeter, a panther, goats and birds. The masks are best described as Bacchic. Some are derived from satyr-play, others from comedy, but there is no sign of any particular reference. They belong to the landscape, to the sanctuary of Dionysos, as suitable decoration for a vessel of a shape that was particularly associated with him. This use of theatrical motifs for the evocation of the sanctuary belongs to the Hellenistic tradition, but neither the maker nor the client was now particularly concerned with having the details accurate in either historical or contemporary terms. The message is a general one, and for the Roman client, possibly as well understood as some of the motifs of Oriental porcelain for us. Among other expensive items, close parallels for this sort of treatment exist for example in the silver cups of the Hildesheim treasure in Berlin, or on a pair of silver kantharoi found in Pompeii in 1836.[27] On the latter, in one case Erotes ride a bull and a lion in a sanctuary setting with *thyrsoi* and masks with closed mouths, and in the other they ride a panther and bull in much the same environment. The masks are part of what makes a sanctuary and are elements of a festive setting.

It is not difficult to find other examples of the same approach. The Seven Sages Mosaic from Torre Annunziata has a border of masks set in a festoon.[28] The theme is one seen earlier, for example in Delos, but the original idea has been lost.[29] Instead of reflecting the cast, or the possible cast of a play, comic masks of somewhat out-of-date type are combined with satyr-masks in an arrangement in which the decorative element is the important consideration: comic masks in the centres of the sides (slave, youth, slave, girl) and satyr-masks at the corners. Other contemporary

Figure 6.6 Sardonyx kantharos with scenes of the sanctuary of Dionysos, perhaps early to mid-first century AD. Paris, Cabinet des Médailles

mosaic borders follow the same pattern.[30]

A further case is that of *oscilla* of the type found in Pompeii and elsewhere that are decorated with masks in low relief. They were designed to be hung in peristyle gardens and to evoke the sanctuary of Dionysos. A number of them depict the masks in a deliberately archaistic fashion – to record a long and old tradition – and others, seemingly through misunderstanding, include 'masks' of Attis and Polyphemos. There is now less precision or specialised knowledge in the use of this kind of material. It belongs to another culture, the details of which do not matter.[31]

The implication of all this is clear. Traditional theatre is a pretension of the wealthier members of society, and even at that level it is no more than a pretension for many.

It is no contradiction that some members of the same society would go to considerable lengths in the pursuit of a learned antiquarianism. A number of the late paintings from Pompeii give the impression that they were created with a concern for their correctness in the theatrical detail and in the accuracy with which they copied their prototypes.[32] They convey no sense of freedom or re-interpretation, and they clearly copy earlier work rather than reflect contemporary theatre. Some of the more leisured classes none the less maintained a genuine interest in the theatrical tradition and for them it often seems to have been more convenient to arrange private performances for members of their own circle, whether of whole plays or of excerpts of famous scenes or passages.[33]

Rome has now become an established and wealthy power and a well-organised one, and she has developed the confidence to create her own identity. Roman art production may use Hellenistic patterns as a language of expression (as it does, for example, in portrait- and other official sculpture), but even in this area it does so in contexts which are more and more distinctively and dynamically Roman rather than translated Greek. Instead of copying the Greek manner and trying to be a member of the Hellenistic world, Rome moves towards using Greek concepts and material for her own purposes. She begins that steady shift away from the Greek tradition, so that when Hadrian at the beginning of the second century plays the philhellene, it is the deliberate and conscious act of a cultured individual, and it is not unreasonable to see him as standing apart from the general trend. The art of his Antonine successors starts to lose touch with the subtleties as well as the know-how of the classical artistic tradition at the same time that other more purely Roman activities, such as architecture in concrete, develop their techniques in important and exciting new directions.

It is interesting to insert into this picture the phenomenon of the *Onomastikon* of Julius Pollux, a work dedicated to Commodus who was emperor from AD 180–192. His chapter on the theatre is a curiosity: the section on comedy can now be demonstrated without any doubt to derive from a source which knew and described the masks and costume of the transition from Middle to New Comedy. He abbreviates what must have been a longer treatment, and from our point of view at least, he does it in a maddeningly cursory fashion, particularly in the later part.[34] He totally fails to take into account changes in practice during the ensuing period, and even includes masks which were disappearing from use in the time of Menander. His chapter was written without reference to contemporary theatre. His section on tragic masks seems to follow much the same pattern, although the part on special masks (IV.141–2) seems to be a casual and unsystematic survey that could have been composed simply on the basis of play titles, summaries or cast lists.[35] In fact many of the masks attributed to abstractions or personifications seem to be more likely to be derived from the (chorus) titles of Old Comedy. In other words, Pollux' section on theatre belongs to a tradition of derivative scholarship and makes no reference to developments in the period of almost half a millennium since Menander. Indeed some of his remarks on staging exhibit an ignorance of the conditions of the theatre he is discussing, and with it, therefore, a lack of concern. As an attitude it is remarkable, and it shows something of the compartmentalisation of life and society at that period.

This separation and variation of activity and expertise is in large part what makes the period of the Empire so difficult to assess. Despite all that we have just noted, it is an observable phenomenon that the style of masks and costumes continued to develop. Such a process is most unlikely to have occurred without the impetus of performance. Indeed it is possible that the appearance of mask and costume may yet be made to reveal something of the nature of performance as they were adapted to suit contemporary needs.

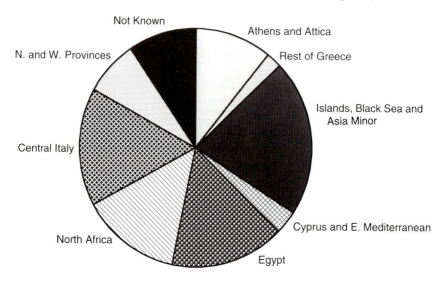

Figure 6.7 The provenances of objects representing comedy, after *c.* AD 180

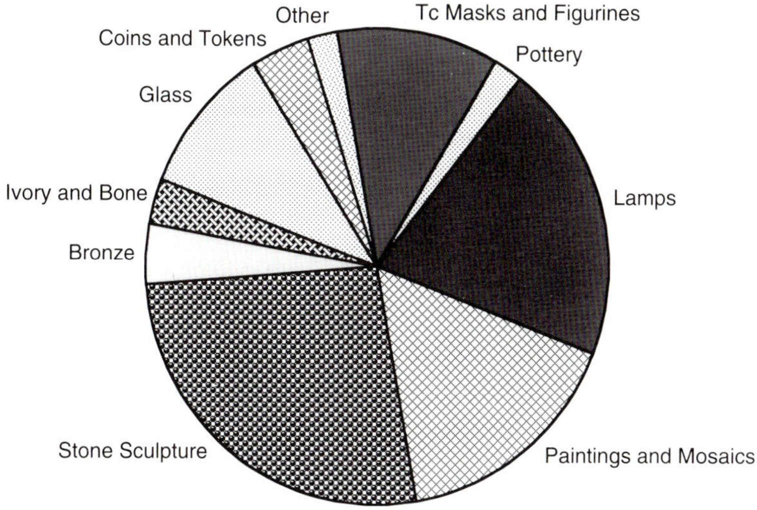

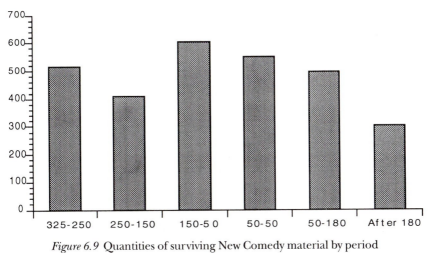

Figure 6.8 The material of surviving objects representing comedy, after *c.* AD 180

Figure 6.9 Quantities of surviving New Comedy material by period
(excluding gems)

In this respect it is interesting to see in Figure 6.7 how Athens' share of the total increases again (as does that of Asia Minor and the Black Sea). In absolute terms the numbers of objects are of course much reduced now. The final column on Figure 6.9 is about 30 per cent shorter than the one before it and yet the time-span involved is about three times greater, lasting to the early sixth century. There is an observable decline in interest from the Latin part of the world during the course of the third century. The fairly

155

large share for North Africa is in part a function of Severan activity in and on behalf of their homeland, and it too drops off quite sharply once their reign comes to an end.

Continuity was without doubt stronger in the Greek-speaking world east of the Adriatic and it was no doubt based not only on continuity in language but in festival and cult where theatre maintained a fairly important role. In the Latin west traditional theatre had been a foreign implant, even if one which played a very important role in Latin culture. In the Greek world it was a native product and, as we saw in discussing the Hellenistic period, it was a focus of Greek identity and so was much more deeply embedded. The competition it faced from other entertainments was of a quite different order. Even so simple a statistic as the comparatively small number of amphitheatres built in Greek-speaking countries is a good indication. The record of festivals, particularly in Greece and Asia Minor, seems to have continued unabated, with continuing investment of money.[36]

There seems little doubt that Lucian, writing in Syria in the third quarter of the second century AD, in addition to his use of theatrical metaphor (which abounded in the Greek language by this date) used contemporary productions as a source of parallels and comment.[37] Thus, for example, in a well-known passage in his *Dream or the Cock* (26) the humble cobbler in observing the problems endured by kings and how his own troubles are minor compared with theirs, uses the analogy of tragic actors:

> And so, when they fall, they are just like tragic actors. You can see many of them who for a while are a Kekrops, a Sisyphos or a Telephos, with diadems and ivory-handled swords, wavy hair and gold-decorated cloaks, but – and this is the kind of thing that often occurs – one of them loses his footing and falls down in the middle of the stage. The audience, of course, breaks into laughter when the mask with its diadem is smashed, the actor's head is bleeding and most of his legs exposed, so that they can see how his undergarments are miserable rags and the [platform] soles of his shoes are ugly and do not fit his feet.

The contrast between appearance and reality is a frequent rhetorical topos, and the whole passage is comparable to others in which the exterior appearance of, say, chryselephantine statues of major gods such as Zeus and Athena is contrasted with their dusty, vermin-infested internal structure.[38] But there is an immediacy to the description here, and the actor's difficulty in moving is a feature of the contemporary tragic stage.

Again in Lucian's *On Dance* (27), which has been argued to have been written in Antioch about AD 162–165:

> We can form an opinion on the nature of Tragedy in the first instance from its appearance. It is such an ugly and at the same time

frightening a spectacle to have a man fitted out to a disproportionate height, mounted up on high footwear, wearing a mask that extends up above his head with a huge gaping mouth, as if he were about to consume the spectators. I don't elaborate on the padding on his chest and belly with which he creates for himself additional and artificial breadth so that his ungainly height isn't made obvious by thinness. Then, inside all that, there is the actor himself, wailing, swaying backwards and forwards, sometimes even delivering his iambics in a sing-song voice, and, what is worst of all, making a song of his calamities, presenting himself as responsible just for his voice: everything else was looked after by the poets who lived long ago. One can put up with his singing so long as he is an Andromache or a Hecuba, but when Herakles himself comes on singing, without regard for his rôle and without respect for either his lionskin or his club, a reasonable man would rightly call the matter a solecism. Then again, the charge that you were bringing against dance, that men imitate women, would be shared by both Tragedy and Comedy: there are more female rôles than male. And then Comedy claims the ridiculousness of the masks themselves as an element in the pleasure it creates, masks of the likes of Daos, Tibios and cooks.

The famous ivory in the Petit Palais (Figure 6.10) is a good and roughly contemporary example of a tragic actor and his use of body language.[39] The part played is that of a young tragic hero. He has the typical boots with high platform soles, the tall mask and the long, very elaborately decorated drapery which on the ivory was picked out in blue and yellow.[40] Such an actor would find it difficult to move quickly, and even from the figurine one has some sense that in tragedy the emphases were on rich costume, turns of the body, hand gestures, diction and delivery. Performance had become highly stylised. A Herakles of much the same period is to be found on the façade of the stage at Sabratha in North Africa. His ferocity, if any, is to be found in his mask. The claim that there are more female roles than male is a difficult one to uphold – unless, of course, Lucian is thinking of recitations of excerpts, of famous passages, in which case the statement could probably be justified from among the classic Euripidean women. As to the comment on Comedy, one thinks of the contemporary emphasis on the frowns and distorted expressions of the slave masks such as he mentions. They may not seem particularly funny to us but in antiquity in general, and more particularly perhaps in this period, types we would find ugly or pathetic were regularly found amusing.[41] There is social comment here too: he picks on the slaves (through the classic names of Daos and Tibios), not the young heroes or heroines, and he verges on another topos, the way the stage elevates the lower orders into figures of importance.

Inherently interesting are the gravestones of theatre performers, like

Figure 6.10 Ivory figurine of a tragic actor in the role of a youthful hero.
Paris, Petit Palais, inv. A. DUT 192. Ht 16 cm

that of Marcus Verenius in Thessalonike (Figure 6.11).[42] It is in the form
of a funerary altar with a relief of the performer on the front, his right
hand raised in salutation. He wears an elaborately decorated costume, on
which colour traces remain. It is in fact very like that of the figurine in
the Petit Palais (Figure 6.10) and is typical of the costume of the period.
The altar may perhaps be dated to the second half of the second century
but it could well belong in the earlier part of the third. Even so, the mask
depicted in the field to the side is of traditional, generic appearance, not
a representation of a mask the actor would have used. This is an interesting
dichotomy. The use of this type of mask must have carried connotations
to the effect that Verenius was a member of an old profession. Although
he himself is made particular (within the limits of the art of the period),
his activity is expressed through a generalisation. Earlier, and perhaps of
the third quarter of the first century, is the grave relief of someone called
Bathyllos.[43] It is Athenian and has the masks of an old man and a slave
in a box on a pillar, representing a dedication in a sanctuary, a theme
with a long tradition. It is probably worth noting that both these

158

Figure 6.11 Detail from the funerary altar of the actor Marcus Verenius, late second to early third century AD. Thessalonike 9815

159

gravestones come from the Greek-speaking world.

An important and fairly recent find is a silver statuette of an actor as a slave standing with his right arm at his side and his left hand holding the cloak which comes over his shoulder (Figure 6.12).[44] It was found at Odessos on the Black Sea coast and has been thought to have originated in Miletos. The mask and costume are of developed type, the *chiton* to mid-calf, the hair brushed up into a crest (i.e. to some extent following the tragic pattern) and with a wig-like treatment at the back where it ends in long tresses coming over his back and shoulders. It is a good example of the growingly conventional nature of the appearance of comic theatre: no one would ever see a real slave looking like this. Some indication of the date to be given to the piece is provided by a series of terracotta figures from the Athenian Agora which look as if they could have been taken from metal originals such as this.[45] They are from contexts of the third quarter of the third century. Such pieces are now produced in small numbers but they often have the appearance of having been made for customers with a genuine interest.

Figure 6.12 Silver statuette from Odessos in the form of a slave from comedy, perhaps AD 250–275. Varna II-5801. Ht incl. base 10.3 cm

The clearest indications of theatrical performances are perhaps theatre tickets. They survive as small lead tokens which under normal circumstances would have been collected, melted down and re-issued with new stamps for new events. The interpretation of the individual stamps often proves very difficult, as does the dating. Very few survive, but it should be remembered that their chances of survival were infinitesimal – that they exist at all is more significant than their number and appearance might suggest. Some simply have representations of masks,[46] but a dozen or so are inscribed *Theophoroumene* (which must refer to Menander's play) and they are plausibly dated to the time of the Herulian sack of Athens in the year AD 267.[47]

Another line of enquiry concerns the physical remains of the theatres themselves and how long they continued in use. One cannot tell, of course, what was performed in them – mime, pantomime, water displays, acrobats, animal hunts or traditional theatre – but theatres remained necessary for the public performance of traditional theatre. The other important point about theatres is that they remained as sanctuaries under the protection of (pagan) gods and that performances continued to take place within such a religious setting, however weak the religion may have been. As we shall see, an element in the objections against theatre raised by early Christian writers rested in precisely this point. Yet, in a very useful survey, Spieser has shown how little Christians interfered with or went about destroying pagan sanctuaries in Greece.[48] The traditional sanctuaries were, rather, in what one might describe as a natural decline which was only partially and temporarily reversed by the vigorous activities of Hadrian. One remembers, for example, that the oracle at Delphi had virtually no role by the Early Imperial period. Many sanctuaries and their structures (including theatres) seem to have been ignored and allowed to fall into disrepair. More significant than the activities of adherents of the new religion were events such as the Herulian invasion in the latter half of the third century AD with its associated widespread destructions.

In the nature of things it is difficult to tell at all precisely when a theatre went out of use, and in any case for too many of the more important theatres very little of the key archaeological evidence remains.[49] Recent work at Corinth suggests that the final abandonment of the theatre took place in the later part of the fourth century and it seems possible to date robbing of the walls for stone for other constructions to the very end of the fourth and the earlier part of the fifth centuries.[50] The theatre at Argos had been an important one since the Early Hellenistic period (when it had the largest *cavea* in Greece). After its conversion to a theatre of Roman type in the Early Empire, it underwent many reconstructions. In the later phases, its *orchestra* was transformed into an arena in the third century AD, and a pool was constructed for aquatic ballets in the fourth. Like the theatre at Corinth, it finally seems to have been abandoned towards the end of the fourth century AD.[51] The evidence for the Theatre of Dionysos at Athens is extremely difficult.[52] The latest element in the sequence of theatre construction is the so-called Phaidros *bema*, the platform-like structure with stairway which remains visible on the site and is constructed of elements taken from the Hadrianic stage building or *scaenae frons*. Alison Frantz has argued that it must belong before AD 345 and was possibly carried out under Constantine. What it was used for is not entirely clear. The area of the stage and *orchestra* seems to have been separated from the rest of the theatre at the same time. Entrance was controlled by doors constructed in the *parodoi* and the marble parapet was built around the *orchestra* using cement of just the same type as in the *bema*. Travlos suggested that the space was now used for meetings but it is not at all impossible that it was used for recitals of items from classical theatre for the restricted audience now interested, particularly in such a small town as Athens now was. Perhaps some time towards the end of the fifth century a basilica was built in the eastern *parodos* and the *orchestra* was used as a courtyard.

Elsewhere in Greece, the theatre at Phlious seems to have been in use until some time in the fourth century, as does the town theatre at Epidauros. That at Philippi seems to have been abandoned at the end of the fourth or in the early fifth century. All this presents a reasonably consistent pattern although there were of course exceptions. The theatre at Vergina, for example, fell into disuse as early as the middle of the second century AD, whereas at Hierapolis in Asia Minor the theatre seems to have survived until the fifth or even the sixth century.[53] Similarly, the theatre at Aphrodisias continued in use until well into the sixth century and possibly even into the seventh when it was severely damaged by an earthquake.[54] In this case it is evident from graffiti on the seats that the kinds of performances put on there were often of the kind to attract the following of the Greens and the Blues, groups one knows better from the circus.[55] Obviously use or non-use was to a large degree dependent on the economic situation in any given area, but it also depends on the interest in directing remaining resources into such activities. And we must remember, too, that many of the performances of the kind we are interested in were produced privately or semi-privately, to invited groups. In this respect it is interesting that the theatre in Alexandria now seems to be a construction dating from towards AD 400.[56] It is in fact a comparatively small structure and might better be considered an Odeion. It would not be at all surprising if it should turn out to be a private construction for some major official and it was certainly built quite lavishly, especially for its period. It seems to have had three main phases, the first of which is thought to have been covered with vaulted roof which collapsed after a relatively short time. The final phase came in the sixth century when the stage building was removed: one can only speculate on its function then. Nevertheless in Rome, even so prominent a landmark as the Theatre of Marcellus must have been in ruins by the end of the fourth century when material from it was used in the construction of the Pons Cestius – and this despite the fact that slightly earlier, in the middle of that same century, Ammianus Marcellinus counted the Theatre of Pompey as one of Rome's finest buildings.[57]

It is perhaps ironic that it is at almost precisely this time, about AD 400, that there was a sudden if brief renewal of interest in figures drawn from the theatre. In Athens, for example, there was a short-lived flurry of lamps with fairly convincing theatre masks.[58] We do not have enough evidence to say if the phenomenon is more than coincidence. The construction of the theatre at Alexandria and the creation of the Mytilene mosaics suggest that the lamps were not an isolated accident. It is all a generation too late to have anything directly to do with Julian the Apostate, but it must have represented a similar looking back to the past and attempted revival.

This is not the place for detailed discussion of the illuminated manuscripts of Terence.[59] The three earliest and best-preserved copies (Cod. Vaticanus Lat. 3868; Cod. Parisinus Lat. 788; Cod. Ambrosianus H. 75) date to the ninth century. It can be argued that they go back to an original of the fourth century, perhaps the middle, and it is interesting to see what the illustrations do and do not get 'right'.[60] Each codex has the six plays with an initial *aedicula* of masks ostensibly showing the characters in order of appearance, but they are often misplaced and interspersed with masks for mute or merely reported persons; then there are drawings of each scene, a total of about 150 miniatures clearly copied from the same original. There is little to show that the original designer had experience of actual performances on the stage, or that he used models from the artistic tradition akin to those of the Mytilene mosaics for the scenes, or carefully composed old mask models for the *aediculae* – rather the contrary. Old men and slaves in the miniatures are more certainly distinguished by costume than by mask: slaves never wear a large mantle, but often one that is small and scarf-like. More often the slave *chiton* is long, though a short *chiton* is sometimes seen (the practice is inconsistent within individual plays). Slave masks may be distinguished as older or younger by the colour of the hair, but they are not otherwise consistently differentiated between types. The hourglass ornament so characteristic of old men's costume in other Late Antique monuments such as the Mytilene mosaics is absent. Nor is there any evidence of the square crowning element found above late masks in the Greek-speaking world. If the manuscript illustrations demonstrate anything for our purposes, it would seem to be that the original designer relied on text rather than performance, and that he relied on a selection of sources of rather uneven relevance and quality. That is, he was working in an area with which he was not fully familiar and attempting to reconstruct the antique mode.

It is instructive to compare with the Terence miniatures other Late Antique depictions of scenes from tragedy and comedy. A set of paintings decorating the walls of a house in Ephesos has been taken to date to the later part of the second century, although it would hardly be surprising if they should prove to be later. They are a series of scenes from tragedy and comedy painted on a red ground. The combination of tragic and comic continues a Hellenistic tradition (such as we saw in Delos) although there need not have been a regular alternation through the series. These are the first such scenes known to us to have labels, and of what may have originally been ten scenes, each about 40–45 cm high, we have *Sikyonioi*, *Oresstes* [*sic*], *Perikeiromene* and *Iphigeneia*. It is difficult to say much of the context, although the same complex had other theatrical motifs added in later years.[61] The scene in a mosaic in Oescus in Bulgaria (labelled Menander's *Achaioi*) is a panel from a larger composition which included pictures of maritime life and fighting cocks with agonistic symbols.[62] The technique of representation (the scene was represented as if seen from above, or with figures standing on sharply sloping ground) suggests a date in the fourth–fifth century. The series of scenes from comedy found in the triclinium and the adjoining portico of the Late Roman villa at Mytilene in Lesbos now known as the House of the Menander is the best preserved of all these sets of scenes.[63] The primary publication argued for a date in the later third century and this has generally been accepted without further discussion, but the recent suggestion by Berczelly of a date in or near the reign of Julian the Apostate (AD 361–363) is perhaps more likely.[64] In terms of its labelling, this series is also the fullest, giving the names of the author, the play, the act the scene is taken from, and in a number of cases (those in the triclinium), the names of the characters. The scenes are all from Menander, from the *Plokion*, *Samia*, *Synaristosai*, *Epitrepontes*, *Theophoroumene*, *Encheiridion* and *Messenia*, and then in the portico the *Kybernetai*, *Leukadia*, *Misoumenos* and *Phasma*. The panels included a Menander portrait and an illustration of Plato's *Phaedo*. Another mosaic found in Chania in Crete is fragmentary and has had only preliminary publication.[65] Two scenes are preserved, one in a reasonably complete state and labelled *Plokion*, the other only partially preserved but identifiable as the *Sikyonioi* even though the label does not survive. One might guess at a date in the fourth century.

These representations are a curious phenomenon and it is not easy to be sure of their function. The first point to be clear about is that in every case one can check, the scenes are not fresh inventions but belong to an iconographic tradition that reaches back to the series of Early Hellenistic scenes discussed in Chapters 4 and 5. Needless to say given the conditions of copying and transmission in Antiquity, they are not exact reproductions of the archetypes, and they are the result of a multiple and recurrent process of up-dating for style of mask, costume and body-language through the intervening years. Nevertheless they are, from the perspective of the period, quotations from the classical past. Even if some elements of the visual language are more or less contemporary, the basis of expression relies on the past. They are not snapshots of the contemporary stage, nor can they be taken as necessarily implying that productions of these plays were put on in these places at these dates. They are the visual equivalent of literary quotations. In this respect the portrait of Menander and the illustration of Plato's *Phaedo* provide useful context.

It will be clear that I see no need to suppose that groups of mosaic illustrations of this kind were created for special-interest groups such as Friends of Menander or Actors' Unions. One would need more than just floor-decorations to demonstrate it, and it would mean supposing that Oescus, Chania and Mytilene all shared these elements. The closest one comes is with the superb second-century AD mosaic floor recently discovered in a room above the Demeter Sanctuary at Pergamon.[66] It has a series of tragic and comic masks set in medallions together with other Dionysiac motifs. The masks are careful up-datings of Early Hellenistic types and are evidence for a sophistication in theatre history and practice. That is they stand apart from the kind of iconographic tradition we have just been considering. In this case the point is reinforced by the fact that the room also contained a large and elaborate *pithos* which also had theatrical decoration. It was a theatre room – for whatever purpose: a guild of actors perhaps.

By this date we need not make too much of the fact that the play-scenes of the mosaics had not needed labels throughout the Hellenistic period but now do. It is a sign of the times. More interesting is the antiquarianism reflected in the Mytilene mosaics with their identification of characters and of the act from which the scene was taken. It is evidence of the shift in function. As we saw earlier, these scenes originally represented key moments from the plays in question, often the name-scenes, but always the evocative scenes. Now one suspects that they have lost that role and that they simply illustrate Menander, or even the Classics. By making the point of reference precise, the labelling gave increased status. It is possible, even probable, that in many cases motifs drawn from scenes such as these had lost their point of reference and simply carried a generalised meaning. Obvious examples where this process had been under way for a long time include slaves seated on altars where the types had been extracted from their original contexts even within the Hellenistic period and used as favourite figures of the comic theatre rather than as slave X from a key scene of play Y. We saw an example in the Getty bronze, Figure 6.5 above (p. 149). An interesting case from later Antiquity is the one illustrated in Figures 6.13, 6.14 and 6.15.[67] We can demonstrate that all three derive from an Early Hellenistic painting which is known to us in two full versions, one a late second- or early first-century BC cameo now in Geneva, and the other the famous marble relief in Naples which is probably of the first century AD (Figures 5.26, 5.27, p. 138). The group we see preserved was already frequently extracted in the Late Hellenistic period. The figure is a young

Figure 6.13 Ivory group of a drunken young man and his slave, perhaps later third century AD. Milan, Museo Teatrale 345. Ht 9.5 cm. (Compare Figures 5.26 and 5.27)

man, drunk after a night on the town, who comes on the scene from the right and needing the support of his slave, while his father, on the left, has to be restrained in his shock and anger by an old friend. We do not know the name of the play, but Menander's *Methe* has been suggested and it would be suitable since the appropriation of the group of young man and slave would imply that the speech he gave at this point became famous.[68] One might then suppose that the figure of youth and slave became associated with the speech as an excerpt, and hazard a guess that the speech was in praise of festivity (as well perhaps as the younger generation) and thus highly appropriate as a symbol of the perceived role of comedy.

Figure 6.13 is an ivory in the Museo Teatrale in Milan, perhaps of the later part of the third century, and it is a good example of the formality of comic costume as it has evolved by this period.[69] The mask has long curling hair falling back over the shoulders and a tall crowning head-piece of a kind that must have been developed as a counterpart to the *onkoi* of tragedy.[70]

Figure 6.14 Contorniate medallion with group of drunken young man and his slave, about AD 400. London, British Museum 79

It is a pity that the face of the small slave-figure is not preserved. Figure 6.14 is a contorniate medallion of about AD 400.[71] The details are unclear but the group clearly belongs to our series. By the figures is an inscription which may possibly be read as ARNODUNIUS, a form of name which would be typical of the period. It could well be the name of the reciter. Figure 6.15 is in many ways more useful for our purposes since it gives us context.[72] It is a diptych now in St Petersburg made for Anastasius when he took up the consulship in Constantinople in AD 517 (and is thus our latest datable object). The costume and mask of the young man have evidently been brought into line with contemporary fashion. The formality and elaboration of costume seen in the Mytilene mosaics and the Milan ivory have now been taken a step further. The mask has now acquired a far more elaborate crowning element than that on the Milan ivory. The slave here is smaller still and he is turned toward the front, his right hand extended. The group of young man and slave is juxtaposed with a juggler and a troupe of acrobats. In the equivalent parts of the other Anastasian diptychs are the usual *venationes*, another juggler, scenes from pantomime, and, in the same position on the diptych in Paris, a scene from tragedy.[73] Grabar has taken these scenes to show the entertainments offered to the public by the consul on the day of his accession,[74] and in broad terms this seems likely enough. What is less certain is how literally we should take them. Given the date and the nature of the other events, it is stretching credulity to suppose that Anastasius staged a full-length performance of Menander's *Methe*. More likely that the group stands for recital of extracts from classical theatre, or even that it simply stands as a symbol for theatre and festivity.

A number of the more convincing masks of these later periods have large deep openings for the eyes and mouth through which the features of the

Figure 6.15 Part of an ivory diptych recording the consulship of Anastasius in Constantinople in AD 517. Various performances including the group of drunken young man and his slave. St Petersburg Ω 263 (Byz 925/16)

actor are clearly seen.[75] The ivory figurine in the Petit Palais (Figure 6.10) already shows the first steps in this process. As Lucian had observed, the performer has become in many ways more important than the medium.[76] The mask is now much less critical as a definer of character. If traditional theatre has largely become a selection of well-known set-pieces of famous speeches, and especially if the performances were often close-up, in the dining room, the character is already determined before the actor appears and the audience already knows. In these cases the mask is now merely a concession to tradition and has little practical purpose. Whether this is true of all late masks is less clear: by no means all have these characteristics. One's view ultimately depends on how literal one believes representations are, if the more traditionally constructed masks are simply following an iconographic pattern. Some of the latter, however, seem to be up to date in other respects and so it is perhaps more likely that two styles of masks were emerging: those for public and those for more intimate performance.

Another respect in which, in the later years, there seems to have been a growing divergence in the appearance of masks is one that seems to have a geographical basis. A number of comic masks from the Greek-speaking half of the Empire (but none so far from the Latin West) have a more and more pronounced crowning element above the forehead. In terms of giving added height to the figure, as well as a greater formality, it is equivalent to the tragic *onkos*. We see it, for example, on the ivory now in Milan, Figure 6.13, perhaps of the later third century (although it could well be of the fourth); on two masks on a bone plaque from a small box from a tomb of the third quarter of the fourth century from Pella in Jordan;[77] as well as on a fragment of tapestry border, probably datable to the fourth century, from Petrie's excavations at Hawara, with the mask of a young girl under a garland.[78] It appears in pronounced form on the diptych of Anastasius, Figure 6.15. Another example of much the same date as the diptych occurs on a marble capital now in the garden of the Istanbul Museum.[79] It is slightly damaged at the top but it too must have had one of these crowning elements. The mask is placed over crossed cornucopiae and one should surely read this as symbolic of the perceived function of masks, even at this late date. One may also wish to take this kind of public representation (and that of a diptych) as evidence that the anti-theatrical propaganda of the early Christian fathers did not have complete success even as late as the early sixth century. Another, if perhaps less remarkable example of the persistence of the old iconography and ways of thinking, is a fifth-century ivory panel in the Louvre showing poets and their Muses.[80] In middle register we find Thalia with a slave mask held on the fingertips of her right hand; she is in the company of a youthful poet who has a marked resemblance to the traditional portraits of Menander.

Papyrus texts seem to have been disappearing about the same time. We have codices of Menander of the fifth and perhaps the sixth century AD, but virtually nothing afterwards. The well-known Bodmer codex containing *Dyskolos* probably dates to the third or else the early fourth century. It had a long life and was twice resewn. The Cairo Menander is probably to be dated to the second half of the fifth century but a century later it was used as wrapping for more precious documents in a jar. The latest texts may belong to the second half of the sixth century, but there seems to have been no new generation of copies.[81]

We may end this survey with a glance at the Christian reaction to theatre and what it was they saw as its chief characteristics. Their railings against the theatre might at times lead one to expect more was being staged than in fact was the case.[82] On analysis, however, most mentions (when they are at all specific and not putting spectacles such as horse-racing and exhibitions of animal-hunting in the same context) refer to mime and other forms of popular theatre (which might well include jugglers and acrobats, much as we think of vaudeville). The other danger in using these texts as evidence is that they may well not be original observations, but simply copied as part of a generic approach given authority by some earlier writer. There is no doubt that they are extremely repetitive. (Indeed they have been taken as evidence that Christians persisted in going to the theatre none the less.) One example from the late third century is Arnobius' *Adversus Paganos* 7.33:

Does Jupiter give up his wrath if the *Amphitruo* of Plautus is acted and spoken, or if Europa, if Leda, if Ganymede or Danae be danced, does he restrain his wrath? Does the Great Mother become calmer, more gentle, if she sees the ancient tale of Attis rehashed by the actors? Will Venus cancel her displeasure if she sees a mime act out the part of Adonis in dancing? Does the anger of Alcaeus' scion [sc. Hercules] grow weak if the tragedy of Sophocles entitled *The Trachinian Women*, or the *Hercules* of Euripides is acted? Or does Flora think she is treated with respect if in her games she sees a portrayal of shameful things and an exodus from the brothels to the theatres?

(Trans. G.E. McCracken)

It is a typical example. The mention of traditional comedy and tragedy is inserted among references to mimes and other performers of mimetic dancing, and then the parade of prostitutes associated with celebration of Floralia. In fact there is no real suggestion here that Arnobius had any particular performance of Plautus or Sophocles in mind. The reference is much more likely to be a generalisation, and the examples chosen quite possibly derive from their use as school texts.

One may none the less contemplate the underlying assumption in this passage: that performances were staged in honour of the gods and even of the figures portrayed. Is this simply a piece of Christian rhetoric, or does it, rather, reflect a viewpoint which had a wider base in the community?

The reasons why early Christians reacted so violently against the theatre are numerous and one should not expect that they were always clearly thought through. An important factor was that they wanted to set themselves apart from the normal population, and so went about finding reasons for not joining popular activities. It is probably for this reason too that the early Christian writers put such strong emphasis on the religious (pagan) aspect of these occasions, something one certainly does not find in other Greek and Roman writers of the period. They could readily add to these the broadly accepted view that actors and other performers (in the Roman world particularly) were dissolute and depraved, belonging to the lowest social strata. More particularly, however, the Christians were obsessed with the power of satan and demons, and they saw this expressed in the creation of dramatic illusion, in the 'otherness' achievable by the actor, as well as in the power the actor could exert over his audience. This is well illustrated by Lactantius early in the fourth century, particularly because he is one of the more intelligent and better educated (*Divine Institutes* 6.20):

In plays, too, I do not know whether there exists more vicious corruption. Even the comedies speak of the defiling of virgins or the love affairs of prostitutes, and the more eloquent the writers who have fashioned those tales of crime, the more do they persuade by the elegance of their sentences, and the more easily will their numerous ornate verses stick in the memory of their hearers. Likewise, the tragic histories put before one's eyes the murders and incests of evil kings and present 'elevated' crimes. The shameless motions of the actors also, what else do they teach and arouse but the passions? Their enervated bodies, softened to womanish step and apparel, belie shameless women with their dishonourable gestures.

What shall I say of the mimes which exhibit the training of seducers, which teach adulteries, while they present the fiction, and make the transition from images of reality? What do young men or maidens do when they see that these things are carried out and willingly watched without shame by all?

(After M.F. McDonald)

Lactantius seems to list the four main types of theatrical performance, comedy, tragedy, pantomime ('shameless motions'), and mime. Even allowing for an element of exaggeration, performances of tragedy and comedy are seen as creating a serious level of reality which can corrupt the viewer. To us this seems curious, not only because many of the myths of tragedy were Greek rather than Roman (even though presented in Latin), and one might have thought by this period so out-dated as scarcely to be taken seriously, but because the settings of comedy also referred to a bygone age and culture. Furthermore costume by this period was form-alised and heavy, and very far from naturalistic, and so too were the masks. It also seems likely that there was now very little stage business; the plays were performed as a comparatively stiff ritual theatre. Despite Lactantius' comments, this style seems to have evolved in part because of a steadily developing reaction against emotive presentation through gesture and movement (that is for traditional theatre, perhaps by deliberate opposition to mime). The performance had moved to something much closer to recitation. It is as if in the constant struggle for territory between the different genres in the theatre that had been going on now for almost a thousand years, movement, song and the more explicit exciting of emotion had been taken over by mime. Traditional theatre was retreating to what remained as secure ground. Lactantius confirms the point and gives a further reason why: the interest now was in the old-fashioned purity and elegance of the words and language.[83] He finds them totally seductive.

NOTES

1 INTRODUCTION

1   M.L. West has cast legitimate doubts on the reliability of the chronology for early theatre (*CQ* 39, 1989, 251–254) as does Connor (*Classica et Mediaevalia* 40, 1989, 7–32) who also argues for a close link between the establishment of tragedy and the establishment of Cleisthenic democracy, although one might have expected later records to make something of it if a direct link existed. On the question of origins (which I find a largely unprofitable pursuit), the standard work is G.F. Else, *Origin and Early Form of Greek Tragedy* [Martin Classical Lectures 1965] (New York 1972). G.A. Privitera, 'Origini della tragedia e ruolo del ditirambo', *SIFC* 84, 1991, 184–195 has recently given a sane and salutary discussion. Also worth reading is W. Burkert, 'Greek Tragedy and Sacrificial Ritual', *GRBS* 7, 1966, 87–121 as well as *DTC*^{2} 60–131.

2   Bruno Snell rather neatly suggested that the available myths became unsuitable for the types of enquiry that were becoming popular, so that the tradition developed by Aeschylus and Euripides was picked up by Socrates and Plato: *Discovery of the Mind* (Oxford 1953), esp. Ch. 5, 'Myth and Reality in Greek Tragedy', and Ch. 6, 'Aristophanes and Aesthetic Criticism' (from *Die Antike* 1944 and 1937 respectively).

3   See also lines 943, 1436, 1448, 1458, 1501. There are useful recent comments on these issues for example in L. Woodbury, 'The Judgment of Dionysos: Books, Taste and Teaching in the *Frogs*', in M. Cropp, E. Fantham and S.E. Scully (eds), *Greek Tragedy and its Legacy. Essays Presented to D.J. Conacher* (Calgary 1986) 241–257, although he argues that teaching as a function of poetry seems to derive from contemporary sophistic ideas, even if at the same time admitting that there is an important element in early, archaic and classical verse that might broadly be called educational or culturally formative: Homer, Hesiod, Solon, Xenophanes, Theognis.

4   On the role of the theatre in a proto-literate society, see C. Segal, 'Tragédie, oralité, écriture', *Poétique* 50, 1982, 131–154; *id.*, 'Greek Tragedy: Writing, Truth, and the Representation of the Self', in H.D. Evjen (ed.) *Mnemai. Classical Studies in Memory of Karl K. Hulley* (Chico, California, 1985) 41–67, or 'Vérité, tragédie et écriture', in M. Detienne (ed.), *Les savoirs de l'écriture en Grèce ancienne* (Lille 1988) 330–358; B. Gentili, 'Tragedia e communicazione', *Dioniso* 54, 1983, 227–240; E.A. Havelock, 'The Oral Composition of Greek Drama', *QUCC* no. 6, 1980, 61–113, and a number of articles in M. Vegetti (ed.), *Oralità scrittura spettacolo* (Turin, 1983). There is now a large literature on the generic differences between so-called oral and literate societies. Basic is Walter J. Ong, *Orality and Literacy* (London and New York, 1982); one may also note the same

author's somewhat over-brief presentation 'Writing is a Technology that Restructures Thought', in G. Baumann (ed.), *The Written Word. Literacy in Transition* (Oxford 1986) 23–50. See too E.A. Havelock *The Literate Revolution in Greece & its Cultural Consequences* (Princeton 1982), together with the comments on it by L. Woodbury in *Échos du Monde Classique* 27, 1983, 329–352. There are also very useful observations (and counterbalance to Havelock) from G.F. Nieddu, 'Testo, scrittura, libro nella Grecia arcaica e classica: note e osservazioni sulla prosa scientico-filosofica', *Scrittura e Civiltà* 8 (1984) 213–261, as well as the same author's earlier 'Alfabetismo e diffusione sociale della scrittura nella Grecia arcaica e classica: pregiudizi recenti e realtà documentaria', *Scrittura e Civiltà* 6 (1982) 233–261; also the fine article by S. Flory, 'Who Read Herodotus' Histories?', *AJP* 101, 1980, 12–28, and J.A. Davison, 'Literature and Literacy in Ancient Greece', *Phoenix* 16, 1962, 141–156 and 219–233. Those committed to a high level of literacy include E.G. Turner, *Athenian Books in the Fifth and Fourth Centuries* B.C. (London 1951, second edn 1971); F.E. Harvey, 'Literacy in the Athenian Democracy', *REG* 79, 1966, 585–635 (with a good collection of references to the literary sources); and A. Burns, 'Athenian Literacy in the Fifth Century B.C.', *JHI* 42, 1981, 371–388. Note recently R. Johne, 'Zur Entstehung einer "Buchkultur" in der zweiten Hälfte des 5. Jahrhunderts v.u.Z.', *Philologus* 135, 1991, 45–54. For what is now a classic article on the effect of literacy on thought processes, see J. Goody and I. Watt. 'The Consequences of Literacy', in J. Goody (ed.), *Literacy in Traditional Societies* (Cambridge 1968) 27–68, as well as his 'Literacy and Achievement in the Ancient World', in F. Coulmas and K. Ehlich (eds.), *Writing in Focus* (Berlin–Amsterdam–New York, 1983) (Trends in Linguistics. Studies and Monographs, 24) 83–98. Further, J. Goody, *The Interface between the Written and the Oral* (Cambridge 1987); W.V. Harris, *Ancient Literacy* (Cambridge, Mass., 1989) although I find the latter somewhat disappointing. Very handy is the summary and critical assessment of views to that date by M. Fantuzzi, 'Oralità, scrittura, auralità. Gli studi sulle techniche della comunicazione nella Grecia antica (1960–1980)', *Lingua e Stile* (Milan) 15, 1980, 593–612.

Current investigation is moving away from determination of generic differences between oral and literate societies to studies of particular reactions to the change in particular cultures.

More generally on the relationship between theatre and society, see J. Gregory, *Euripides and the Instruction of the Athenians* (Ann Arbor 1991), esp. Introduction; and B. Knox, 'Sophocles and the Polis', in *Sophocle: Entretiens sur l'antiquité classique* xxix (Vandœuvres-Geneva 1983) 1–27, together with other items listed in the Bibliography.

5   M. Detienne, *The Creation of Mythology* (Chicago 1986) (= *L'invention de la mythologie*, Paris 1981), Ch. 2; see also Rosalind Thomas, *Oral Tradition and Written Record in Classical Athens* (Cambridge 1989). Note also Aeschylus, *Supplices* 946–949.

6   Fr. 578 N^2.

7   *Suda*, s.v. Pericles: 1180 Adler (quoted by Woodbury, op. cit.).

8   But see recently T. Dorandi, *Prometheus* 16, 1990, 225–226.

9   One could look, for example, at Aristophanes' and other comic poets' complaints about the stealing of ideas and material, even if their complaints seem a quasi-formulaic way of asserting their own originality when competing for the prize in the theatre.

10 Something of this idea had already occurred to Denniston, *CQ* 21, 1927, 117–119. It is interesting that a century earlier, according to Athenaeus (3A),

notable collectors of books were the tyrants Polykrates and Peisistratos. For pictures of people with rolls of papyrus, see H.R. Immerwahr, 'Book Rolls on Attic Vases', in *Classical, Medieval, and Renaissance Studies in Honor of B.L. Ullman*, i (*Storia e Letteratura* 93, 1964) 17–48, and 'More Book Rolls on Attic Vases', *AntK* 16, 1973, 143–147; or G.M. Parassoglou, 'Dexia cheir kai gonu. Some Thoughts on the Postures of the Greeks and Romans when Writing on Papyrus Rolls', *Scrittura e Civiltà* 3, 1979, 5–21, and 'A Roll upon his Knees', *YCS* 28, 1985, 273–275. The problem here rests in identifying the sorts of people depicted and the sorts of buyer the vases were aimed at.

The perception of books as status symbols has parallels in the medieval period, especially in the production of lavish books for particular patrons, for example in and around Chaucer's circle. Again the rise of a status-seeking merchant class in fourteenth-century London has been connected with the appearance of ateliers for producing manuscripts.

11 *Gnomol.Vat.* 743 St. (41 A4 D.-K.).

12 This is not a book on comparative ethnography, but I cannot help but recall that the Australian aborigines, who as hunter-gatherers used to cover vast tracts of land that we would regard as featureless and inhospitable, had poems which described and fixed the geography of areas perhaps 150 km across. This was of course a particular response to particular needs, but it is a fine example of a possible and very practical use of oral poetry.

13 Plato's negative reaction to the emotions expressed in the theatre as being habit-forming seems an instinctive recognition of this function.

14 See W. Burkert, *Greek Religion. Archaic & Classical* (London 1985), *passim.*

15 For a good example, see W. Burkert, 'The Making of Homer in the Sixth Century B.C.: Rhapsodes versus Stesichorus', in *Papers on the Amasis Painter and his World* (Colloquium ... Getty Museum, Malibu 1987) 43–62. Note too the challenging book by B. Gentili, *Poetry and its Public in Ancient Greece from Homer to the Fifth Century* (Baltimore 1988). This is a somewhat revised version of his *Poesia e pubblico nella Grecia antica da Omero al V secolo* (Rome–Bari 1984). Note too the story preserved in Plutarch, *Solon* 8, 1–2, of Solon and the Salamis crisis and the way that he appeared in the Agora in a traveller's cap (*pilidion*), stood upon the Herald's Stone and delivered his poem beginning: 'I come as a herald from lovely Salamis ...'. On the other hand one has to admit that, according to Plutarch's account, he had pretended to have taken leave of his senses. See also n. 1 in the next chapter.

16 It was long thought that the number of comedies at the Dionysia and Lenaia was reduced to three during the period of the Peloponnesian War, but W. Luppe seems persuasive in his arguments that this is a misconstruction: *Philologus* 116, 1972, 53–73 and *Nikephoros* 1, 1988, 185–189.

17 See Pickard-Cambridge, *Festivals*[2] 80, and recently J.M. Bremer, 'Poets and their Patrons', in H. Hofmann and A. Harder (eds), *Fragmenta dramatica. Beiträge zur Interpretation der griechischen Tragikerfragmente und ihrer Wirkungsgeschichte* (Göttingen 1991) 39–60.

18 For the reality of tragedy as performed and perceived, see my article in *GRBS* 32, 1991, 15–50. For ancient willingness in general to believe in the part played, see W.R. Connor on Peisistratos and Phye and other similar cases in *JHS* 97, 1987, 42–47, or the forthcoming article by Rebecca Sinos on epiphanies. On broader issues of the Dionysia, see for example, S. Goldhill whose article 'The Great Dionysia and Civic Ideology' has appeared in three forms, in *JHS* 107, 1987, 58–76, in P. Ghiron-Bistagne (ed.), *Anthropologie et théâtre antique* (Cahiers du GITA 3, 1987), and in J.J. Winkler and F.I. Zeitlin (eds), *Nothing to Do with*

Dionysos? Athenian Drama in its Social Context (Princeton 1989) 97–129. Note the useful linking with democracy by W.R. Connor, above, n. 1.

19   I do not know of much that has been done recently on these aspects of festivals, but note from the trade viewpoint, L. De Ligt and P.W. De Neeve, 'Ancient Periodic Markets: Festivals and Fairs', *Athenaeum* 66, 1988, 417–426.

20   There are worthwhile things to read on performance beyond that of the theatrical type discussed here. One thinks particularly of Victor Turner and such books as *From Ritual to Theatre: The Human Seriousness of Play* (New York 1982) or such articles as 'Dramatic Ritual/Ritual Drama: Performative and Reflexive Anthropology', in J. Ruby (ed.), *A Crack in the Mirror: Reflexive Perspectives in Anthropology* (Philadelphia 1982) 83–97, and 'Liminality and the Performative Genres', in J.J. MacAloon (ed.), *Rite, Drama, Festival, Spectacle* (Philadelphia 1984) 19–41; or of Richard Schechner, e.g., *Essays on Performance Theory* (New York 1977), or (with M. Schuman), *Ritual, Play and Performance* (New York 1976).

Turner is also useful in pointing out that the level of competitiveness present in 'primitive' performances is high, as individuals jockey for position in their community. One could argue that the competitiveness of Greek theatre was a formal development of such patterns of behaviour.

21   E. Tsirivakos, 'Iniochos technis tragikis', *ADelt* 29, 1973–74 (1977), 88–94. The piece is also discussed by N.W. Slater, 'Vanished Players: Two Classical Reliefs and Theatre History', *GRBS* 26, 1985, 333–344. I do not share their interpretation of the piece, despite Slater's attractive argument that this is a young poet with mask: I do not see evidence that that motif has evolved by this date, rather the contrary.

22   J.J. Winkler, 'The Ephebes' Song: *Tragoidia* and *Polis*', in Winkler and Zeitlin, op. cit., 20–62.

23   Performance in all three tragedies and the satyr-play of a set would not have been an impossible task for a boy in his later teens, but it would have been a severe test given the complexity of words, music and dance. Since not all tragedies were arranged in a trilogy or connected sequence of three, continuity is not a strong argument. Chorusmen in a satyr-play, which came at the end of the sequence, needed to be fresh and vigorous. On chorus numbers, see Pickard-Cambridge, *Festivals*² 234–236.

24   Despite all that has been written, the size of the audience in the fifth-century Theatre of Dionysos is unknown and probably unknowable: the physical remains of the structure are too unclear. On issues of principle, see L. Gallo, 'La capienza dei teatri e il calcolo della popolazione. Il caso di Atene', in I. Gallo (ed.), *Studi salternitani in memoria di R. Cantarella* (Salerno 1981) 271–289.

25   For the arrangement of the audience, see in the first instance Pickard-Cambridge, *Festivals*² 263ff. – more recent discussions have not added anything new. On participation in choruses, D.M. MacDowell, 'Athenian Laws about Choruses', in *Symposion 1982. Vorträge zur griechischen und hellenistischen Rechtsgeschichte (Santander, 1.–4. September 1982)* (Cologne 1989) 65–77. On the chorus and the part of *ephebes*, J.J. Winkler, 'The Ephebes' Song: *Tragoidia* and *Polis*', *Representations* 11 (1985) 26–62, and the revised version in Winkler and Zeitlin, op. cit., 20–62. I do not believe however that they can have been *ephebes* in the fourth century. On the interaction of writer and actor, Z. Pavlovskis, 'The Voice of the Actor in Greek Tragedy', *Classical World* 71, 1977, 113–123; F. Jouan, 'Réflexions sur le rôle du protagoniste tragique', in *Théâtres et spectacles dans l'antiquité. Actes du colloque de Strasbourg, 5–7 novembre 1981* (Leiden 1983) 63–80.

The question of the dramatist writing with his actors in mind has been pursued further by M. Damen, 'Actor and Character in Greek Tragedy,' *Theatre Journal* 41, 1989, 316–340.

26 James Redfield, 'Drama and Community: Aristophanes and Some of his Rivals', in Winkler and Zeitlin, op. cit., 314–335. On theatre and current affairs, there is a sane statement by W.G. Forrest, 'The Stage and Politics', in M. Cropp, E. Fantham and S.E. Scully (eds.), *Greek Tragedy and its Legacy. Essays Presented to D.J. Conacher* (Calgary 1986) 229–239. Also M. Heath, *Political Comedy in Aristophanes* (*Hypomnemata* 87, Göttingen 1987). Recently: Chr. Meier, 'Politik und Tragödie in 5. Jahrhundert', *Philologus* 135, 1991, 70–87.

27 *Témoignages sur le théâtre* (Paris 1952), 133.

28 This said, Edith Hall, *Inventing the Barbarian. Greek Self-Definition through Tragedy* (Oxford 1989), is useful in pointing up the use of foreigners within the restricted theme of surviving tragedies.

29 Note R. Brock, 'The Emergence of Democratic Ideology', *Historia* 40, 1991, 160–169 where he points out (161) that 'imagery applied favourably to the demos is hard to find', but we should realise that democratic ideology and support for the *demos* is by no means the same thing as civic ideology and support for Athens (at least in Aristophanes' eyes).

30 For tragedy, see more recently C.A. Müller, *Zur Datierung des sophokleischen Oedipus* (*AbhMainz* 1984 no. 5) 60ff. For comedy, A.C. Cassio, 'I tempi di composizione delle commedie attiche e una parafrasi di Aristofane in Galeno (Ar.Fr. 346 K.-A.)', *RFIC* 115, 1987, 5–11. The latter contains the implication that a lot of the work was done after the award of the chorus. Similarly, J. Henderson on the need to re-write *Lysistrata* in the light of the rapidly changing events of 411 BC, in the Introduction to his edition.

31 See for example the article by Parassoglou mentioned above in n. 10.

32 On the unreliability of the biographical material, M.R. Lefkowitz, *The Lives of the Greek Poets* (London 1981). On the club of which Aristophanes was a member, see *IG* II² 2343, and for discussion, (among others) H. Lind, *MusHelv* 42, 1985, 249–261. More generally, P. Ghiron-Bistagne, *Recherches sur les acteurs dans la Grèce antique* (Paris 1976). D.F. Sutton, 'The Theatrical Families of Athens', *AJP* 108, 1987, 9–26, has a useful collection of material although he does not deal with Euaion. For Euaion, see recently A. Shapiro, 'Kalos-Inscriptions with Patronymic', *ZPE* 68, 1987, 107–118.

33 There are good comments on the institution of the prize and what it implies by N.W. Slater, 'The Idea of the Actor', in Winkler and Zeitlin, op. cit., 385–395.

2 THE EARLY PERIOD AND THE FIFTH CENTURY

1 For the role of the poet in the performance of non-theatrical poetry, see n. 15 in Chapter 1; W. Mullen, *Choreia: Pindar and Dance* (Princeton 1982) 3–45; R.P. Martin, *The Language of Heroes: Speech and Performance in the Iliad* (Ithaca–London 1985); T.J. Figueira and G. Nagy (eds), *Theognis of Megara: Poetry and the Polis* (Baltimore 1985); G. Nagy, *Greek Mythology and Poetics* (Ithaca–London 1990) (e.g. Chapter 11 on the performance of Tyrtaeus and the context of that performance).

2 The exception is of course the Prologue which can briefly set out the background and setting, but even this is delivered not by the poet as poet but by a devised character. One remembers none the less that in the early years the

poet often participated in his own performances – as an actor. See on this Charles Segal, 'Tragic Beginnings: Narration, Voice, and Authority in the Prologues of Greek Drama', *YCS* 29, 1992, 85–112, together with his *Interpreting Greek Tragedy: Myth, Poetry, Text* (Ithaca N.Y., 1986) 70ff.

E.W. Handley points out to me at the same time that what is so striking about much of the Homeric epics is the amount of direct speech, and the consciousness, reflected in (say) *Iliad* 3.204–225, that one man's manner of speech differs radically from another's. Since this goes on in lyric narrative, and since in personal poetry the poet may assume both a persona and the direct speech to go with it, we are interestingly on the way to dramatic delivery and hence drama via narrative role-playing: see e.g. Archilochus 1.23, 196a West.

3   This tradition is not necessarily to be believed. The evidence is presented clearly and conveniently in Pickard-Cambridge, *Festivals*[2] 130f. and 190f. See also Chapter 1, n. 1, above.

4   See below pp. 45–6 with n. 60, and pp. 77–80, on the power of masks. It is possible that something of this is what was referred to by Aristotle as the *satyrikon*, his second element in the formation of tragedy (*Poetics* 1449 a 8–30). See recently the article by Privitera mentioned above in Chapter 1, n. 1.

5   Basle BS 415. The primary publication is M. Schmidt, 'Dionysien', *AntK* 10 (1967) 70, pl. 19, 1–2; see also H. Froning, *Dithyrambos und Vasenmalerei in Athen* (Würzburg 1971) pl. 7, 2; E. Simon, *Das antike Theater* (Heidelberg 1972), pl. 2; *ead. The Ancient Theatre* (London 1982) pl. 2; *CVA* (3) pl. 6, 1–2, pl. 7, 3–5 (with further refs.). See the discussion in *GRBS* 32, 1991, 42ff. with its listing of the other three vases. On the Aeschylean version, see conveniently O. Taplin, *The Stagecraft of Aeschylus* (Oxford 1977) 105–106 and 114ff. In view of the history of the motif, it is worth observing how Aeschylus withholds mention of what will be done until very shortly before the scene itself.

6   It also shows the interaction between group and individual, between rank-and-file and leader, between problem-explanation and problem-solving.

7   There is an excellent treatment of the theme in literature by F. Jouan, 'L'évocation des morts dans la tragédie grecque', *RHR* 98 (1981) 403–421. For the copying of Phrynichus, Aesch. *Persae* arg. It is worth noting that Simonides also used the theme (in this case Achilles appearing from his tomb to the Greeks as they were about to begin their homeward voyage), and that Pseudo-Longinus (*De Sublimitate* 15.7) found his version superior even to that of Sophocles (*Polyxena*) in the vividness of its presentation.

8   See in the first instance O. Taplin, 'Aeschylean Silences and Silences in Aeschylus', *HSCP* 76, 1972, 57–97. Achilles in *Phrygians or Ransom of Hector* and Niobe in *Niobe* were two notorious cases. Silent figures are of course one way of creating spectacle without using an (extra) actor. Handley points out to me a Euripidean echo of the technique in *Tro*, with Hekabe present from the beginning, highlighted by 36ff., eventually speaking in lament 98ff.

9   It is of course possible that the memory was reinforced by occasional re-performances at country festivals in the meanwhile, but that would have affected only part of the total audience that saw *Frogs*.

10 (a) Red-figure hydria, British Museum 1843.11–3.24 (E 169), *ARV*[2] 1062 (workshop of the Coghill Painter), 1681; *MTS*[2] 117, AV 56; *AJA* 72 (1968), pl. 6, 11–12; *IGD* III.2, 3.
    (b) Red-figure pelike, Boston 63.2663, *Paral.* 448 (Kensington Painter and Kensington Class); *MTS*[2] 117, AV 54; *AJA* 72 (1968) pl. 7, 13; *IGD* III.2, 2.
    (c) Red-figure bell-krater, Caltanisetta V.1818, *MTS*[2] 117, AV 55; *AJA* 72 (1968) pl. 6, 14.

(d) Red-figure calyx-krater, Basle BS 403, ARV^2 1684, 15 bis, 1708 (Kleophon Painter); CVA (3) pl. 10, 1–6 (with refs.)

(e) White-ground calyx-krater, Agrigento AG 7, ARV^2 1017, 53 (Phiale Painter); MTS^2 116, AV 53; AJA 72 (1968) pl. 7, 15; IGD III.2, 1; J.H. Oakley, *The Phiale Painter* (Mainz 1990) no. 53, pl. 37, with further refs.

For discussion, see most recently *GRBS* 32, 1991, 42ff.

11 For the evidence on all this and useful discussion, see S. Rutherford Roberts, *The Attic Pyxis* (Chicago 1978) 182–184; I. Jenkins, 'Is There Life after Marriage?', *BICS* 30, 1983, 137–146; I.S. Mark, *Hesperia* 53, 1984, 309–312. For interesting modern parallels: M. Alexiou and P. Dronke, *Studi Mediaevali* (Spoleto) 12(2), 1971, 819–863; L.M. Darnforth, *The Death Rituals of Rural Greece* (Princeton 1982), Chapter 4.

12 Green, *GRBS* 32, 1991, 42ff. The vase-painters can be shown to be reacting to what they saw in the theatre and not copying from each other (or from some other source such as a votive plaque) by the variety in the moment chosen: Andromeda led to the spot while stakes are set up (no. 1), Andromeda being tied to the stakes (no. 2), Andromeda standing tied to the stakes (nos. 3, 4, 5). Different moments are chosen from an evolving tableau. Note the ambiguity in no. 3 where Andromeda stands tied to a stake but an attendant in still digging a hole for the stake.

13 *GettyMJ* 14, 1986, 193 fig. 61; *RVSIS* ill. 44. The painter has shown the general effect rather than any individual moment. Thus Perseus is present already, in conversation with Kepheus.

14 M. Guarducci, *MonAnt* 33, 1929, 5–38; *MTS²* 150–151; *IGD* II, 8–10; Simon, in *The Eye of Greece*, 145–146.

15 On visual symbolism in Sophocles, see C. Segal, *CW* 74, 1980, 125–142, and more generally on his use of stage space; O. Taplin, *EntrHardt* xxix, 1983, 155–174. Also D. Seale, *Vision and Stagecraft in Sophocles* (London 1982). On the bow, see also recently J.A. Johnson, 'Sophocles' *Philoctetes*: Deictic Language and the Claims of Odysseus', *Eranos* 86, 1988, 117–121.

16 Berlin inv.3237, *MTS²* 50, AV 34; *IGD* III.3, 10. See also K. Schefold, 'Der Andromeda des Nikias', in *Studies in Honour of A.D. Trendall* (Sydney 1979) 155–158, where he argues that the Berlin vase is derivative from the Andromeda by the painter Nikias, of which a later copy is that in the Casa dei Dioscuri.

17 The same was surely true of masks as well. There are good analogies for this in so-called primitive societies.

18 There is still a long way to go in the exploration of this topic, but some very useful groundwork has been provided by Rudolph Wachter, 'The Inscriptions on the François Vase', *MusHelv* 48, 1991, 86–113. It will be worth pursuing this mnemonic role of visual depictions. It is surely significant that ancient systems for training the memory to recall complex series of facts relied on mental data-banks of visual images of places into which people or events were set as *aides-mémoire*: see the *Ad Herennium* III.xvi–xxiv, Cicero, *De Oratore* II.lxxxvii–lxxxviii, and Quintilian, *Inst.Or.* XI.xx.17ff. It is interesting, too, that many of the examples given in these discussions seem originally to have been drawn from the stage. For an introductory discussion of the technique (which has now become a classic), see F.A. Yates, *The Art of Memory* (London 1966), Chapters 1–2, and the brief comments of P. Rossi in *La memoria del sapere. Forme di conservazione e strutture organizzative dall'antichità a oggi* (Rome–Bari 1988) esp. 225ff. There is helpful discussion on a broader basis in Jan Vansina, *Oral Tradition as History* (Madison, Wisconsin, 1985) 44ff. (Ch. 2 Performance and

NOTES

Tradition, (d) Mnemotechnic Devices).

19 Berlin-Charlottenburg inv.3223, by an Undetermined Earlier Mannerist, *ARV*² 586, 47; *MTS*² AV 15; Pickard-Cambridge, *Festivals*² 182, fig. 35; A. Greifen-hagen, *Führer durch die Antikenabteilung* (Berlin 1968) 126, pl. 65b; E. Simon, *The Ancient Theatre* (London 1982) pl. 1; Green, *GRBS* 32, 1991, 33–34 and pl. 5a–b. There is excellent discussion by Beazley in *Hesperia* 24 (1955) 312–313.

20 From a large bibliography, see D. Bain, *Actors and Audience. A Study of Asides and Related Conventions in Greek Drama* (Oxford 1977) and 'Some Reflections on the Illusion in Greek Tragedy', *BICS* 34, 1987, 1–14.

21 Fundamental is G.M. Sifakis, *Parabasis and Animal Choruses. A Contribution to the History of Attic Comedy* (London 1971) 7–14; see also R. Crahay and M. Delcourt, 'Les ruptures d'illusion dans les comédies antiques', *Mélanges Henri Gregoire* iv (*AIPhO* 12, Brussels 1952) 83–92; *RE* Suppl. xii (1970) 1538ff. (Gelzer); K.J. Dover, *Aristophanic Comedy* (London 1972) 55–59; F. Muecke, 'Playing with the Play: Theatrical Self-Consciousness in Aristophanes', *Antichthon* 11 (1977) 52–67; A.M. Wilson, 'Breach of Dramatic Illusion in the Old Comic Fragments', *Euphrosyne* 9 (1978–79) 145–150; G. Roux, 'Aristophane au théâtre', in *Stemmata. Mélanges de philologie, d'histoire et d'archéologie grecques offerts à Jules Labarbe* (*Ant.Class.* Suppl., Liège–Louvain 1987) 91–100; and the survey of examples by G.A.H. Chapman, 'Some Notes on Dramatic Illusion in Aristophanes', *AJP* 104 (1983) 1–23. There is also much useful comment in Taplin, 'Fifth-Century Tragedy and Comedy: a Synkrisis', *Journal of Hellenic Studies* 106, 1986, 163–174; see, too, T. Kowzan, 'Les comédies d'Aristophane, véhicule de la critique dramatique', *Dioniso* 54 (1983) 83–100.

22 Cf. Ar. *Frogs* 1ff; *Wasps* 58–59; *Plutus* 797–799; also *Peace* 960–966.

23 Whatever one says about the origins of the large *phallos* worn by comic actors lying in the celebration of fertility festivals, there must be at least a semi-conscious rejection of the conventions of contemporary art with its 'heroic nudity' and where the male genitalia are shown as small (unless the nature of the depiction demands otherwise).

24 Whip *Frogs* 630ff.; stick e.g. *Clouds* 541f. and the self-conscious variant at Menander, *Epitr.* 248f. Arnott. Scene with stick, see e.g. the old man pursuing fleeing slave on New York, coll. Fleischman, F 98 *RVAp* Suppl.ii, 74 no. 11/133b, pl. 12, 5–6.

25 For a good expression of the traditional view, based simply on the evidence of the texts, see A.M. Wilson, 'The Individualized Chorus in Old Comedy', *CQ* ns 27, 1977, 278–283; my view developed in 'Birds', with full illustrations of surviving depictions of earlier comic choruses.

26 See the comments on this phenomenon in the last chapter. Berlin F 1697, *ABV* 297, 17 (Painter of Berlin 1686); Bieber, *Theater*² fig. 116; Ghiron-Bistagne fig. 113, 'Birds' no. 3. For good treatment of the Italian versions of such helmets, see more recently A. Bottini, 'Apulische-korinthische Helme', in H. Pflug (ed.), *Antike Helme* (Mainz 1989) 107–136; id., 'Gli elmi apulo-corinzi: proposta di classificazione', *AION* 12, 1990, 23–38; id., *Gli strumenti della guerra in Basilicata fra VIII e III secolo a.C.* (Bari 1991).

27 J.R. Green, 'A Representation of the *Birds* of Aristophanes', *The J. Paul Getty Museum. Greek Vases* 2 (Malibu 1985) 95–118, with further comments in *GRBS* 32, 1991, 15–50; A.H. Sommerstein, *Aristophanes, Birds* (1987), frontispiece. Taplin, *PCPS* 213 (ns 33), 1987, 92–104, somewhat revised in *Dioniso* 57, 1987, 95–109, argues that these should be the Just and Unjust Arguments of *Clouds*. (He was followed by D. Fowler, *CQ* 39, 1989, 257–259.) This cannot be: the grammar and syntax of the iconography is quite clear that we are dealing with

179

a chorus. See now his Appendix in *Comic Angels* (Oxford 1993).

28   *MMC*³ 118–119, AS 3–4, with references. Also G.M. Sifakis, 'Aristotle E.N. IV,2, 1123a19–24, and the Comic Chorus in the Fourth Century', *AJP* 92, 1971, 410–432; and R.L. Hunter, 'The Comic Chorus in the Fourth Century', *ZPE* 36, 1979, 23–38.

29   London B 509 by the Gela Painter, Haspels, *ABL* 214 no. 187; Bieber, *Theater*² fig. 123; 'Birds' no. 8 fig. 11a–c.

30   'Birds' no. 11, fig. 14. with refs.

31   This practice of ringing the changes with what could be regarded as a common pool of material is well brought out by M. Heath, 'Aristophanes and his Rivals', *Greece & Rome* 37, 1990, 143–158.

32   'Birds' no. 6 fig. 9; *ARV*² 1622, 7 bis; *Paral.* 259, 326; Greifenhagen, *Pantheon* 23, 1965, 1–7.

33   *BICS* 14 (1967) 36–37.

34   'Birds' nos. 13–17 (with refs.) together with another from the Dechter Collection: K. Hamma (ed.), *The Dechter Collection of Greek Vases* (San Bernardino 1989) 42–43 no. 22 (ill.).

35   Athens, Kerameikos 5671. *ABV* 518 (Theseus Painter); Brommer *AA* 1942, 31 figs. 4–5; 'Birds' no. 13.

36   The possible exception is a poorly published red-figure lekythos in Athens: *ADelt* 25 (1970) Chron.47, pl. 51d. It shows a figure as Polyphemos and could be from satyr-play.

37   M. Crosby, *Hesperia* 24, 1955, 76–84; *MMC*³ 33–34, AV 10–14, and e.g. Pickard-Cambridge, *Festivals*² 122–123 with figs 82–84 and 86–87 as well as the forthcoming edition of *PhV.* For the possibility of recognising Eupolis, *Taxiarchoi*, see more recently Kassel-Austin, *PCG* V (1986) 452ff. (with refs.).

38   *MMC*³ 31, AV 5, 32, AV 8–9, and the comments of H. Metzger in *Recherches sur l'imagerie athénienne* (Paris 1965) 57–58. For a recent overall examination of choes, their iconography and relationship to the Athenian festival of the Anthesteria, see Richard Hamilton, *Choes and Anthesteria. Athenian Iconography and Ritual* (Ann Arbor 1992).

39   *MMC*³ 45ff., AT 9–23; *BICS* 27, 1980, 123–131. Further additions could now be made.

40   *MMC*³ 47–48, AT 10.

41   For Aristophanes being atypical, Erich Segal, 'The *physis* of Comedy', *HSCP* 77 (1973) 129–136. For this and the selection we have of Aristophanes, E.W. Handley, *CambHistClassLit* i, 391ff., and in his introductory notes to *POxy* 3540.

42   See Chapter 1 and n. 25 there.

43   Among more recent general works on satyr-play, see N.E. Collinge, 'Some Reflections on Satyr-Plays', *PCPS* ns 5 (1958–59) 28–35; L.E. Rossi, 'Il dramma satiresco attico: forma, fortuna e funzione di un genere letterario antico', *DArch* 6 (1972) 248–302; D.F. Sutton, 'A Handlist of Satyr Plays', *HSCP* 78 (1974) 107–143; id., 'A Complete Handlist to the Literary Remains of the Greek Satyr Plays', *AncW* 3 (1980) 115–130; id., The Greek Satyr Play (Meisenheim am Glan 1980); id., 'Satyr-Play', *CambHistClassLit* i, 346–354. On representations of satyr-play, see *MTS*² and O. Jahn, 'Perseus, Herakles, Satyrn auf vasenbildern und das satyrdrama', *Philologus* 27, 1868, 1–27; E. Buschor, *Satyrtänze und frühes Drama* (Munich 1943); F. Brommer, *Satyrspiele. Bilder griechischer Vasen* (2nd edn, Berlin 1959) with additions in *GettyMJ* 6/7 (1978–79) 144–146 and *GVGetty* 1 (1983) 115–120; E. Simon, 'Satyr-Plays on Vases in the Time of Aeschylus', in D. Kurtz and B.A. Sparkes (eds), *The Eye of Greece. Studies in the Art of Athens* (Cambridge 1982) 123–148 (with an up-dated German version in B. Seiden-

sticker (ed.), *Satyrspiel* (Wege der Forschung 579, Darmstadt 1989); C. Bérard, 'Le corps bestial (les métamorphoses de l'homme idéal au siècle de Périclès)', in C. Reichler (ed.), *Le corps et ses fictions* (Paris 1983) 43–54; D.F. Sutton, 'Scenes from Greek Satyr Plays Illustrated in Greek Vase-Paintings', *AncW* 9 (1984) 119–126; F. Lissarrague, 'Pourquoi les satyres sont-ils bons à montrer?', *Anthropologie et Théâtre antique. Cahiers du GITA* 3, 1987, 93–106 = 'Why Satyrs Are Good to Represent' in J.J. Winkler and F.I. Zeitlin (eds.) *Nothing to Do with Dionysos? Athenian Drama in its Social Context* (Princeton 1990) 228–236). The last is very reluctant to see the influence of theatre on scenes on pots. By contrast, see now G.M. Hedreen, *Silens in Attic Black-Figure Vase-Paintings. Myth and Performance* (Ann Arbor 1992) who is much more ready to see reflections of satyr-play than I am.

44 Few from many: M. Gluckmann (ed.), *Essays on the Ritual of Social Relations* (Manchester 1962); M. Bakhtin, *Rabelais and his World* (Cambridge, Mass., 1968); V. Turner, *The Ritual Process. Structure and Anti-Structure* (Chicago–London 1969); I. Donaldson, *The World Upside-Down, Comedy from Jonson to Fielding* (Oxford 1970); N.Z. Davis, *Society and Culture in Early Modern France* (Stanford 1975), Ch. 2; B.A. Babcock, *The Reversible World. Symbolic Inversion in Art and Society* (Ithaca N.Y., 1978); M.D. Bristol, *Carnival and Theater: Plebeian Culture and the Structure of Authority in Renaissance England* (London–New York 1985); T. Castle, *Masquerade and Civilization. The Carnivalesque in Eighteenth-Century English Culture and Fiction* (Stanford 1986). See also the article by Bérard mentioned in the last note.

45 See n. 43 above.

46 (a) London, British Museum E 65, *ARV²* 370, 13 and 1649 (Brygos Painter); *Paral.* 365; *Addenda²* 224; Buschor, *Satyrtänze* figs. 76–77; Simon *Eye of Greece* pl. 30. (b) Berlin F 2591, *ARV²* 888, 150 (Penthesilea Painter); Brommer, *Satyrspiele²* 26 fig. 18; *CVA* (1) (DDR 3) pl. 33, 1–3. (c) Boston 08.30a, *ARV²* 135 (a) (Wider Circle of the Nikosthenes Painter); *Addenda²* 177; Brommer, *Satyrspiele²* 26 fig. 17; *AntK* 12, 1969, pl. 10, 3. Rohde in the Berlin *CVA* compares a vase formerly on the Freiburg market, Galerie Gunter Puhze, *Kunst der Antike* 4 (1982) no. 200. Simon in *The Eye of Greece* suggests that the offering on the London vase is a tongue, but Van Straten, 'The God's Portion in Greek Sacrificial Representations: Is the Tail doing Nicely?', in R. Hägg *et al.* (eds), *Early Greek Cult Practice. Proceedings of the Fifth International Symposium of the Swedish Institute at Athens, 26–29 June, 1986* (Stockholm 1988) 51–68, argues for the old view that it is a tail, probably rightly. It is undoubtedly a tail on the Berlin vase.

47 See the useful collection of material by J. Boardman, *LIMC* V, 155–160, s.v. Herakles. The remains of a somewhat mysterious play on this theme were published from PBodmer XXVIII by E.G. Turner, *MusHelv* 33, 1976, 1–23; see H.-J. Mette, *Urkunden dramatischer Aufführungen* (Berlin 1977) 150ff.

48 *AA* 1941 54–5, figs. 1–2 (Brommer); Brommer, *Satyrspiele²* 42 figs 38–39; *Eye of Greece* pl. 35b (Simon).

49 *Das Satyrspiel Sphinx des Aischylos* (Heidelberg 1981) as well as in *The Eye of Greece* 141–142. The play was produced as part of his Theban tetralogy, which also included the *Seven Against Thebes*.

50 Cambridge GR 2.1977, R.V. Nicholls in *Annual Report of the Fitzwilliam Museum Syndicate* (Cambridge 1977) pl. 2; L. Burn in *Proceedings of the 3rd Symposium on Ancient Greek and Related Pottery* (Copenhagen 1988) 99–106; Green, *GRBS* 32, 1991, 45ff.

51 Nor am I clear if the Amazon shown on the inside of the cup has anything to

do with the scene on the outside; she makes the idea of Theseus the more tempting.

52 F. Brommer, *Satyrspiele*² (Berlin 1959) no. 115, fig. 67. Curiously, the figure is taken by N.H. Young, 'The Figure of the Paidagogos in Art and Literature', *Biblical Archaeologist* 53, 1990, 80–86 (the skyphos p. 84) as a human *paidagogos*.

53 Boston 03.788, probably from Greece. *ARV*² 571, 75; *Paral.* 390; *Addenda*² 261; CB iii, 51–52 no. 151, pl. 86; Brommer, *Satyrspiele*² no. 1, fig. 6; *MTS*² 46, AV 14; Pickard-Cambridge, *Festivals*² fig. 40.

54 Vienna IV 985. *ARV*² 591, 20; Brommer, *Satyrspiele*² fig. 20; Pickard-Cambridge, *Festivals*² 184, fig. 41; *MTS*² 47, AV 16; F. Brommer, *Hephaistos, der Schmeidegott in der antiken Kunst* (Mainz 1978) pl. 3, 1; *CVA* (3) pl. 101, 1–2 (with further refs.).

55 K. Schefold, *Die Göttersage in der klassischen und hellenistischen Kunst* (Munich 1981), 128–129, provides a good and convenient discussion of Returns in the fifth century; see also recently M. Halm-Tisserant, *AntK* 29 (1986) 8–22.

56 Bonn 1216.183+. *ARV*² 2–3 (Painter of the Athens Dinos); *MTS*² 49, AV 23–24; *CVA* (1) pl. 32, 11–13; Pickard-Cambridge, *Festivals* ¹fig. 31, ²figs 45–46; Brommer, *Satyrspiele*² 11, fig. 3.

57 Pausanias II, 13, 6; Diogenes Laertius II, 133.

58 *POxy* 2162; Radt, *TrGF* iii, Fr.78a. See further H. Lloyd-Jones in the Loeb edition *Aeschylus* ii (Cambridge, Mass., 1957) 541–556, with refs; H.J. Mette, *Der verlorene Aischylos* (Berlin 1963) 164–170; D.F. Sutton, *The Greek Satyr Play* (Meisenheim 1980) 29–33. The translation is based on that by Lloyd-Jones.

59 See Gloria Ferrari, *RevArch* 1986, 19–20. The suggestion had been made already by Mette (op. cit.). Sutton (op. cit.) also takes these effigies as masks but, following Fraenkel and Lloyd-Jones, sees them as possibly for use as antefixes.

60 Note the use of the term *mormolykeion* in, e.g., Aristophanes fr.131K=130K-A and the fact that there the masks are said to be hung in the Dionysion. Extant examples in art are rather later, but one still within the fifth century is that shown on the small chous in Eleusis, *MTS*² 49, AV 26; G. Mylonas, *To dytikon nekrotapheion tis Eleusinos* (Athens 1975) pl. 362, no. 726. See also the next chapter.

61 New York. coll. Fleischman F 93; A.D. Trendall, 'Farce and Tragedy in South Italian Vase-Painting', in T. Rasmussen and N. Spivey (eds), *Looking at Greek Vases* (Cambridge 1991) 164–165, fig. 67; O. Taplin, *Comic Angels and Other Approaches to Greek Drama through Vase-Paintings* (Oxford 1993) 55–63, pl. 9.1; *RVAp* Suppl.ii, 7 no. 1/124, pl. 1, 3. By the Choregos Painter who was also responsible for the Cleveland bell-krater with slave and *papposilenos* about the head of Dionysos, and the well-known bell-krater in Milan with on one side the comic scene of an old man and a woman eating from a tray while a slave hides a cake in his tunic and on the other Herakles supporting the world while satyrs make off with his weapons, *PhV*² no. 45, pl. 2a; Bieber, *Theater*² fig. 509; *IGD* IV, 18; *RVAp* Suppl.ii, no. 1/123. Note that the *choregoi* on our vase are dressed as actors, not chorusmen as Taplin suggests.

62 E.W. Handley points out to me some interesting coincidences: (1) that Phrynichus' *Mousai* was staged in competition with Aristophanes' *Frogs*; (2) that it too may well have been concerned with the staging of tragedy, given the nature of the reference to the recently dead Sophocles in fr. 32 (see Kassel-Austin *PCG* VII (1989) 409ff; (3) that the one occasion we know of when there really were two *choregoi* rather than one was this same year. It is usually assumed that the use of two *choregoi* was due to shortage of funds and difficulties around the end of the Peloponnesian War. This play may, therefore, have picked up on

this event, have developed the idea that in the chaos of the time a slave could be Archon or Judge, and at the same time used the theme of the contrast between the conservative old and the supporters of the new school.

63 See for example Taplin, *JHS* 106, 1986, 165.

3 THE LATE FIFTH AND THE FOURTH CENTURIES

1 H.D.F. Kitto, in 'Aristotle and Fourth Century Tragedy', in M. Kelly (ed.), *For Service to Classical Studies. Essays in Honour of Francis Letters* (Melbourne 1966) 113–129. See also T.B.L. Webster, 'Fourth-Century Tragedy and the *Poetics*', *Hermes* 82, 1954, 294–308; J. Jones *On Aristotle and Greek Tragedy* (Oxford 1962); and the relevant parts of D.A. Russell and M. Winterbottom (eds.), *Ancient Literary Criticism: The Principal Texts in New Translations* (Oxford 1972); D.A. Russell, *Criticism in Antiquity* (London 1981). There is a lively characterisation of fourth-century tragedy by B.M.W. Knox in *CambHistClassLit* i, 339–345.

2 Fr. 191 K/189 K–A. For recent discussion of the use of the crane, see, among others, H.-J. Newiger, 'Ekkyklema e mechané nella messa in scena del dramma greco', *Dioniso* 59, 1989, 173–185 (= 'Ekkyklema und Mechané in der Inszenierung des grieschischen Dramas', *WürzJbAltWiss* 16, 1990, 33–42); D.J. Mastronarde, 'Actors on High: The Skene Roof, the Crane, and the Gods in Attic Drama', *ClAnt* 9(2), 1990, 247–294; and A.L.H. Robkin, 'That Magnificent Flying Machine. On the Nature of the 'Mechane' of the Theater of Dionysos at Athens', *ArchNews* 8, 1979, 1–6. The mechanics of the device are still not fully understood.

3 *Poetics* 13.7 (1453a). We shall see below from the evidence of vase-paintings that in fact some rare and even extraordinary myths were brought into service. We might suppose that he means rejection of myths of the wrong style, because they were either grotesque or did not offer the right scope for contemporary interests.

4 Aristotle, *Poetics* IX (1451b).

5 On the other hand, we should remember that we are more likely to pick up allusions to plays whose texts are preserved, and no fourth-century tragedies survive. On the staging of tragedies and what we can deduce of audience familiarity with them, see A.G. Katsouris, 'The Staging of Palaiai Tragodiai in Relation to Menander's Audience', *Dodone* 3, 1974, 173–204; also his *Tragic Patterns in Menander* (Athens 1975). The best treatment of fourth-century tragedy is G. Xanthakis-Karamanos, *Studies in Fourth-Century Tragedy* (Athens 1980). On Menander and tragedy, see also n. 7.

6 J. Bousquet, 'Inscriptions de Delphes', *BCH* 116, 1992, 183–186.

7 See T.B.L. Webster, 'Scenic Notes II', in R. Hanslik, A. Lesky and H. Schwabl (eds), *Antidosis. Festschrift für Walter Kraus* (Vienna 1972) 454–457, and for the paintings, V.M. Strocka, *Die Wandmalerei der Hanghäuser in Ephesos (Forschungen in Ephesos* VIII.1, Vienna 1977) 45ff., pl. 62ff.; *MNC*[3] 6DP 1.1–2. On Menander's use of tragedy, see recently A. Hurst, 'Ménandre et la tragédie', in E.W. Handley and A. Hurst (eds), *Relire Ménandre* (Geneva 1990) 93–122 (with refs). Note E.W. Handley, *The Dyskolos of Menander* 6: 'it is perhaps mildly amusing, but certainly not ridiculous, to find a charcoal-burner quoting myth as seen in tragedy as part of his case in an argument with a shepherd'.

8 Aristotle, *Poetics* 1455a22–29; see most recently Green, *GRBS* 31, 1990, 281–285.

9 Fr. 14, from his *Oineus*. See Collard, *JHS* 90, 1970, 22–34.

10 For a very useful critical view, see J.-M. Moret, *L'Ilioupersis dans la céramique italiote*, Rome 1975 (Bibl. Helvetica Rom., xiv), and *Oedipe, la Sphinx et les Thébains. Essai de mythologie iconographique*, Rome 1984 (Bibl. Helvetica Rom., xxiii).

11 For a handy list, see *MTS*² 159–160. I do not know of any further examples that have come to light since. For discussion, see A. Cambitoglou, *AntK* 18, 1975, 56–66.

12 For other views of the function of such scenes, see A. Novellone, 'Il valore contentutistico delle rappresentazioni vascolari di miti', *PdP* 26, 1971, 205–220; M. Schmidt, in M. Schmidt, A.D. Trendall and A. Cambitoglou, *Eine Gruppe apulischer Grabvasen in Basel* (Basle 1976) 40–49; E. Keuls, *MededRom* 40, 1978, 83–91; *ead. ZPE* 30, 1978, 41–68; and E. Vermeule in *Studies in Classical Art and Archaeology … P.H. von Blanckenhagen* (Locust Valley, N.Y., 1979), 185–188; *Peintre de Darius* 268.

13 'The Mourning Niobe', *RevArch* 1972, 309–316; and 'An Apulian Loutrophoros Representing the Tantalidae', *GVGetty* 3, 1985, 129–144. Note too H.M. Fracchia, *EMC/CV* 31, 1987, 199–208.

14 Sydney 71.01; *IGD* III.1, 23; *RevArch* 1972, 310, fig. 1; *RVSIS*, fig. 305; *LCS* Suppl. 2, 223, no. 3/340a, pl. 38, 4, by the Libation Painter.

15 Worth noting that this is *her* tomb, not the tomb of her children as seems to have been the case in Aeschylus' play. For the literary remains, see Lloyd-Jones' Appendix in the revised Loeb edition, ii, 1983, 556–562 (with 430–434). In Sophocles' play of the same name, Niobe returned to her native Lydia after the death of her children in Thebes, but there is no sign of a foreign context here.

16 For a good survey and discussion of Alcestis scenes, see M. Schmidt, *LIMC* I, s.v. Alkestis.

17 Basle S 21, M. Schmidt, A.D. Trendall and A. Cambitoglou, *Eine Gruppe apulischer Grabvasen in Basel* (Basel 1976) pl. 21; *RVSIS*, fig. 196; *RVAp* ii, 482, no. 18/16, pl. 171, 4, near the Laodameia Painter.

18 W.M. Calder III, 'The Alkestis Inscription from Odessos: *IGBR* I² 222', *AJA* 79, 1975, 80–83.

19 See C. Robert, *Bild und Lied. Archäologische Beiträge zur Geschichte der griechischen Heldensage* (Philologische Untersuchengen v, Berlin 1881) 150ff., and more recently the good survey and discussion by I. McPhee, *LIMC* III, s.v. Elektra I. On the staging of Electra scenes, see recently D. Malhadas, 'La rencontre d'Oreste et d'Electre. Espace et mise en scène', *Dioniso* 59, 1989, 361–363.

20 *LCS* Suppl. 3, 199 nos. 304e f, pl. 23, 1 and 3.

21 The reference should be to Aeschylus' play but it is rarely so specific: compare *RVAp* i, 436 no. 14a, of the early fourth century, where she is shown examining the lock of hair. Note that the theme is the subject of a Tarentine grave relief of the later fourth century: H. Klumbach, *Tarentiner Grabkunst* (Reutlingen 1937) no. 63, pl. 12; J.C. Carter, *The Sculpture of Taras* (Philadelphia 1975) no. 123.

 Carcinus and Theodectes in the fourth century also wrote plays entitled *Orestes*, and Alexis and Autocleides seem to have written comedies around the theme. In this context one recalls the Berlin neck-amphora by the Boston Orestes Painter which seems to confuse or compound the stories of Orestes and Electra at the tomb of Agamemnon, the priestess Theano handing over the Palladion to Odysseus, and Orestes' meeting with Iphigeneia among the Taurians: cf. *RVP* 254.

22 Geneva, coll. Sciclounoff, *Peintre de Darius*, 190–199 (ill.) and colour-plate; *RVSIS* fig. 210; by the Underworld Painter, third quarter of the fourth century.

The prologue of Euripides' play is preserved (though somewhat inadequately) and it is the primary source for Melanippe's family background. Euripides evidently needed to give it a fairly full explanation. See most recently W. Luppe, 'Zum Prolog der "Melanippe Sophe"', *WürzJbAltWiss* 15, 1989, 83–95.

23 This was a family with a history of problems. Melanippe's mother was the daughter of a centaur who had apparently been tricked into motherhood by Aiolos and had herself transformed into a horse (taking on the name Hippe or Hippo). Thus perhaps the horse in this scene which is being given a wreath by Kretheus. She is mentioned briefly in the Prologue. It seems that in Euripides' play, the children were thought to be monsters. Here they look quite normal. The interest of Athena in these events is noticeable and it is possible that she imposed some resolution of the situation at the end of the play.

24 A.D. Trendall, 'The Daughters of Anios', in E. Böhr and W. Martini (eds), *Studien zur Mythologie und Vasenmalerei. Festschrift für Konrad Schauenburg* (Mainz 1986) 166–168.

25 G.M. Sifakis, *Studies in the History of Hellenistic Drama* (London 1967) 7; P. Bruneau in *LIMC* I, s.v. Anios.

26 He was also the father of Andros, Mykonos and Thasos.

27 Note for example his Medea at Eleusis on a volute-krater in Princeton; A.D. Trendall, 'Medea at Eleusis on a Volute Krater by the Darius Painter', *Princeton University Art Museum Record* 43(1), 1984; and M. Schmidt, 'Medea und Herakles – zwei tragische Kindermörder' in E. Böhr and W. Martini (eds), *Studien zur Mythologie und Vasenmalerei. Festschift für Konrad Schauenburg* (Mainz 1986) 169–174. See also Trendall's comments in *RVAp* ii, 484.

Erika Simon has related the Adonis scene on the Baltimore Painter's name vase to the play of that name by Dionysius of Syracuse: 'Dramen des älteren Dionysios auf italiotischen Vasen', in *Aparchai Arias*, ii, 479–482.

28 See in general the excellent treatment by W.B. Stanford, *Greek Tragedy and the Emotions* (London 1983).

29 There is more work to be done on the place and function of *paidagogos* figures in the scenes. See *RVSIS* 12 and 262 for observations by Trendall. Chamay and Cambitoglou, *AntK* 23, 1980, 40–42 give a list of 31 examples, to which some additions could now be made, including the one illustrated here. But note in the first instance Robert, *Bild und Lied* 42. J.H. Oakley, ' "The Death of Hippolytus" in South Italian Vase-Painting', *NumAntCl* 20, 1991, 63–83 has recently pursued this same line in relation to the series of eight vases showing the scene of the death of Hippolytos.

30 Melbourne, coll. Geddes, A 5(4), *LIMC* III, pl. 503, 6; *RVSIS* fig. 211, together with Trendall's full discussion in *Enthousiasmos. Essays on Greek and Related Pottery presented to J.M. Hemelrijk* (Amsterdam 1986) 157–166. Compare the name vase of the (Sicilian) Dirce Painter of the early fourth century, Berlin F 3296; *LCS* 203, 27; *IGD* III.3, 15; *LIMC* I, pl. 681, Antiope I 6. For general coverage of the archaeological material, see F. Heger, *LIMC* III, s.v. Dirke.

31 By far the best treatment of these issues is M. Kaimio, *Physical Contact in Greek Tragedy. A Study of Stage Conventions* (Annales Academiæ Scientiarum Fennicæ, Ser. B, 244, Helsinki 1988).

32 The passage from Chaeremon noted above must also have been designed for expressive delivery.

33 Galerie Günter Puhze (Freiburg), *Kunst der Antike. Katalog 10* (1993) no. 220 (colour ill.). Another example of the *paidagogos* shown alone is to be found on the slightly later kantharos in the Jatta Collection in Ruvo (inv. 1394, *Iapigia* 3, 1932, 289, fig. 41; Pickard-Cambridge, *Festivals*[1] fig. 47; *MTS*[2] TV 1). He too

raises his hand in the characteristic speaking gesture.

34 On 'running slaves', see more recently Csapo, *Phoenix* 41, 1987, 399–419; *CQ* 39, 1989, 148–163; and *AntK* 36, 1993, 41–58.

35 Syracuse 66557, from Syracuse. *LCS* Suppl. 3, 276 no. 98a; *IGD* III.2, 8; *RVSIS* fig. 429. Gibil Gabib Group in the Lentini-Manfria Group. See also the tragic scene with a messenger relating dreadful news to a group of women, also set on a stage, Caltanissetta from Capodarso, *LCS* 601 no. 98, pl. 235, 2–3; *MTS*² SV 2; also from the Gibil Gabib Group.

36 G.M. Sifakis, 'Children in Greek Tragedy', *BICS* 26, 1979, 67–80.

37 Athenaeus XI, 482D quoting Ephippus fr. 16K = 16K–A. On treatment of the texts, see R. Hamilton, 'Objective Evidence for Actors' Interpolations in Greek Tragedy', *GRBS* 15, 1974, 387–402 (with refs). It is of course more difficult to detect what has disappeared from surviving texts.

38 For the remodelling of the Theatre of Dionysos at Athens, see Pickard-Cambridge, *ToD* 134ff; R.F. Townsend, *Hesperia* 55, 1986, 421–438; Polacco, *Teatro* 174ff.; on Epidauros, A. von Gerkan and W. Müller-Wiener, *Das Theater von Epidauros* (Stuttgart 1961); Polacco, *NumAntCl* 7, 1978, 83–93.

39 For a recent examination of the situation and people's reaction to it, see Barry S. Strauss, *Athens after the Peloponnesian War: Class, Faction and Policy 403–386 B.C.* (Ithaca, N.Y. 1986), or on more particular aspects, A. López Eire, 'Comedia politica y utopia', *Cuadernos de Investigación filológica* 10, 1984, 137–174; M. Dillon, 'Topicality in Aristophanes' Ploutos', *ClAnt* 6, 1987, 155–183, and the useful comments of S.D. Olson, 'Economics and Ideology in Aristophanes' *Wealth*', *HSCP* 93, 1990, 223–242.

40 'The Art of the State in Late Fifth-Century Athens', in M.M. MacKenzie and C. Roueché (eds), *Images of Authority. Papers Presented to Joyce Reynolds on the Occasion of her Seventieth Birthday* (*ProcCambPhilSoc*, Suppl. 16, Cambridge 1989) 62–81.

41 For discussions of Middle Comedy, see more recently the excellent survey by E.W. Handley, 'Comedy. From Aristophanes to Menander', *CambHistClassLit* i (1985) 398–414; H.-G. Nesselrath, *Die attische mittlere Komödie. Ihre Stellung in der antiken Literaturkritik und Literaturgeschichte* (Berlin 1990).

42 See for example T.B.L. Webster, *Studies in Later Greek Comedy* (Manchester ¹1953, ²1970) 23ff., 37ff., 102ff., and the comments of S.M. Burstein on Menander, *Halieis*, in S.M. Burstein and L.A. Okin (eds), *Panhellenica. Essays in Ancient History and Historiography in Honor of Truesdell S. Brown* (Lawrence, Kans. 1980) 69–76; or, on allusions to politics by contemporaries of Menander, A.W. Gomme and F.H. Sandbach, *Menander. A Commentary* (Oxford 1973) 24, n. 1. The latter provide a useful warning against over-simplifying the contemporary socio-political situation. For mention of contemporaries, see Gomme-Sandbach on *Samia* 603 (for the parasite Chairephon and others). Chairephon is also particularised by Alexis. See Arnott, *GRBS* 9, 1968, 161–168.

43 On 'Phlyax' vases as showing Athenian comedy, besides the earlier arguments of Webster, see more recently E.W. Handley, *CambHistClassLit* i, 398; my own comments, for example in *Lustrum* 31, 1989, 75–78 and *NumAntClass. Quaderni Ticinesi* 20, 1991, 49–56, or the lively presentation by Oliver Taplin, *Comic Angels and Other Approaches to Greek Drama through Vase-Paintings* (Oxford 1993). A new edition of A.D. Trendall, *Phlyax Vases* is in preparation and should appear directly.

44 *RVAp* i, 65 no. 4/4a. For initial publication and linking with the play, see A. Kossatz-Deißmann, 'Telephos travestitus', in H.A. Cahn and E. Simon (eds), *Taenia. Festschrift Roland Hampe* (Mainz 1980) 281–290; for identification and

discussion of the scene, see the important article by E. Csapo, *Phoenix* 40, 1986 [1988] 379–392; and O. Taplin, *PCPS* 213 (ns 33), 1987, 92–104; *Dioniso* 57, 1987, 95–109. For more general (earlier) discussion, C. Bauchhenss-Thüriedl, *Der Mythos von Telephos in der antiken Bildkunst* (Würzburg 1971).

45 Her name, Mikka, is a familiar and diminutive one, doubtless implying someone young and likeable, even attractive.

46 R. Aélion, *Euripide, héritier d'Eschyle* i (Paris 1983) 31–42, gives a useful survey and discussion of the handling of the theme. The fact that we know so little of Sophocles' *Telephia* should not obscure the fact that he too will have made a contribution. Agathon also wrote a play of the same name.

47 The example in Germany is published by K. Stähler, *Griechische Vasen aus westfälischen Sammlungen* (Münster 1984) 159–160 no. 58. Naples Stg 368, *CVA* (2) pl. 23, 1 and 27, 1 (with earlier refs.).

48 Comic scenes with figures on altars on vases include:
   (1) Berlin F 3045, bell-krater. *PhV²* 21; Bieber, *Theater²*, fig. 493; *IGD* IV, 29; *RVAp* i, 78 no. 4/92. Priam seated on altar and gesturing towards Neoptolemos who approaches with raised sword. Apulian; related to the Eton Nika Painter; first quarter of the fourth century.
   (2) Rome, coll. Rotondo, oinochoe. Hermes as slave (or slave as Hermes) seated on altar. *PhV²* no. 124, pl. 7e. Apulian; unattributed; second quarter of the fourth century.
   (3) Taranto, from Canosa(?) (1923), calyx-krater. Old man with torch and stick approaching slave seated on altar, branch in hand. *CVA* (1) pl. 17, 1; *PhV²* no. 89. Apulian; unattributed; c. 340–330 BC.
   (4) Taranto 29020, from Taranto, Viale Virgilio, oinochoe. *Atti del 22° Convegno di studi sulla Magna Grecia, Taranto 1982* (1983) pl. 39, 1; *RVAp* Suppl. ii, 41 no. 7/V2. Slave and old man about an altar. Apulian; Felton Painter; mid-fourth century. Probably related to this theme.
   (5) Rio de Janeiro, Museu Nacional 1500, bell-krater. Female piper standing between man and another seated on altar. *AJA* 66, 1962, 323ff., pl. 87; *LCS* 486 no. 4/334, pl. 187, 6; *PhV²* no. 56, pl. 4c. Campanian; Painter of New York GR 1000; third quarter of the fourth century.
   (6) Malibu 86.AE.412 (ex Bareiss 404), calyx-krater fragment. Part of male seated on altar waving scabbard; before him old slave and baggage. *Greek Vases. Molly and Walter Bareiss Collection* (Malibu 1983) 84 no. 216; *Wandlungen. Studien ... Homann-Wedeking* (Waldsassen 1975) pl. 37c (Schauenburg). Sicilian; unattributed; second quarter of the fourth century.
   (7) Gela 8255–6, from Gela, fragments of bell-krater. Old man (L) by door; man seated on altar. *PhV²* no. 77; *RVP* 47 no. 102 (Painter of Louvre K 240); G. Pugliese Carratelli (ed.), *Megale Hellas* (Milan 1983) fig. 630. Sicilian; unattributed; mid-fourth century.
   (8) Gela 643, from Manfria, fragment of skyphoid krater. Old man leaning on stick before slave seated on altar. *NSc* 1958, 312 no. 1, fig. 17; *MonAnt* 44, 1958, col. 645, fig. 267; *LCS* 595 no. 69, pl. 231, 2. Sicilian; Manfria Group; c. 340–330 BC.
   (9) Gela, from Monte Saraceno, fragment of skyphoid krater. Stage with steps; on it, altar and legs of male. *PHV²* no. 101; *LCS* 596 no. 73. Sicilian; Manfria Group; c. 340–330 BC.

49 Worth noting here too that Euripides was reacting to the staging of an earlier *Andromeda*, that of Sophocles, discussed in the last chapter. On being tied to a plank, see D. Clay, in *Studi in onore di Adelmo Barigazzi* i (Rome 1986) 174. It was not totally unlike crucifixion: the victim was stripped naked and attached by

arms, legs and mouth or jaw to a plank, raised to an upright position and left to die of exposure. See the photographs of excavated victims in *ADelt* 2, 1916, 53–54, figs 57–58.

50 See the useful list of comic playwrights by C. Austin *ZPE* 14, 1974, 201–225. Isocrates (*De Pace* (8).14) comments on comic poets broadcasting their fellow-citizens' mistakes to all Greece: cf. Handley, *CambHistClassLit* i, 405. Niall Slater points out to me that the large numbers of tragedies from the pens of Astydamas and Carcinus (see this chapter, p. 51) indicate that they were writing for an export market too – one could hardly have had so many performance opportunities at Athens.

51 Compare Plutarch, *Moralia* 854A: 'Some dramatists write for the common people, some for the few ... But Menander ...' But his view arises out of the perspective of his own time and place as well as from the place he is seeking to give Menander's work in the culture of his period.

52 Much of the detail of this section is based on the material provided in *MMC³*, together with the additions published in *BICS* 27, 1980, 123–131, and then a few modifications and additions of more recent material. The various mask types of Middle Comedy are defined (with illustrations) in *MMC³* 13–26. The mask types of New Comedy, referred to below, are described by Pollux, *Onomasticon* IV, 143–154, and this description forms something of the basis for the identification of the various types with the surviving archaeological evidence. He was writing in the second century AD and his book is full of curious facts culled, not always with understanding, from a wide range of sources. In Book IV he includes an account of theatre masks and costume, some passages of which betray a bizarre view of the classical theatre of 600 years earlier. The section on comic masks, however, though abbreviated to the point of obscurity in some places, can be demonstrated to derive from a reliable account of masks at the transition from Middle to New Comedy. See further *MNC³*, chapter on 'Costumes and Masks', and H.-G. Nesselrath, *Die attische mittlere Komödie. Ihre Stellung in der antiken Literaturkritik und Literaturgeschichte* (Berlin 1990) 83ff.

53 The continuing manufacture in England of Toby jugs may be a reasonable analogy.

54 *Hydria* (212K/210 K-A), quoted and translated by Handley, *CambHistClassLit* i, 411.

55 While writing this book in North Carolina, I met a man who told me the converse of this story, a fine, salt-of-the-earth kind of man. Blacks had started to move into his neighbourhood, but although he felt some concern initially, he soon realised they were ex-servicemen, so that was all right. What was more worrying was that they were married to white women, but he realised after a while, and when he travelled he confirmed it, that they had met these women in Europe, so that was all right as well: they were not American.

56 On the variety of stage *hetairai*, see P.G.McC. Brown, 'Plots and Prostitutes in New Comedy', *Papers of the Leeds International Latin Seminar* 6, 1990, 241–266.

57 The contrast with Wives is instructive. Handley, *Dyskolos of Menander* 11f. and *CambHistClassLit* i, 419, points out that Knemon, the character around whom the whole play *Dyskolos* revolves, is only on stage for a quarter of the play, and much of that in a concentrated sequence.

58 On cooks, G. Berthiaume, *Les rôles du mágeiros* (*Mnemosyne* Suppl. 70, 1982); H. Dohm, *Mageiros* (Zetemata 32, Munich 1964); A. Giannini, 'La figura del cuoco nella commedia greca', *Acme* 13, 1960, 135–216. For a splendid piece written for a cook and only recently published, see W.H. Willis, *GRBS* 32, 1991, 331–353.

59 I have not included the Boeotian black-figure Kabeirion vases in this count either.
60 E.H. Gombrich, *Art and Illusion* (London 1958), esp. chapters IV–V, and his article 'The Mask and the Face. The Perception of Physiognomic Likeness in Life and in Art', in M. Mandelbaum (ed.), *Art, Perception & Reality* (Baltimore 1972) 1–46. See further the ideas and important documentation in I. Eibl-Eibesfeldt, *Human Ethology* (New York 1989) esp. 666ff. (trans. from *Die Biologie des menschlichen Verhaltens. Grundriss der Humanethologie* [Munich 1984]).
61 Worth noting that almost the only reaction shown in profile faces in archaic art is by the open mouth, often with teeth showing; emotions and reactions are otherwise expressed by gesture, which the artist finds easier to control and generalise.
62 See Y. Korshak, 'Frontal Faces in Attic Vase Painting of the Archaic Period', *AncW* 10 (1984) 89–105, or her book of the same title (Chicago 1987). There has been a great deal of work on masks from Lévi-Strauss (see *La voie des masques*) and his successors. Compare F. Frontisi-Ducroux, 'Idoles, figures, images', *RevArch* 1982, 81–108; 'Au miroir du masque', in C. Bérard and J.-P. Vernant (eds), *La cité des images. Religion et société en Grèce antique* (Lausanne-Paris 1984) 147–161 (= *City of Images* [Princeton 1989] 151–165); 'Face et profil: les deux masques', in C. Bérard, C. Bon and A. Pomari (eds), *Images et société en Grèce ancienne. L'iconographie comme méthode d'analyse.* (Actes du Colloque int., Lausanne, 8–11 février 1984. Cahiers d'archéologie romande, no. 36, Lausanne 1987) 89–102; and 'Prosopon, le masque et le visage', in P. Ghiron-Bistagne (ed.), *Anthropologie et Théâtre antique. Cahiers du GITA* 1987, 383–392, also F. Frontisi-Ducroux and J.-P. Vernant, 'Figures de masques en Grèce ancienne', *Journal de psychologie* 80, 1983, 53–69, and 'Divinités au masque dans la Grèce ancienne', in O. Aslan and D. Bablet (eds), *Le masque. Du rite au théâtre* (Paris 1985) 19–26; and the useful recent discussion by Claude Calame, 'Facing Otherness: The Tragic Mask in Ancient Greece', *History of Religions* 26, 1986, 125–142, although I cannot accept it in all details. Also Chs 4 and 5 in his *Le récit en Grèce ancienne. Enonciations et représentations de poètes* (Paris 1986).
63 See, for example, the illustrations towards the end of *Le masque. Du rite au théâtre* mentioned in the last note. It is of course well known that a carefully designed mask on the head of a good actor will appear to change expression according to the angle at which it is held to the light, the shift of the shoulders, and so on. See for example the comments of D. Wiles, *Masks of Menander* 104ff.
64 This is particularly true of the early or proto-comic material and of the so-called padded dancers and the spirit-beings they often seem to have represented. Tragedy as a masked performance was a relatively late invention.
65 Fragment 131K (= 130K-A), see also 31K (= 31K-A). Mormo was a monster or bogey, particularly invoked to frighten children.
66 From tomb Theta 17. G.E. Mylonas, *To dutikon nekrotapheion tes Eleusinos* (Athens 1975) 81–82 no. 726, pl. 362; *MTS*² 49, AV 26.
67 Plutarch, *Moralia* 600E. The notion of transference to children was picked up also by Frontisi-Ducroux and Vernant in *Le masque. Du rite au théâtre* 21. On Eros with mask, see the still valuable article by W. Deonna, 'Notes archéologiques. I. Eros jouant avec un masque de Silène', *RevArch* 1916, 74–97; L. Hadermann-Misguisch, 'L'image antique, byzantine et moderne du putto au masque', *Rayonnement Grec. Hommages à Charles Delvoye* (Brussels 1982) 513–552. Little cupids play with a satyr mask on one of the cups from the Boscoreale treasure in the Louvre: BJ 1912, F. Baratte, *Le trésor d'orfèvrerie romaine de Boscoreale* (Paris 1986) 61–63 (with earlier refs.); *id. Il tesoro di Boscoreale* (Exhib.Cat., Milan 1988)

42–45, 58 no. 13; L. Pirzio Biroli Stefanelli, *L'argento dei Romani. Vasellame da tavola e d'apparato* (Rome 1991) 143 (colour ill.). Vollenweider, *Deliciae Leonis*, 68 no. 99, has a clay impression from the Merz collection in Berne of a gem of the first century BC with Eros using a mask as a frightener. The recent London (but not New York) version of the Mantegna exhibition contained a drawing (Paris, Louvre inv. 5072, after Mantegna) with a *putto* wearing a mask and adding to the frightening effect by poking his hand forward through the mouth, and thus terrifying another who has fallen to the ground: J. Martineau (ed.), *Andrea Mantegna* (London–New York 1992) 457–458 no. 149 (colour ill.). He presumably picked it up from some such piece as the Roman statuette of perhaps the first century AD in which a *papposilenos* mask is used: B. Palma, in A. Giuliano (ed.), *Museo Nazionale Romano. Le sculture I.6. I marmi Ludovisi dispersi* (Rome 1986) 96–98, fig. 111, 3. One may note that Ekserdjian is misguided in his catalogue entry to suppose that this motif originated as late as the Late Hellenistic period.

68 I owe this observation to Mr William K. Zewadski who is preparing a study of these depictions.

69 With satyric masks: Athens, National Museum 4531, from Dioniso (Attica); E. Mitropoulou, *Attic Votive Reliefs of the Sixth and Fifth Centuries B.C.* (Athens 1977) 75 no. 159; Green, *RevArch* 1982, 244–245 fig. 7, with arguments for the date and identification, but note that the spellings seem old-fashioned. With tragic masks: Athens, National Museum 1750; *MTS*[2] 34, AS 5; Ghiron-Bistagne, 74 fig. 24; S. Karouzou, 'Bemalte attische Weihreliefs', in G. Kopcke and M.B. Moore (eds), *Studies in Classical Art and Archaeology . . . P.H. von Blanckenhagen* (Locust Valley, N.Y., 1979) 111–116. It was found in the area of the Theatre of Dionysos. The reverse had painted decoration, but we do not know with what. With comic masks: Athens, National Museum 13262, from Aixone (of 340/339 rather than 313/12 BC); *MMC*[3] 118, AS 2; *IGD* IV.8a; Ghiron-Bistagne, 87 fig. 34; Mette, 136, III B 5, 2.

The relief is a reminder of the competitive spirit developed by *choregoi*. He commissioned it as a reminder of his successful expenditure. The sums involved could be substantial: already in the later fifth century, Lysias xxi.4 mentions 1600 drachmas 'for the comedies together with the dedication of the equipment' (one drachma was a day's wage for a skilled workman), and there are hints that expenditure increased with time. Plutarch (*Moralia* 348–349) notes that if the Athenians had spent as much on 'defence' as they did on theatre, their destiny would have been quite different. The dramatic competitions put on by Alexander the Great in Tyre also seem to have involved its *choregoi* in substantial expenditure: see pp. 106–7.

70 *MMC*[3] 117, AS 1. Ht. 1.19 m. The primary publication is that by E. Strong, 'Three Sculptured Stelai in the Possession of Lord Newton at Lyme Park', *JHS* 23, 1903, 356–359, pl. 13, after which it passed rapidly into the literature. On its interpretation, see G. Dontas, *Eikones pneumatikon anthropon* (Athens 1960) 19–20, pl. 3b; and T.B.L. Webster, 'The Poet and the Mask', in M.J. Anderson (ed.), *Classical Drama & its Influence: Studies . . . Kitto* (London 1965) 5–13. I must admit to having followed Webster and others in supposing it was found in the Kerameikos cemetery, but Strong reports Thomas Legh's account that he excavated it in May 1811 'at a short distance from the walls of the city [Athens] on the western side of the road that leads to Thebes'.

71 See *MNC*[3] 3AS 5a–c. Illustrated is Princeton, 51–1. See also Vatican 9985 (ex Lateran), e.g. Bieber, *Theater*[2] fig. 317; G.M.A. Richter, *Portraits of the Greeks* (London 1965) fig. 1527; Berlin SK 951, from Aquileia, *AM* 26 (1901) 136 fig. 3

(Krüger); Richter, op. cit., fig. 1524.

72 St Petersburg B 201 (St. 1538); *ARV²* 555, 95; *AntK* 10, 1967, 78, pl. 19 (Schmidt); A.-B. Follmann, *Der Pan-Maler* (Bonn 1968) 36 and pl. 5, 1; *LIMC* iii, pl. 401, 846. I am exploring the evidence of the vase more fully in a forthcoming article. Note the similarity of the chorusmen to those on the Basle vase (Figure 2.1, p. 17), except that these play the part of older men.

73 Naples inv.81673 (H 3240); *ARV²* 1336, 1; *Paral.* 480; *Addenda²* 365–366.

74 For discussion of Himeros, as well as a detail illustration of this piece, see *LIMC* v.

75 For a very useful listing, see A. Kossatz-Deißmann, 'Satyr- und Mänadennamen auf Vasenbildern des Getty-Museums und der Sammlung Cahn (Basel) mit Addenda zu Charlotte Fränkel, *Satyr- und Bakchennamen auf Vasenbildern* (Halle, 1912)', *GVGetty* 5 (Malibu 1991) 131–199, esp. 147ff. Mimos as satyr at an elaborate symposion of Dionysos, with Athena: Würzburg H 5708 (ex Langlotz); *ARV²* 1339, 5 (near or by the Talos Painter); *Addenda²* 367; *Pantheon* 36, 1978, 199–206 (Simon); *AA* 1979, 512 (Brommer); Kannicht and Snell, *TrGF* ii, Fr. 3f; *CVA* (2) pls 42–44.

76 See T.B.L. Webster, *Hellenistic Art* (London 1966) 49; and for the dating F. Salviat, 'Vedettes de la scène en province. Signification et date des monuments chorégiques à Thasos', *Thasiaca* (*BCH* Suppl. 5, Paris 1979) 155–167 (with earlier refs).

77 Samothrace 65.1041; *RevArch* 1982, 237–241, figs 2–4, with further refs.

78 Ferrara T 161C (inv. 20483), from Spina, F. Berti and C. Gasparri (eds), *Dionysos. Mito e mistero* (Bologna 1989) 132–133 no. 63 (ill.).

79 Cleveland 89.73, *Bulletin of the Cleveland Museum of Art* 78(3), 1991, 73; *RVAp* Suppl. ii, 493 no. 1/125 (Choregos Painter). This material has been presented in detail in my forthcoming article 'Theatrical Motifs in Non-Theatrical Contexts'. For general background, and some discussion of methodology, see my 'Dedications of Masks', *RevArch* 1982 237–248.

80 See B.A. Sparkes, 'Treading the Grapes', *BABesch* 51, 1976, 47–64; and C. Gasparri, *LIMC* iii, 1, 459, nos. 404–412.

4 THE TRANSITION TO THE HELLENISTIC WORLD

1 On Asteas, see *RVP* 136ff (ch. 7) and *RVSIS* 202–3.

2 Richmond 82.15: *RVP* 158 no. 271, pl. 100c–d.

3 Madrid 11028. *RVP* 124 no. 177, pl. 73c–d (Asteas); *PhV²* no. 42. The vase was earlier attributed to Python. Other examples with just the same motif include the bell-kraters (i) Geneva, priv. coll., *RVP* 72 no. 36, pl. 26a (Asteas [early]); (ii) Paestum 24294, from Contrada Andriuolo (1970), t. 147. *RVP* 123 no. 172, pl. 71e (Asteas); (iii) formerly Paris, market, *PhV²* no. 54, *RVP* 159 no. 282, pl. 102f (Python).

4 Sydney 47.04. Trendall, *Paestan Pottery* no. 116, pl. 20d; *PhV²* no. 171; *EAA* iii, 712 fig. 874; *RVP* 158 no. 269, pl. 99c–d. Compare, *inter alia*, the bell-krater also by Python recently on the market, Trendall *NumAntCl* 19, 1990, 133 fig. 14; NFA Classical Auctions Inc., *Sale Cat.*, New York, 11 December 1991, no. 96 (colour ill.), not in *RVP*.

5 See *Peace* 1317, *Frogs*, 1525, *Eccles.* 1150, *Clouds* 1490; also *Birds* 1274f. Worth noting that even as late as Menander, the chorus could be described as revellers, e.g. *Perik.* 71–72/191–192, *Epitr.* 33–35/169–171 and elsewhere, with possible antecedents in Middle Comedy: see the commentators on *Dysk.* 230ff. (which is a special case of the same motif) and H.-D. Blume, quoted in n. 7.

6   See for example Richard Schechner and Willa Appel (eds), *By Means of Performance. Intercultural Studies of Theatre and Ritual* (Cambridge 1990) 5.

7   Cf. Menander, *Dyskolos* 963: 'someone give us wreaths and a torch', or *Samia* 731–732: 'here, someone bring us a torch and wreaths, so we can set off on our procession'. See H.-D. Blume, in E. Handley and A. Hurst (eds.), *Relire Ménandre* (Geneva 1990) 17f. with nn. 10–11.

8   New York 1989.11.4. Sotheby (New York), *Sale Cat.* 23 June 1989, no. 196 (ill.).

9   The vase reminds me also of the story of Kleobis and Biton serving as the oxen pulling the cart at the Hera festival in Herodotus i.31. In fact the theme of appropriate figures pulling the cart that carried (an image or impersonation of) the god or goddess is a fundamental one.

10   E.E. Rice, *The Grand Procession of Ptolemy Philadelphus* (Oxford 1983). Her discussion of the date of the Procession is at pp. 182–187 together with the addendum on p. vi.

11   Ibid. 67, 83ff.; P. Goukowsky, *Essai sur les origines du mythe d'Alexandre*, ii. *Alexandre et Dionysos* (Nancy 1978–81).

12   Plutarch, *Demetrius* 12.1. See W.R. Connor, *Classica et Mediaevalia*, 40, 1989, 19, for discussion and further references.

13   Note the statistics given in the last chapter. A full list will be given in PhV^3. For masks included in other scenes, note in the first instance the basic discussions and listings by A.D. Trendall, 'Masks on Apulian Red-Figured Vases', in *Studies Webster* ii, 137–154; 'Vasi apuli raffiguranti maschere femminili con viso bianco', in *Ricerche e Studi* (Quaderni del Museo Archeologico Provinciale 'Francesco Ribezzo' di Brindisi) 12, 1980–87, 43–55.

14   The pieces are listed in MNC^3 under the catalogue number 3AS 5 where fuller references are quoted. (a) Vatican 9985 (ex Lateran), Bieber, *Theater*[1] fig. 223, [2]fig. 317; G.M.A. Richter, *Portraits of the Greeks* (London 1965) fig. 1527; G. Dontas, *Eikones kathemenon pneumatikon anthropon* (Athens 1960) 83, pl. 33. (b) Princeton 51-1, F.F. Jones, *The Theater in Ancient Art* (Princeton 1951) no. 29 (ill.); Bieber, in *Festschrift A. Rumpf* (Krefeld 1952) 14, pl. 5; ead., *Theater*[2] fig. 316; Richter, op. cit., fig. 1526. Note the (modern) copy of the Vatican piece from Landsdowne House, Michaelis 457–8 no. 72; Sotheby, *Sale Cat.*, 15 July 1980, no. 206 (withdrawn) *Sale Cat.*, 14–15 December 1981, no. 354. See also the gems MNC^3 4XJ 92a–b.

15   'Motif-Symbolism and Gnathia Vases', in H.-U. Cain, H. Gabelmann and D. Salzamann (eds), *Beiträge zur Ikonographie und Hermeneutik. Festschrift für N. Himmelmann-Wildschütz* (Mainz 1989) 221–226.

16   We have good evidence that this happened in life as well as on vases, for example from the excavations at Priene: see Th. Wiegand and H. Schrader, *Priene* (Berlin 1904), 361 figs. 446–450. Compare the group of three masks from a house at Delos; *BCH* 85, 1961, 915–917 figs. 7–9.

17   F. Tiné Bertocchi, *La pittura funeraria apula* (Naples 1964) 71–77. She gives further examples.

18   On the game of *kottabos*, see in the first instance Jahn, *Philologus* 26, 1867, 201ff., Heydemann, *Annali* 1868, 217ff., Robert *JdI* 3, 1887, 178ff.; then B.A. Sparkes, *Archaeology* 13, 1960, 202ff., and among several more recent discussions, E. Csapo and M.C. Miller, *Hesperia* 60, 1991, 367–382.

19   One may note that the couch does not have legs (despite the fringe that Python shows hanging down at each end) but is a mattress-like object laid out along the ground. This is evident in the whole iconographic tradition of such scenes, from the early part of the century, even if in time the arrangement becomes more and more assimilated to that of regular couches.

20 Franz Studniczka, *Das Symposion Ptolemaios II* (Sächs. Abh. xxx.2, 1914). See
    more recently F.E. Winter, 'The Symposium-Tent of Ptolemy II: A New
    Proposal', *EMC/CV* 29, 1985, 289–308; G. Grimm, 'Orient und Okzident in der
    Kunst Alexandriens', in *Alexandrien. Kulturbegegnungen dreier Jahrtausende im
    Schmeltztiegel einer mediterranen Großstadt* (Mainz 1981) 13–25; E. Salza Prina
    Ricotti, 'Le tende conviviali e la tenda di Tolomeo Filadelfo', in R.I. Curtis
    (ed.), *Studia pompeiana et classica in Honor of Wilhelmina F. Jashemski* (New
    Rochelle 1989) ii, 199–239; and the comments of H. von Hesberg, "Temporäre
    Bilder oder die Grenzen der Kunst. Zur Legitimation frühhellenistischer
    Königsherrschaft im Fest', *JdI* 104, 1989, 61–82.

21 For Attic and Attic-derived examples of the Early Hellenistic period (Period 1),
    see *MNC*³ 1AT 35–37, 39–41, 43–45, 51–53, 55, 58, 60, 67–70, 74, 82 (for Old
    Style), and 1AT 38, 42, 46, 50, 54, 56–57, 59, 61, 62–66, 71–73, 75–80 (for New
    Style), together with the discussion in the chapter 'Costumes and Masks'.

22 See for example, T.B.L. Webster, *An Introduction to Menander* (Manchester 1974)
    44ff.

23 See the important article by G. Krien, 'Der Ausdruck der antiken Theater-
    masken nach Angaben im Polluxkatalog und in der pseudoaristotelischen
    "Physiognomik,"' *JhOAI* 42, 1955, 84–117. Earlier, T.B.L. Webster, in 'The Masks
    of Greek Comedy', *Bull. Rylands Library* 32, 1949, 13, then N. Yalouris, 'Die
    Anfänge der griechischen Porträtkunst und der Physiognomon Zopyros', *AntK*
    29, 1986, 5–7. B. Kiilerich, 'Physiognomics and the Iconography of Alexander
    the Great', *Symbolae Osloenses* 63, 1988, 51–66 failed to take Krien's article into
    account, thereby ignoring the critical place of theatre masks in this whole
    process. E.C. Evans, *Physiognomics in the Ancient World* (*TransAmPhilSoc* 59(5),
    Philadelphia 1969) does not have much that is directly relevant, but note now
    Wiles, *Masks of Menander* 85–88, 152ff.

24 Paris, Louvre MA 436 (the Azara herm) and Dresden Skulpturensammlung.

25 Figure 4.8 is Copenhagen NM 7367, from Agrigento, *MNC*³ 1AT 51a, ht.
    0.069 m. Note also *MNC*³ 1AT 49 and 50, and the Transitional 1AT 2 and 1AT
    29, as well as the Campanian (1NT 7) and Sicilian versions (1ST 28–29). The
    mask has Middle Comedy antecedents (Mask Z) where again it seems to have
    been applied to a vigorous character.

26 *MNC*³ 1AT 41, note that the nose is restored). See also 1BT 5, the Kavalla
    plaque; also 1AT 42 (New Style), 1BT 6, 1DA 3, 1ST 11–12.

27 See, for example, I. Eibl-Eibesfeldt, *Der vorprogrammierte Mensch. Das Ererbte als
    bestimmender Faktor im menschlichen Verhalten* (Kiel, rev. edn 1985), or the same
    author's *Human Ethology* mentioned in n. 60 in Chapter 3.

28 There are good comments in Wiles, *Masks of Menander*, e.g. 98–99.

29 It should be remembered, however, that they became fossilised at this point,
    even to the extent of preserving the fashions of the age in women's hairstyles,
    hairbands, etc.

30 Some think that the slave's joke at Plautus, *Rudens* 429 implies a reference to
    a visibly phallic costume; if so, in the original by Diphilus, it is perhaps to be
    seen as an echo of tradition, like the chorus (if it is to be so called) of fishermen
    at 290ff., with a special entrance-song.

31 *Moralia* VII.8, 712B.

32 *OCD*² 670. On moral values as expressed in Menander, see W.G. Arnott, 'Moral
    Values in Menander', *Philologus* 125, 1981, 215–227. There are excellent
    observations by Handley, 'Menander and the New Comedy', *CambHistClassLit*
    i, 414–425. Note also G. Bodei Giglioni, *Menandro o la politica della convivenza.
    La storia attraverso i testi letterari* (Como 1984) and T.B.L. Webster, *An Introduction*

to Menander (Manchester 1974) 'The Social Code' and 'The Ethical Code', pp. 25–55.

5 THEATRE IN THE HELLENISTIC WORLD

1 See for example T.J. Dunbabin, *The Western Greeks* (Oxford 1948) p. vii (on the early settlement in Sydney), or P.D. Curtin, *Death by Migration* (Cambridge 1989), although he is mostly concerned with the plight of European military in tropical countries. One thinks too of the first winter of the migrants of the *Mayflower*, or of the experience of early farmers in the American Midwest. Naphthali Lewis, *Greeks in Ptolemaic Egypt* (Oxford 1986) gives a fascinating and instructive set of case studies.

2 Plutarch gives an abbreviated version of both stories in *Moralia* 334E. See further Ghiron-Bistagne, 162. Athenodoros had presumably undertaken to perform at the Dionysia in Athens and then defaulted. Fines in such circumstances could be considerable, and understandably so. See Pickard-Cambridge, *Festivals*[2] 280, 282, 300. Both were winning prizes in the tragic competition at Athens in this period: see conveniently Pickard-Cambridge, *Festivals*[2] 108–109.

3 These kinds of objects must primarily have been personal possessions, a pattern which slowly changes, as we shall see.

4 *MNC*[3] 1SJ 1–2.

5 See the gold ear-rings with Erotes holding masks, *MNC*[3] 1BA 1–3, 1DA 1, 1DA 7, 1KA 1a–b; or the necklace with gold masks, *MNC*[3] 1DA 2–6.

6 Taranto I.G. 22436. *MNC*[3] 1TA 2; illustrated in colour in E.M. De Juliis, *Il Museo Nazionale di Taranto* (1983) 61 fig. 131, and E. De Juliis and D. Loiacono, *Taranto, Il Museo Archeologico* (1985) 322 fig. 380.

7 *MNC*[3] 1CB 1; W. Züchner, *Griechische Klappspiegel* (*JdI* 14.Ergh., Berlin 1942) 86 no. 144, fig. 48.

8 *MNC*[3] 1TA 1.

9 Naples 9985, from Pompeii, 'Villa of Cicero' (found in 1763), ht 0.437 m, e.g. Bieber, *Theater*[1] fig 239,[2] fig. 346; Webster, *Hellenistic Art* (London 1967) 117, pl. 33; *BICS* 16 (1969) 88ff. (Handley); *Mytilène* 48f., pl. 6, 2; *IGD* 145, V. 3, frontispiece; *MNC*[2] 183, NM 2. Handley associated the scene with the Mytilene mosaic and with papyrus fragments of *Theophoroumene*. Restoration affects the two figures on the left.

10 One may also note another contemporary if fragmentary mosaic that seems to go back to an Early Hellenistic archetype, Naples 6146, from the Santangelo Collection, e.g. Bieber, *Theater*[1] fig. 262, [2]fig. 401; *aavv.*, *Le collezioni del Museo Nazionale di Napoli* (Rome 1986) 118–119 no. 28 (ill.); *MNC*[3] 3NM 1. Slave seated on altar, leaning right and supported on right hand, left hand on lap. At left edge, traces of another actor. At right edge, unmasked boy in *chiton*. Above, festoons with suspended tambourine (sanctuary). The slave is of a well-known type.

11 Chr. Dedoussi, 'Fr.246 (PSI 847): An Illustrated Fragment of Menander's Eunouchos', *BICS* 27, 1980, 97–102. See also *POxy* 2652 (Turner) for an ink sketch of Agnoia, the prologue-figure of Menander, *Perikeiromene*; cf. also 2653.

12 *MNC*[3] 1AS 1.1–3 together with 1AS 2, Athens NM 1751, 1752, 1754, and Agora S 600; *MNC*[3] 1AS 3.1–4, Athens, Acropolis Museum, inv. 2291, 2296, 2298 (from the Theatre).

13 *MNC*[3] 1BT 5, Kavalla 240 (E 489), Webster, *Hellenistic Art* (London 1966) 60,

Appendix pl. 4; M.B. Sakellariou (ed.), *Macedonia. 4000 Years of Greek History and Civilization* (Athens 1983) 171 fig. 108 (colour).

14 Webster, *GTP* 86.

15 For examples, see note 5, above. Paphos, Cyprus, 1931, *MNC*[3] 1KA 1a; *BCH* 93 (1969) 478 fig. 90, pl. 10.

16 For the theme of Erotes carrying such objects, see the useful article by D.K. Hill, 'Bacchic Erotes at Tarentum', *Hesperia* 16, 1947, 248–255. For Erotes driving a panther-chariot, see for example the well-known Gnathia krater from Oria, Naples 81007; *BCH* 35, 1911, pl. V; *MemAccNapoli* 1940, pl. 1,1; *CVA* (3) pls. 54–55; Adriani, *Coppa paesistica* pl. 5, 15; *JhOAI* 50, 1972–73, 153–154; *LIMC* iii, pl. 623, 271 (detail). A good example of Erotes with symposion equipment is the Gnathia krater Göttingen ZV 1964.140, Münzen und Medaillen, *Auktion XXVI* (1963), pl. 59, 167; *AA* 1967, 441–444, figs 37–39; *CVA* pls. 39–40; M. Benz and F. Rumscheid, *Gr. Vasen aus Unteritalien*, (Göttingen 1987) 54–55 no. 27 (ill.); *CVA* (1) pls. 39–40; *Forschungen und Berichte* 28, 1990, 86.

17 See my 'Motif-Symbolism and Gnathia Vases', in H.-U. Cain, H. Gabelmann and D. Salzmann (eds), *Beiträge zur Ikonographie und Hermeneutik. Festschrift für N. Himmelmann-Wildschütz* (Mainz 1989) 221–226.

18 The fundamental treatments remain those by Paul Wolters 'Zu griechischen Agonen', *30. Programm d. Kunstgeschichtl. Museums Univ. Würzburg* (1901) 5–9, and 'Faden und Knoten als Amulett', (Suppl. *ArchivRelWiss* 8, Leipzig 1905), but a new study is being prepared by Ann M. Nicgorski.

19 A further complication, which I am ignoring here, is the connection with the afterlife; but wishes for a blessed afterlife were based on what was wished for on earth and I do not see convincing evidence that the one was not applicable to the other. Useful in all this is M. Schmidt, 'Beziehungen zwischen Eros, dem dionysischen und dem "eleusinischen" Kreis auf apulischen Vasenbildern', in C. Bérard, C. Bon and A. Pomari (eds), *Images et société en Grèce ancienne. L'iconographie comme méthode d'analyse (Actes du Colloque int., Lausanne, 8–11 février 1984. Cahiers d'archéologie romande*, no. 36, Lausanne 1987) 155–167. On Eros and Dionysos, see Metzger, *Représentations*, 129–133. Note the presence of Himeros on the Pronomos Vase.

20 Basle BS 468, Schweizerische Kunst- und Antiquitätenmesse (Basle 9–19 May 1974), *Cat.* p. 5 (ill.); *RVAp* ii, 480 no. 13, pl. 170, 3; *Studies … Webster* ii, 153 no. 2; *RVSIS* fig 194. For this theme of Dionysos and Ariadne, see Metzger, *Représentations* 115ff., and H. Cassimatis, 'Amours légitimes? Rêves d'amour? dans la céramique grecque', *BABesch* 62, 1987, 75–84. On an early vase by Asteas in a private collection in Naples, Eros presents Dionysos with a mask: *RVP* 64 no. 9, pl. 17e.

21 Würzburg H 5771, *Aparchai Arias* pl. 128, 1 (Schauenburg); Termer, *Kunst der Antike, Kat. 1* (1982) no. 51 (ill.); *RVP* 159 no. 278, pl. 102c. Third quarter of the fourth century. Note also the similar scene on Hanover R 1906.160, *PhV*[2] no. 28; *RM* 79, 1972, pl. 18b (Schauenburg); *RVP* 159 no. 279, pl. 102e. Third quarter of the fourth century.

22 London F 150, *PhV*[2] no. 36; Bieber, *Theater*[2] fig. 501; *JhOAI* 54, 1983, 68 fig. 11; *RVP* 72 no. 45, pl. 28a–b (with refs) (Asteas, early). Soon after the middle of the fourth century. Note also the well-known bell-krater also by Asteas in the Vatican with Zeus carrying a ladder on a love adventure with Hermes as guide carrying an oil-lamp: Vatican U 19 (inv.17106); *PhV*[2] no. 65; Bieber, *Theater*[2] fig. 484; *IGD* iv, 19; *RVP* no. 2/176, pl. 73a (with refs) (Asteas); *RVSIS* fig. 364. C. 350–340 BC. For a general discussion of the theme of women in windows, see Schauenburg, *RM* 79, 1972, 1–15.

23 See MNC^3 1BT 17–29 (with further references and discussion). They continue to be popular in Middle Hellenistic. On Tanagras in general, see G. Kleiner, *Tanagrafiguren: Untersuchungen zur hellenistischen Kunst und Geschichte* (new edn, rev. K. Parlasca, Berlin–New York, 1984), and R.A. Higgins, *Tanagra and the Figurines* (London–Princeton 1986).

24 One would exclude areas such as Etruria from such a statement.

25 See MNC^3 2AV 13–49. For general discussion, see the fundamental work by S.I. Rotroff, *The Athenian Agora xxii. Hellenistic Pottery, Athenian and Imported Moldmade Bowls* (Princeton 1982) and on issues of chronology and the introduction of the series, ead., 'Silver, Glass and Clay. Evidence for the Dating of Hellenistic Luxury Tableware', *Hesperia* 51 (1982) 329–337.

26 Athens, Agora P 590. *Hesperia* 3 (1934) 379 no. D 35, fig. 66 (H.A. Thompson); *Hesperia* 29 (1960) 278, 283 no. C 22 (Webster); MNC^3 2AV 13e.

27 See MNC^3 2BV 1–5 (for Delphi) and 2CV 7 (for Corinth).

28 See MNC^3 2DV 1–5, and for figures, especially 4–5.

29 See MNC^3 2BV 6–7, 2CV 2–6, 2DV 14, 2RV 1, 2SV 1, 2TV 1–6 and 8–10.

30 Metaponto 141 P (PZ80), (J.C. Carter) *Excavations in the Territory, Metaponto, 1980* 16 fig. 13; id., *1981*, pl. 5 below.

31 New York 1981.11.18 and 1982.11.12. *BMMA*, Summer 1984, 59–60 nos. 105–106 = D. von Bothmer, *A Greek and Roman Treasury* (New York 1984) 59–60 nos. 105–106 (colour ills.); MNC^3 2XA 1–2. See also P.G. Guzzo, 'Proposta di attribuzione alla Daunia di un gruppo di argenti al Metropolitan Museum of Art di New York', *Annali Pisa* 21, 1991, 166–173 and pl. 21.

32 Corinth C-48-126, preserved ht 25.5 cm. *Hesperia* 18 (1949) 152, pl. 17, no. 23; *Corinth* vii.3, no. 647, pls. 26 and 61; MNC^2 60, AV 32; MNC^3 2XV 3a. This is a near-complete piece and it was taken by Edwards (*Corinth* vii.3, 119) as a local imitation of a foreign type. The mask type is that of the wavy-haired slave (Mask 27). It should antedate the destruction of 146 BC.

An arbitrary selection of other published examples of the same series includes Copenhagen, Ny Carlsberg Glyptotek, 988, from Taranto, V. Poulsen, *Catalogue des terres cuites grecques et romaines* (Copenhagen 1949) no. 87, pl. 47; once coll. M. Bieber, from Naples, Bieber, *Theater²* fig. 391; Princeton 50.69, F.F. Jones, *The Theater in Ancient Art* (Princeton 1951) no. 41; Heraclea Minoa 697, *NSc* 1958, 276 no. 8, fig. 38c; Copenhagen NM ABb 327, N. Breitenstein, *Catalogue of Terracottas, Cypriot, Greek, Etrusco-Italian and Roman (Danish National Museum)* (Copenhagen 1941) no. 629, pl. 75; Leiden I 1934/11.21, from South Italy?, P.G. Leyenaar-Plaisier, *Les terres cuites grecques et romaines* (Leiden 1979) no. 1523, Bari 1830, from Bari, E.M. De Juliis, *Archeologia in Puglia* (Bari 1983) 70 fig. 123 (colour); and among the many in Alexandria from Alexandria, E. Breccia, *Terrecotte figurate greche e greco-egizie del Museo di Alessandria*, i (*Monuments de l'Egypte gréco-romaine* ii.1) (Bergamo 1930), pl. 37, 4, 6, 8 and 9, pl. 38, 2, 4 and 7, pl. 46, 2 and 17.

33 See MNC^3 2XV 3, and add to them for example those from Carthage: *Karthago* 13 (1967) 15f. and pl. 3, nos.12–15; also *Cahiers de Byrsa* 5 (1955) pl. 82, 156.

34 For this series in general, see MNC^3 3XV 15–17, together with further examples from Carthage: *Karthago* 13 (1967) pl. 10; see also *Cahiers de Byrsa* 9, 1960–61, nos. 502–504.

35 Delos B 3718. *BCH* 76 (1952) 623 fig. 25; *BCH* 85 (1961) 496ff., figs 26–28; *AE* 1953–54, 121ff. (Rumpf); MNC^3 3XV 5.

36 It is easy to forget that they did not have photographs or other ready means of knowing such things at second hand. On all this J.J. Pollitt's 'The Impact of Greek Art on Rome', *TAPA* 108, 1978, 155–174 is of enormous value; see also his *Art in the Hellenistic Age* (Cambridge 1986) 150–163.

37 See J.-P. Morel, 'Céramiques d'Italie et céramiques hellénistiques (150–30 av. J.-C.)', *Hellenismus in Mittelitalien (Abh. der Akademie der Wissenschaften in Göttingen,* no. 97, 1976) 471–501, and 'Céramiques à vernis noir d'Italie trouvées à Délos', *BCH* 110 (1986) 461–493, as well as M. Leiwo, 'Why Velia survived through the Second Century B.C. Remarks on her Economic Connections with Delos', *Athenaeum* 63 (1985) 494–498.

28 There is a good discussion together with a comprehensive bibliography on the two mosaics by M. Donderer, *Die Mosaizisten der Antike und ihre wirtschaftliche und soziale Stellung* (Erlangen 1989) 59–61.

39 Naples 22248–9, ht 1.11 m and 1.15 m. H. von Rohden, *Terrakotten von Pompeji* (1880) 46, pl. 35; A. Levi, *Terrecotte figurate del Museo Nazionale* (Florence 1926) nos. 871–872, pl. 14, 1–2; *Pompeii AD 79* (London 1976) nos. 312–313 (with earlier refs); *MNC³* 3NT 1.1–2.

40 Once Paros, coll. Dellagrammati, preserved ht 0.115 m. *Arch.Epigr.Mitt.aus Oest.Ungarn* 11 (1887) 183–184 fig. 17, pl. 5, 3; *MNC³* 3DT 46i.

41 *MNC³* 3NT 2–8.

42 See *MNC³* 2NV 4–8 (nine examples), 3DV 14–19, 3NV 1–9 (23 examples). Many of the so-called plastic vases were collected by R.A. Higgins in an article in *British Museum Yearbook* 1 (1976), to which J.G. Szilágyi added useful comments in *Etudes et Travaux* 13 (Warsaw 1983) 358–364. See further, M. Sguaitamatti, 'Vases plastiques hellénistiques de Grande Grèce et de Sicile', *NumActClass* 20, 1991, 117–146.

43 For this process, see my 'Drunk Again. A Study in the Iconography of the Comic Theatre', *AJA* 89, 1985, 465–472.

44 Australian National University 79.05, ht 11.1 cm. Sotheby, *Sale Cat.,* 10 July 1979, no. 226 (ill.); *MNC³* 3NV 8b.

45 One should also reckon that a good number of gems should also belong to this period: they have not been counted here because of the difficulty of arriving at a secure chronology for them.

46 *Délos* xxvii, 168ff., pls. 21–25 (with earlier refs.); V.J. Bruno, *Hellenistic Painting Techniques. The Evidence of the Delos Fragments* (Leiden 1985) 22–30, pls. 3–7 (colour); *MNC³* 3DP 2.

47 *MNC³* 3DP 2.3; *Délos* xxvii, pl. 22, 7; Bruno, op. cit., pl. 4, 5a. See also *MNC³* 'Illustrations of Plays', XZ 21–23.

48 *Perikeiromene*: *MNC³* 3DP 2.4 18–19; *Délos* xxvii, pl. 22, 8, details pl. 23, 5–8; Bruno, op. cit., pls. 3, 5b. *Aspis*: *MNC³* 3DP 2.5 and 'Illustrations of Plays', XZ 4; *Délos* xxvii, pl. 24, 3. Note that we seem to have another version of the *Perikeiromene* scene in the series of wall-paintings in Ephesos: *MNC³* 6DP 1.2.

49 See E.W. Handley, 'Plautus and his Public: Some Thoughts on New Comedy in Latin', *Dioniso* 46 (1975) 117–132, and Frances Muecke, 'Plautus and the Theater of Disguise', *Classical Antiquity* 5, 1986, 216–229.

50 On the series in general, see D. Burr, *Terracottas from Myrina in the Museum of Fine Arts* (Vienna 1934) and S. Besques, *Catalogue raisonné des figurines et reliefs en terre-cuite grecs, étrusques et romains,* ii. *Myrina* (Paris 1963). For a list and classification of the actor-figures, *MNC³* 3DT 1–46. For the question of their inspiration, *AJA* 89, 1985, 465–472, and *MNC³* 'Illustrations of Plays' XZ 2, 19, 32, 33, 39, 40, 50.

51 Athens 5060 (Misthos 543), ht 0.19 m. A Philadelpheus, *Pelina eidolia ek Myrines* (Athens 1928) pl. 24, 5; Bieber, *Theater¹* fig. 240, ²fig. 342; Webster, *Hellenistic Art* (London 1966) 130 fig. 35; *IGD* 146, V.10; *CAH, Plates to Vol. VII.1,* no. 203a (ill.); *MNC³* 3DT 17a. The left foot and the base are restored; there is mauve on the wreath and fillet, red-brown for the flesh, yellow on the drapery.

52 Berlin TK 7969, from Myrina, e.g. Bieber, *Theater²* fig. 341; Webster, *Hellenistic*

Art (London 1966) 131 fig. 36; E. Rhode, *Griechische Terrakotten* (Berlin 1970) pl. 35; *MNC*³ 3DT 16.

53 Athens 5029 (Misthos 428), ht *c*.0.18 m. A. Philadelpheus, *Pelina eidolia ek Myrines* (Athens 1928) pl. 24, 9; Bieber, *Theater*¹ fig. 271; Pickard-Cambridge, *Festivals*¹ fig. 125; *AJA* 89 (1985) pl. 53, 4a–c (Green); *MNC*³ 3DT 42. There is red-brown on the face, mauve on the wreath, fillet and cloak, and there was once yellow on the *chiton*. The curved seat is separate and could well be alien.

54 Naples 9035, dimensions 0.39 × 0.40 m. Bieber, *Theater*¹ fig. 228, ²fig. 328; *MAAR* 23 (1955) 155, pl. 52, 2; *AJA* 89 (1985) pl. 53, 5; *MNC*³ 5NP 6a. The companion-piece, Naples 9037, listed as 5NP 5b in *MNC*³, is a scene with an old slave, a young woman and a youth (e.g. Bieber, *Theater*¹ fig. 238; Pickard-Cambridge, *Festivals*¹ fig. 97). Another version of the same picture is better known: Pompeii I.vi.11, Casa dei Quadretti Teatrali. A Maiuri, *Roman Painting* (Geneva 1953) 95; Bieber, *Theater*² fig. 395; C.L. Ragghianti, *Pittori di Pompei* (Milan 1963) 69 (colour). Our scene too was once known in another copy: Pompeii VII.xii.23: K. Schefold, *Die Wände Pompejis* (Berlin 1957) 202.

55 Naples 6633, from Pompeii, ht 0.295 m; e.g. Th. Schreiber, *Hellenistische Reliefbilder* (1894) pl. 99; Bieber, *Theater*² fig. 562; *Pompeii AD 79* (London 1976) no. 80; *AntK* 21 (1978) pl. 9, 3; *RM* 88 (1981) 287 no. 158 (Dwyer); *BJb* 188 (1988) 200 no. 45, 140 figs 33–34 (Cain, with refs.); *MNC*³ 3AS 2b. 3AS 2a in the Vatican, perhaps from Ostia (Bieber, *Theater*² fig. 564; *AntK* 21 (1978) pl. 9, 5; *BJb* 188 (1988) 209–210 no. 89, 141 figs. 35–36 [Cain]) shows the same masks in mirror-image.

56 For discussions of the type, see Picard, *AJA* 38 (1934) 137–152; Watzinger, *JdI* 61–62 (1946–47) 76–87; Webster, *Hellenistic Art* (1967) 169ff; B. Hundsalz, *Das dionysische Schmuckrelief* (Munich 1987) 21–26 and 148–155, nos. K 24–35; A. Kruglov, *SoobErmit* 52, 1987, 33–36. The five examples which include masks have been listed as *MNC*³ 3AS 4.

57 Oxford 1968.777. *JEA* 50 (1964) 147, pl. 15 (D.B. Thompson); *JHS* 93 (1973) 104ff., pl. 1 (E.W. Handley); *RM* 95 (1988) 102–103, pl. 41, 3 (H. Wrede); *MNC*³ 3EA 1. Kabul, from Begram, J. Hackin (ed.), *Nouvelles recherches archéologiques à Bégram* (1954) 136 no. 226, fig. 310; A. Adriani, *Una coppa paesistica* (1959) pl. 20, 5–6; *MNC*³ 3EA 2. It was found with a relief tondo of a tragic poet and Muse (*MTS*² 67, ET 15). Two late relief-jugs (*MNC*³ 6DV 2a–b) have a design apparently based on the same original.

58 Note also the palm-tree of the London version of the Ikarios reliefs.

59 Naples 9991, from Pompeii VI.12, e.g. T. Kraus and L. von Matt, *Lebendiges Pompeii* (1973) 83 fig. 103; Bieber, *Theater*² fig. 565 (detail); *aavv.*, *Le collezioni del Museo Nazionale di Napoli* (Rome 1986) 116–117 no. 7 (ill.), and 32 (colour ill.), *MNC*³ 3NM 2a.

60 Naples 114281, from Pompeii, VIII.ii.34, e.g. *JdI* 78 (1963) 264 fig. 2 (Parlasca); A. De Franciscis, *Museo Nazionale di Napoli* (Cava dei Tirreni 1963) pl. 22; *aavv.*, *Le collezioni del Museo Nazionale di Napoli* (Rome 1986) 118–119 no. 17 (ill.); *MNC*³ 3NM 2b.

61 Naples *MEFRA* 92 (1980) 249ff., figs. 1–5; *MNC*³ 3NM 3.

62 *MNC*³ 3DM 5, from the House of Masks, e.g. *Délos* xiv, pls. 4–6; *Délos* xxix, 57ff., 245ff., no. 215, figs 184–195; *IGD* 122, IV, 8c, and *MNC*³ 3DM 6, from the Ilot des bijoux, e.g. *BCH* 93 (1969) 261ff., esp. 289ff. with figs 25–31 (Bruneau and Siebert); *Délos* xxix 156ff. no. 68, figs. 55–79, and pl. A, 3–4 (colour).

63 M.-F. Boussac, 'Sceaux déliens', *RevArch* 1988, 337 fig. 68.

64 Geneva 1974/21133. Vollenweider 294f., no. 312, pl. 95 and colour pl. VIII; *AJA* 89 (1985) 465ff., pl. 52, 2 (Green); *MNC*³ 4XJ 1.

65 Naples 6687, e.g. Th. Schreiber, *Hellenistische Reliefbilder* (Leipzig 1894) pl. 83; Bieber, *Theater*[1] fig. 225 [2] fig. 324; Pickard-Cambridge, *Festivals*[1] fig. 94, [2]fig. 110; Pickard-Cambridge, *ToD* fig. 77; *WS* 85 (1972) 226ff. (Brein) *AJA* 90 (1985) 465ff., pl. 52, 1 (Green); *MNC*[3] 4XS 1. Not from Pompeii.

66 There is a list of 16 examples in *MNC*[3] under 4XJ 10.

67 The 'pottery' segment in Figure 5.20 includes the figures and masks modelled in the form of vessels together with braziers, but compare Figure 5.16.

68 See the recent publication by P. Bruneau, 'La céramique pergaménienne à reliefs appliqués de Délos', *BCH* 115, 1991, 561–577; he also presents a very useful discussion of the subject-matter of the decoration in general, thus making clear the function of theatrical material on pottery of this kind at this period (the late second and the first half of the first century BC).

69 *MNC*[3] 3DL 1–27. They are Broneer's types 13 ('Knidian') and 19 ('Ephesian'); the former probably began before 150 BC, the latter go beyond 50 BC.

70 Note the well-known set of masks of this period from Priene and now divided between Istanbul and Berlin (*MNC*[3] 3DT 90). They comprise a slave, a young man, a *pornoboskos*, a girl and perhaps a cook; there may also have been a second slave. The masks hung between *boukrania* on the walls of a symposion-room which must therefore have had overtones of a festal sanctuary. The *pornoboskos* mask is illustrated in Th. Wiegand and H. Schrader, *Priene* (Berlin 1904) 361 fig. 447; Bieber, *Theater*[2] fig. 387; J. Raeder, *Priene. Funde aus einer griechischen Stadt* (Berlin 1984) no. 19, pl. 4b (colour).

71 *MNC*[3] 3DL 29–47.

72 Paris, Louvre S 1724, length 0.23 m. O. Touchefeu-Meynier, *Le théâtre antique* (Musées Nationaux, n.d.) no. 34; *Goût du théâtre* no. 36; *MNC*[3] 3EL 2.

73 Note, however, that six often seems to be the number of masks depicted, as on the Kavalla plaque.

6 CONVENTIONS AND THE CLASSICS

1 The *theatrum terra exaggeratum*, built up on flat ground by means of an earth embankment. See D. Mertens, 'Metaponto: Il teatro-ekklesiasterion, I', *BdA* 67(16), 1982, 1–57. There is a somewhat earlier example at Elis. On the Latin and Campanian theatres, see the surveys and discussions by W. Johannowsky, 'La situazione in Campania', in *Hellenismus in Mittelitalien* (Abh.d.Akad.d. Wiss.Göttingen 97, 1976) 272, and in the same volume, H. Lauter, 'Die hellenistischen Theater der Samniten und Latiner in ihrer Beziehung zur Theaterarchitektur der Griechen' (pp. 413–430), and A. La Regina, 'Il Sannio' (pp. 219–254). Much of the material is collected in K. Mitens, *Teatri greci e teatri ispirati all'architettura greca in Sicilia e nell'Italia meridionale, c. 350–50 a.C. Un catalogo* (*AnalRomInstDan* Suppl.13, Rome 1988).

Polacco has argued for the importance of the theatre at Syracuse as a model for Roman theatres, 'Il teatro greco di Sirausa, modello al teatro romano', *NumAntClass* 6, 1977, 107–117.

Rome itself, of course, relied on temporary theatres erected for specific festivals and occasions, as Livy 34.54.3 (194 BC), 40.51 (179 BC), 41.27 (174 BC), and epit. 48 (155 BC).

2 Much has been written on all this. See in particular E. Fraenkel, *Plautinisches im Plautus* (Berlin 1922) and the revised version *Elementi plautini in Plauto* (Florence 1960); G.E. Duckworth, *The Nature of Roman Comedy* (Princeton

1952); K. Abel, *Die Plautusprologe* (Mülheim 1955); E.W. Handley, *Menander and Plautus: A Study in Comparison* (London 1968); id., 'Plautus and his Public: Some Thoughts on New Comedy in Latin', *Dioniso* 46, 1975, 117–132; E. Segal, *Roman Laughter. The Comedy of Plautus* (2nd edn, Oxford 1987).

3   Persius (v.161), however, recalls the scene with Menander's character names – a shift which is significant.

4   According to Plutarch, *Vit.Pomp.* 42. See also Tertullian 10.5, Aulus Gellius *NA* 10.1.6–7, Pliny *NH* 8.20, Suetonius *Claudius* 21.2. As late as AD 357 Ammianus Marcellinus counted it as one of Rome's finest buildings (inter decora Urbis).

5   For the story of the Theatre of Pompey, A.M. Capoferro Cercetti, 'Variazioni nel tempo dell' identità funzionale di un monumento. Il teatro di Pompeio', *RdA* 3, 1979, 72–85; F. Coarelli, 'Il complesso Pompeiano del Campo Marzio e la sua decorazione scultorea', *RendPontAcc* 44, 1972, 99–122; A.M. Reggiani, 'Ipotesi di recupero del Teatro di Pompeio', in *Roma. Archeologia nel centro* 2 (Rome 1985) 369–374. L. Richardson Jr., *AJA* 91, 1987, 123–126 has thrown considerable doubt on the normal reconstruction and in particular the prominence of the Temple of Venus Victrix. Parts of the bottom levels remain, embedded in more recent buildings. The masks from the Theatre of Marcellus have only recently been identified and published: P. Ciancio Rossetto, 'Le maschere del teatro di Marcello', *BullComm* 88, 1982–83 [1984], 7–49; ead., 'Le maschere del teatro di Marcello a Roma', in Chr. Landes (ed.), *Spectacula II. Le théâtre antique et ses spectacles* (Lattes 1992) 187–191. See also R. Cohon, 'An Early Augustan Throne in San Pietro in Vincoli', *Boreas* 8, 1985, 92–104, for an interesting suggestion that an early Augustan marble throne of very traditional appearance originally came from the Theatre of Marcellus.

6   For a good and useful discussion of the principles of choice in the evocation of earlier art in work of the Early Empire, see T. Hölscher, *Römische Bildsprache als semantisches System* (Abh. Heidelberg 1987).

7   Athens 3373. A. Brückner, in *Skenika* (75.*BerlWP*, 1915) 32ff., pls. 4–6; Bieber, *Theater*² fig. 810; Pickard-Cambridge, *Festivals*¹ fig. 137; *Studies Webster* ii (1988) 72 (Krien-Kummrow); *MNC*³ 4AS 3. Ht 0.34 m.

8   Rome, Museo Barracco 187. C. Pietrangeli, *Museo Barracco di scultura antica. Guida* (2nd edn, Rome 1960) 102. Preserved ht 0.28 m.

9   See M. Fuchs, *Untersuchungen zur Ausstattung römischer Theater* (Mainz 1987) 116 and 147ff.

10   On the importance of theatre-construction at this period, see the very useful article by G. Bejor, 'L'edificio teatrale nell'urbanizzazione augustea', *Athenaeum* 57 (1979) 126–138. See also P. Gros, 'La fonction symbolique des édifices théâtraux dans le paysage urbain de la Rome augustéenne', in *L'Urbs, espace urbain et histoire. Actes du colloque . . . l'École française de Rome, 8–12 mai 1985* (*Coll. de'École fr.* no. 98, Rome 1987) 319–346, and 'Un programme augustéen. Le centre monumental de la colonie d'Arles', *JdI* 102, 1987, 339–363; M. Verzár-Bass, 'I teatri nell'Italia settentrionale', in *La città nell'Italia settentrionale. Morfologie, strutture e funzionamento dei centri urbani delle Regiones X e XI. Atti del convegno . . . Trieste et Rome, 13–15 marzo 1987* (*Coll. École fr. de Rome* no. 130, Trieste–Rome 1990) 411–440, and more generally the implications of the papers in W. Trillmich and P. Zanker (eds), *Stadtbild und Ideologie. Die Monumentalisierung hispanischer Städte zwischen Republik und Kaiserzeit. Kolloquium in Madrid vom 19. bis 23. Oktober 1987* (*AbhMünchen* NF 103, 1990).

11   E.J. Jory and the writer are at present engaged in a project on this issue.

12   See in the first instance Livy 7.2; Val.Max. 2.44.

13   See for example the Canino Group (*MNC*³ 3RT 1–4) and associated pieces, well

known through their illustration in e.g. Bieber, *Theater*[1] figs 410–412, [2]figs. 551–553.

14 There are three important recent articles on the historical and literary evidence for Roman theatrical activity at this period: E. Fantham, 'Roman Experience of Menander in the Late Republic and Early Empire', *TAPA* 114 (1984) 299–310; E.J. Jory, 'Continuity and Change in the Roman Theatre', in *Studies Webster* i, 143–152; and E. Rawson, 'Theatrical Life in Republican Rome and Italy', *BSR* 53 (1985) 97–113.

15 C.P. Jones, 'Dinner Theater', in W.J. Slater (ed.), *Dining in a Classical Context* (Ann Arbor 1991) 185–198. See also the useful information collected by G. Prosperi Valenti, 'Attori-bambini del mondo romano attraverso le testimonianze epigrafiche', *Epigraphica* 47, 1985, 71–82, although not all relates to the performance of pieces from traditional theatre.

16 See S.F. Bonner, *Education in Ancient Rome* (London and Berkeley 1977) 215–218 and 224. On this sort of issue and the principles involved, there are also very useful observations by E. Fantham, 'Quintilian on Performance: Traditional Personal Elements in *Institutio* 11.13', *Phoenix* 36, 1982, 243–263.

17 *MNC*[3] 4RT 5–12 and 4RT 13a–q.

18 Note that many elements of this architectural style, which is also repeated in the façades of Petra, are not taken up in Roman architecture proper until the time of Hadrian when it comes in as part of the hellenising movement. Note also in this context Augustus' enthusiasm for having a major library.

19 See the useful list of the various motifs in G. Koch and H. Sichtermann, *Römische Sarkophage* (Munich 1982) 231ff.

20 See the type of *MNC*[3] 5RL 7, with mask of an old man, of which a published example comes from Nikopolis (Actium); *ADelt* 30, 1975, B 2, 215, pl. 125a (not a miniature mask as stated there).

21 See in *MNC*[3] 5EG 1ff., 5WG 1–2 and 6EG 1ff.

22 87.AB.143. A.P. Kozloff and D.G. Mitten, *The Gods Delight. The Human Figure in Classical Bronze* (Exhib. Cat., Cleveland 1988) 299–302 no. 54 (ill.); *GettyMJ* 16, 1988, 141 no. 2 (ill.). Ht 23.2 cm.

23 See *MNC*[3] 1NT 4, 2NV 7, 3DP 2, 3NM 1, 3NV 6, 4RT 1a–d, 4XS 4a–g, 4XJ 32, 4XJ 33, 4XB 11a–e, 5XB 1a–b, 5XB 7.

24 See *MNC*[3] frontispiece.

25 87.AB.144. Kozloff and Mitten 303–306 no. 55 (ill.); *GettyMJ* 16, 1988, 142 no. 3 (ill.). Ht 19 cm.

26 Ht 0.084 m. E.g. E. Babelon, *Catalogue des camées antiques et modernes de la Bibliothèque Nationale* (Paris 1897) 201ff., no. 368; A. Adriani, *Divagazioni intorno ad una coppa paesistica* (Rome 1959) 22, pls. 30–31; H.P. Bühler, *Antike Vasen aus Edelsteinen* (Mainz 1973) 45ff., no. 18, pl. I (colour); *Le trésor de Saint-Denis* (Exhib. Cat., Louvre 1991) 83ff.; *MNC*[3] 4XJ 37.

27 Berlin 3779.13–14, from Hildesheim, e.g. E. Pernice and F. Winter, *Der Hildesheimer Silberfund* (Berlin 1901) 37ff., pls. 13–16; U. Gehrig, *Hildesheimer Silberfund in der Antikenabteilung Berlin* (Berlin 1967) 24f., figs. 23–26; L. Pirzio Biroli Stefanelli, *L'argento dei Romani. Vasellame da tavola e d'apparato* (Rome 1991) 178 figs 170–171 (colour), 272 no. 93; *MNC*[3] 4XA 2.1–2. The kantharoi, Naples 25380–1, e.g. *aavv., Le collezioni del Museo Nazionale di Napoli* (Rome 1986) 209 nos. 30–31. Note also the use of the masks on the silver kantharoi from the House of the Menander at Pompeii, Naples 145508–9, e.g. A. Maiuri, *La Casa del Menandro e il suo tesoro di argenteria* (Rome 1932) pls. 39–40; Biroli Stefanelli, op.cit. 159 (colour ills.) and 267 no. 72; *MNC*[3] 4XA 1.

28 Naples 124545, e.g. G.M.A. Richter, *Portraits of the Greeks* (London 1965) 82

fig. 316; *Le collezioni del Museo Nazionale di Napoli* (Rome 1986) 116–117 no. 15 (ill.); *MNC*³ 4NM 2.

29 See, for example, *MNC*³ 3DM 6, e.g. *BCH* 93 (1969) 261ff., esp. 289ff. with figs 25–31 (Bruneau and Siebert); *Délos* xxix 156ff. no. 68, figs 55–79 and pl. A, 3–4 (colour).

30 Rome, Terme, from Priverno (fragmentary). *AA* 1976, 370 fig. 30; L. Guerrini (ed.), *Scritti . . . Becatti* (*StudiMisc* 22, Rome 1976) pl. 37, 2 (Morricone); *Enea nel Lazio. Archeologia e mito* (Rome 1981) 79f., no. A 128; *MNC*³ 4RM 1. Imola, from Imola (fragmentary), e.g. *NSc* 1897, 55 figs 4–5; *MAAR* 8 (1930) 145 pl. 46, 4; F. Mancini *et al.*, *Imola nell' Antichità* (Rome 1957) 190 no. 76, pls. 2 and 22, 1–2, cover; *MNC*³ 4RM 2. Both combine comic with satyr-masks. A further example is that from the Piazza della Vittoria in Palermo, *MonAnt* 27 (1921) 181ff., pl. 3 (Gabrici); D. von Boeselager, *Antike Mosaiken in Sizilien: Hellenismus und römische Kaiserzeit* (Archaeologica 40, Rome 1983) 47ff., pls. 11–13, figs. 21–26 (with further refs.); *MNC*² 180, SM 1; *MNC*³ 4SM 1. It includes a curious dark-haired winged mask and what seems to be a satyr-mask alongside the comic.

31 See the remarks by J.-M. Pailler on the inclusion of Attis and Polyphemos masks among tragic on the low-relief 'oscilla': 'Attis, Polyphème et le thiase bacchique: quelques représentations méconnues', *MEFRA* 83 (1971) 127–139. One should note, however, that masks of Attis and Polyphemos are also prominent in Gallo-Roman contexts, as for example at Lyons. On *oscilla* more generally, see E.H. Dwyer, 'Pompeian Oscilla Collections', *RM* 88, 1981, 247–306 (with rather high dating), and J.M. Pailler, 'Les *oscilla* retrouvés. Du recueil des documents à une théorie d'ensemble', *MEFRA* 94, 1982, 743–822.

32 See *MNC*³ 5NP.

33 See the article by Jones mentioned in n. 15 above.

34 See the section on 'Costumes and Masks' in *MNC*³ for an approach based on the archaeological evidence; for a literary approach, see H.-G. Nesselrath, *Die attische Mittlere Komödie. Ihre Stellung in der antiken Literaturkritik und Literaturgeschichte* (Berlin 1990) 83–88.

35 D.F. Sutton, 'Pollux on Special Masks', *AntClass* 53, 1984, 174–183, offers preliminary discussion.

36 See recently, for example, M. Wörrle, *Stadt und Fest in kaiserzeitliche Kleinasien. Studien zu einer agonistischen Stiftung aus Oenoanda* (Vestigia xxxix, Munich 1988), and S. Mitchell, 'Festivals, Games, and Civic Life in Roman Asia Minor', *JRS* 80, 1990, 183–193. Note also A.J.S. Spawforth, 'Agonistic Festivals in Roman Greece', in S. Walker and A. Cameron (eds), *The Greek Renaissance in the Roman Empire* (*BICS* Suppl. 55, 1989) 193–197, who remarks on the proliferation of such events in the third century, but there is no mention of anything theatrical. See earlier A. Müller, 'Das Bühnenwesen in der Zeit von Constantin d. Gr. bis Justinian', *NJbb* 23, 1909, 36–55, and C. Caprizzi, 'Gli spettacoli nella legislazione di Giustiniano', in *Spettacoli conviviali dall'antichità classica alle corti italiane del '400* (Atti del VII Convegno di Studio, Viterbo, 27–30 Maggio 1982, Centro di Studi sul Teatro Medioevale e Rinascimentale, Viterbo 1983) 91–118. There is good discussion too in E.G. Turner, 'Dramatic Representations in Graeco-Roman Egypt: How Long do They Continue?', *AntClass* 32, 1963, 120–128.

37 M. Kokolakis, *Lucian and the Tragic Performances in his Time* (Athens 1961) (= *Platon* 23/24, 67–109). It is interesting to compare Plutarch whose interest in tragedy has a more literary-philosophical basis, even if the two of them share certain attitudes, such as the condemnation of false appearances, a view with

a history going back to the fourth century BC. See A.M. Tagliasacchi, 'Plutarco e la tragedia greca', *Dioniso* 34, 1960, 124–142.

38   In his day their internal structure was doubtless often visible after the removal of some of the sheets of gold, as state assets were either stolen or utilised to balance budgets.

39   Paris, Petit Palais, inv. A. DUT 192. Ht 16 cm. Bieber, *Theater*² fig. 799; Pickard-Cambridge, *Festivals*² fig. 63; *MTS*² 93, II 1; *Goût du théâtre* 135 no. 15 (with early bibl.). The piece is not from Rieti, as is commonly supposed, but from Rome. It cannot be dated accurately but is generally taken to be second to third century AD.

40   On the practice of colouring ivory, see C.L. Connor, 'New Perspectives on Byzantine Ivories', *Gesta* 30, 1991, 100–111.

41   A good example is the series of red-glazed souvenir wine-jugs in the form of an ageing female alcoholic. The type echoes the Later Hellenistic statue of the Drunken Old Woman by Myron of Thebes, and they sometimes have an amusing inscription on the bottom: see, for example, A. Carandini, *MEFR* 82, 1970, 781–783; Ulrich Hausmann in *Antiken aus rheinischem Privatbesitz* (Exhib. Cat., Bonn 1973) no. 168, pl. 79; also J.W. Hayes, *Ancient Lamps in the Royal Ontario Museum* I (Toronto 1980) 142 no. 563, pl. 57. The manufacture is North African, but for an example from Ostia, which came from a context of about AD 240, see E. Fabbricotti, *Studi Miscellanei* 13 [1969] pl. 63, fig. 882. Other examples have appeared recently on the market: Charles Ede Ltd (London), *Antiquities 142* (1987) no. 18 (ill.) (the vase now in the Australian National University, Canberra); and Fortuna Fine Arts Ltd (New York), *Earth and Metal. Terracottas and Bronzes* (New York 1990) no. 58 (ill.). For a recent photograph of the Munich copy of the Hellenistic original, free from restorations, see *RM* 98, 1991, pl. 40.

42   Thessalonike 9815, *Thessalonike apo ta proïstorika mechri ta christianika chronia* (Athens 1986) 136 and 139 no. 145 (colour ill.). Another example is *CIL* V 5889, the altar to Theocritus Pylades with the record of his pantomime victories in the Ambrosiana collection in Milan.

43   Verona, Museo Maffeiano. A. Conze (ed.), *Die attischen Grabreliefs*, iv (Lieferung 19, Berlin 1922) no. 2113, pl. 463; *JdI* 76 (1961) 106 fig. 6 (Webster); T. Ritti, *Iscrizioni e rilievi greci nel Museo Maffeiano di Verona* (Rome 1981) no. 70; *MNC*³ 5AS 16.

44   Varna II-5801, from Odessos. *Arkheologia* 1981 45ff., figs 1–2 (Minchev); *Bull.du Musée National de Varna* (*Izvestia na Narodniya Muzei Varna*) 17(32) (1981) 64–74, pl. 2 (Minchev); *MNC*³ 6DA 1. Ht 0.103 m incl. base.

45   Athens, National Museum(?), from Athens, *ADelt* 21 (1966) B(1), 68, pl. 79b; *MNC*³ 6AT 1a–b (from the same burial as the next in the National Museum); Athens, Agora T 3074, *Agora* vi, no. 505, pl. 11; *Hesperia* 21 (1952) 110, pl. 30b; *AJA* 66 (1962) 334, pl. 88, 4; *MNC*³ 6AT 2a (from a context of debris from the Herulian destruction); Athens, National Museum(?), from Athens, *ADelt* 21 (1966) B(1), 68, pl. 79b; *MNC*³ 6AT 2b (stunted version, with short stubby body). Slave mask with flame hair, uneven brows. From the same burial as 6AT 1: for the accompanying pottery, the best parallels belong to *Agora* v, Group M. Layer 5, which is dated *c.* AD 250–267.

46   For example Athens, O. Benndorf, *Beiträge zur Kenntnis des attischen Theaters* (Vienna 1875) 78, no. 21; *MNC*³ 5AC 1 with frontal slave mask; Athens, Benndorf op. cit., 78 no 22; Pickard-Cambridge, *Festivals*¹ fig. 206, 3; *MNC*³ 5AC 2 with mask of old man; Corinth MF 1241, *Corinth* xii, no. 929, pl. 68; *MNC*³ 5CC 1, with female mask. One may also note three others in the

Numismatic Collection of the National Museum in Athens: Benndorf no. 26; MNC^3 6AC 2 with mask of youth; Benndorf no. 29; MNC^3 6AC 3 with cook mask?; Benndorf no. 25; MNC^3 6AC 4 with female mask. The date of these is uncertain.

47　MNC^3 6AC 1, Athens, National Museum (Numismatic Collection), O. Benndorf, op. cit., 78 no. 23; Pickard-Cambridge, *Festivals*[1] fig. 206, 4; Athens, Agora IL 1311, *Agora* x (1964) 122, L 329, pl. 30; Pickard-Cambridge, *Festivals*[2] fig. 140; *Mytilène* 49, pl. 25, 6; Athens, Agora IL 1312, *Mytilène* pl. 25, 7; Athens, Agora IL 1313. *Agora* x, 122, L. 329, pl. 30; *Mytilène* pl. 25, 8.

48　J.M. Spieser, 'La christianisation des sanctuaires païens en Grèce', in U. Jantzen (ed.), *Neue Forschungen in griechischen Heiligtümern* (Symposion Olympia 1974, Tübingen 1976) 309–320. Note the useful observations in G. Traversari, *Gli spettacoli in acqua nel teatro tardo antico* (Rome 1960).

49　This topic has not, to my knowledge, had any systematic study. J.-Ch. Moretti, 'L'Architecture des théâtres en Grèce (1980–1989)', *Topoi* 1, 1991, 7–38, and 'L'Architecture des théâtres en Asie Mineure (1980–1989)', *Topoi* 2, 1992, 9–32, has provided useful and well-informed surveys of the literature on theatre-buildings in these areas published in the decade 1980–1989, and although he seems to have been unable to gain access to a number of English-language publications, his first-hand knowledge of the Asia Minor theatres in particular makes his work the more valuable. I attempted a more restricted coverage in *Lustrum* 31, 1989, 14ff., and will do so again in my next survey. Note also S. Gogos, 'Das antike Theater in der Periegese des Pausanias', *Klio* 70, 1988, 329–339. He examines the place of theatres in Pausanias and points out that although Pausanias shows a knowledge of certain Greek dramas and demonstrated an interest in some authors, he gives no particular emphasis to theatres in his Description.

50　See, for example, *Archaeological Reports 1984–85*, 18.

51　See recently J.-Ch. Moretti, *REG* 102 (1989) xiv–xv; see also *BCH* 111, 1987, 603–607; *BCH* 122, 1988, 716–720; *BCH* 113, 1989, 717–722; *BCH* 114, 1990, 866–872.

52　For a convenient summary, see J. Travlos, *Pictorial Dictionary of Ancient Athens* (London 1971) 538. Also A. Frantz, 'The Date of the Phaidros Bema in the Theater of Dionysos', in *Studies in Athenian Architecture and Topography ... H.A. Thompson* (*Hesperia* suppl. 20, Princeton 1982) 34–39, and the Hadrianic material, M. Sturgeon, 'The Reliefs on the Theatre of Dionysos in Athens', *AJA* 81, 1977, 31–53.

53　See *Lustrum* 31, 1989, 15 for further references; and for Philippi, *Archaeological Reports 1984–85*, 49; for Hierapolis, *Archaeological Reports 1984–85*, 95.

54　K.T. Erim, 'Recent Work at Aphrodisias 1986–1988', in Ch. Roueché and K.T. Erim (eds), *Aphrodisias Papers. Recent Work on Architecture and Sculpture* (*JRA* Suppl. 1, Ann Abor 1990) 9–36 (esp. 30–32).

55　Ch. Roueché, 'Aphrodisias in Late Antiquity. The Late Roman and Byzantine Inscriptions' (*JRS* Monographs, 5, London 1989) 223–226. I have not seen the same author's *Performers and Partisans at Aphrodisias in the Roman and Late Roman Periods* (*JRS* Monograph 6, 1993).

56　I am grateful to the excavator, Professor Rodziewicz, for his on-site briefing on his work there.

57　See above, n. 4.

58　Athens, Agora, *Agora* vii, no. 872, pl. 19; MTS^2 32, on AL 1: MNC^3 6AL 1a; Corinth IPL 72–79, from Isthmia, Roman Baths, *Hesperia* 50 (1981) 127 no. 5, pl. 34; MNC^3 6AL 1b. Perlzweig in *Agora* vii dated the Agora lamp to the mid-fourth century, but there is a good context of *c.* AD 400–420 for the Isthmia lamp. See also *MNC*³ 6AL 2–3.

59 L.W. Jones and C.R. Morey, *The Miniatures of the Manuscripts of Terence* (Princeton 1931); Robert 87ff.; Bieber, *Theater*¹⁻² 153f.; K. Weitzmann, *Illustrations in Roll and Codex* (Princeton ¹1947, ²1970) 73, 109f., 158f.; *id.*, *Ancient Book Illumination* (Cambridge, Mass. 1959) 85ff.; *Mytilène* 102f.; J.N. Grant, *CQ* 23 (1973) 88–103; Weitzmann and Turner, *AntK* 24 (1981) 39ff.; J.N. Grant, *Studies in the Textual Tradition of Terence* (*Phoenix* Suppl. 20, 1986) 18–59; *MNC*³ 6XP 1a–c.

60 On fourth-century interest in Terence, see A. Alföldi, *Die Kontorniaten* (Leipzig 1942–3) 72.

61 V.M. Strocka, *Die Wandmalereien der Hanghäuser in Ephesos* (*Forschungen in Ephesos*, viii. 1, 1977) 45ff., pl. 62ff.; *MNC*³ 6DP 1.1–3.

62 Oescus, e.g. T. Ivanov, *Une mosaïque romaine de Ulpia Oescus* (Monuments de l'Art en Bulgarie ii, Sofia 1954) pl. 2, 8–13; *AJA* 60 (1956) 80f. (Bieber); *RevArch* 47 (1956) 220ff. (Ch. Picard); K. Weitzmann, *Ancient Book Illumination* (Cambridge, Mass. 1959) 83; Bieber, *Theater*² fig. 315; *Mytilène* 98f., pl. 27, 1; *MNC*³ 6DM 1.

63 *Mytilène* (*passim*); *MNC*³ 6DM 2.1, 6DM 2.6, 6DM 2.8, 6DM 2.11.

64 *BICS* 35, 1988, 119–126.

65 Chania, *ADelt* 32 (1977) B(2), 326ff., pl.198; *MNC*³ 6DM 3; S. Markoulaki, 'Psephidota "Oikias Dionyson" sto Monseio Chanion', *Pepragmena Diethn. Kretol. Synedriou* (*24–30 Avg. 1986*), I.i (Chania 1990) 449–463.

66 D. Salzmann, 'Mosaiken und Pavimente in Pergamon. Vorbericht der Kampagnen 1989 und 1990', *AA* 1991, 433–456.

67 For earlier discussion, see Green, *AJA* 89 (1985) 465–472, and *MNC*³, 'Illustrations of Plays' XZ 41.

68 Worth noting is that the slave was almost certainly mute in this scene (the two other speakers being the old men), and it is for this reason that his physical size was diminished in the iconographic tradition.

69 Milan, Museo Teatrale 345, *Collection théâtrale de M. Jules Sambon. Catalogue des antiquités* (Paris 1911) no. 467; M.M. Roberti, in *Museo Teatrale alla Scala* (ed. gen. C. Pirovano, *Musei e gallerie di Milano*) 1975–76, vol. i, no. 232, fig. 170; *AJA* 89 (1985) 471, pl. 54, 9; *MNC*³ 6XI 1.

70 It should imply a similar stateliness and frontality in performance, since such a crowning element is far less effective in side view. One thinks of the growing importance of frontality for key figures in contemporary relief sculpture and the increasing rejection of three-dimensionality in non-classicising work.

71 London, British Museum 79, A. & E. Alföldi, *Die Kontorniat-Medaillons* i (Berlin–New York 1976) 177 no. 582, pl. 101, 6; *MNC*³ 6RC 1. The reading of the inscription is due to J.P.C. Kent.

72 St Petersburg Ω 263 (Byz 925/16), R. Delbrück, *Die Consulardiptychen und verwandt Denkmäler* (Berlin–Leipzig 1927–29) 125 no. 18, pl. 18; W.F. Volbach, *Elfenbeinarbeiten der Spätantike und des frühen Mittelalters*³ (Mainz 1976) 36 no. 19, pl. 9l; Bieber, *Theater*² fig. 835; *AJA* 89 (1985) pl. 54, 10; *MTS*² 93 (on II 2); *MNC*³ 6DI 1.

73 E.g. Volbach pls. 8–9, no. 21; Bieber, *Theater*² fig. 834.

74 *DOPapers* 14, 1960, 139 (reprinted in his *L'art de la fin de l'antiquité et du Moyen Age* (Paris 1968) 243).

75 Good examples include the marble head of actor as slave, Athens, Agora S 995, *MNC*³ 6AS 1; marble figure of slave standing with legs crossed, hands clasped before belly, (a) Istanbul 1768 from Tralles, G. Mendel, *Catalogue des sculptures*

ii (Constantinople 1914) 283 no. 560; Simon 80, 173, 191 n. 62; Bieber, *Theater*[1] fig. 420, [2]fig. 584; *MNC*[3] 6DS 1a; (b) (head) London 1914.2–21.1, *MNC*[3] 6DS 1b; (c–f) Kos, from Kos, *ASAtene* 33–34 (1955–56) 137 nos. 178–181 (Laurenzi); *MNC*[3] 6DS 1c–f; mask of youth with loose wavy hair, Paris, Louvre MNC 1582, from Carthage, Bieber, *Theater*[1] fig. 537, [2]fig. 804; A. Rumpf in *Mimus und Logos. Eine Festgabe für Carl Niessen* (Emsdetten 1952) 166; *RevArch* 1970, 254 fig. 1 (Ghiron-Bistagne); *MNC*[3] 6FS 8. See also the bronze figurine of a slave (not, as commonly suppposed, soldier), Athens, Agora B 332, *Hesperia* 6 (1937) 351 fig. 15; Pickard-Cambridge, *Festivals*[1] fig. 161; Bieber, *Theater*[2] fig. 369a–b; *Mytilène* 75, pl. 25, 3–4; *MNC*[3] 6XB 1.

76 Representations of actors are more numerous in Late Antiquity, and in relative terms are more common among the surviving material than in any period except Late Hellenistic.

77 Sydney, from Pella of the Dekapolis, tomb 39A, *Pella in Jordan* i (Canberra 1982) 92 no. 91, pl. 44, 3; *MNC*[3] 6HI 1. The mask types are not entirely certain but could well be the traditional grouping of a *kolax* and a wavy-haired youth.

78 Manchester MM 378.1968, from Hawara, *MNC*[3] 6EW 1.

79 From Istanbul?, A. Grabar, *Sculptures byzantines de Constantinople, IVe–Xe siècle* (Paris 1963) pl. 19, 1; *MNC*[3] 6DS 14. Grabar notes that another capital of the same series (Istanbul, Mendel no. 755) was re-carved with an inscription naming Heraclius (610–641); the companion-piece has a local provenance. On the group from which it comes, see E.D. Maguire, *AJA* 84 (1980) 221.

80 J. Natanson, *Early Christian Ivories* (London 1953) pl. 27; W.F. Volbach, *Elfenbeinarbeiten der Spätantike und des frühen Mittelalters*[3] (Mainz 1976) 58 no. 69, pl. 40; *MNC*[3] 6XI 5.

81 See Handley, in E. Handley and A. Hurst (eds), *Relire Ménandre* (Geneva 1990) 143–148.

82 See generally Th. Baumeister, 'Das Theater in der Sicht der Alten Kirche', in *Theaterwesen u. dramatischen Literatur. Beiträge zur Geschichte des Theaters* (Tübingen 1987) 109–125; H. Jürgens, *Pompa Diaboli. Die lateinischen Kirchenväter und das antike Theater* (Stuttgart 1972); W. Weismann, *Kirche und Schauspiele* (Cassiacum XXVII, Würzburg 1972); K. Sallmann, 'Christen vor dem Theater', in J. Blänsdorf (ed.), *Theater und Gesellschaft im Imperium Romanum* (Mainzer Forschungen zu Drama und Theater, 4, Tübingen 1990) 243–259, and, in the same volume, J. Blänsdorf, 'Der spätantike Staat und die Schauspiele im Codex Theodosianus', 261–274. See more generally A.D. Momigliano (ed.), *The Conflict between Paganism and Christianity in the Fourth Century* (1963), and, for a sceptical point of view, J. O'Donnell, 'The Demise of Paganism', *Traditio* 35 (1979) 45–88.

83 Compare somewhat earlier, Tertullian, *De Spectaculis* 27.4, where he argues that the 'grace, sweetness and simplicity' of the plays is 'bait used by the Devil'. See W. Weismann, *Kirche und Schauspiele* (Würzburg 1972) 110f.

BIBLIOGRAPHY

This is a very selective bibliography and leans to the general and interpretive. It does not include everything mentioned in the footnotes, and particularly not references to publications of individual objects unless they have wider significance. Furthermore, given the practice currently fashionable with some scholars of publishing the same article as often as possible, I have normally only mentioned one of such a series. I should also refer to my annotated bibliography of publications related to Greek theatre production between 1971 and 1986 in *Lustrum* 31, 1989; a survey of more recent publications on the subject will appear before long.

aavv., *Scena e spettacolo nell' antichità. Atti del Convegno internazionale di studio, Trento 28–30 marzo 1988* (Florence 1989).
———— *Théâtres et spectacles dan l'antiquité. Actes du colloque de Strasburg, 5–7 novembre 1981* (Leiden 1983).
Adrados, F.R., *Festival, Comedy and Tragedy. The Greek Origins of Theatre* (Leiden 1975).
———— 'Rite, mythe et théâtre en Grèce ancienne', *Anthropologie et Théâtre antique, Cahiers du GITA* 3, 1987, 37–52.
Adriani, A., *Divagazioni intorno ad una coppa paesistica del Museo di Alessandria* (Rome 1959).
Aélion, R., *Euripide héritier d'Eschyle*, i–ii (Paris 1983).
Allen, J.T., 'Greek Acting in the Fifth Century B.C.', *UnivCalifPublClassPhil* 2:15, 1916, 279–89.
———— *The Greek Theater of the Fifth Century before Christ* (Berkeley 1919).
Altheim, F., 'Persona', *ArchivRelWiss* 27, 1929, 35–52.
Anti, C. and L. Polacco, *Il teatro antico di Siracusa* (Padua 1976).
Arnott, P.D., *Greek Scenic Conventions in the Fifth Century B.C.* (Oxford 1962).
———— *Public and Performance in the Greek Theatre* (London 1989).
Arnott, W.G., *Menander, Plautus and Terence (Greece and Rome)* New Surveys 9, Oxford 1975.
———— 'Moral Values in Menander', *Philologus* 125, 1981, 215–27.
Austin, C., 'Catalogus comicorum graecorum', *ZPE* 14, 1974, 201–25.
Babcock, B.A., *The Reversible World. Symbolic Inversion in Art and Society* (Ithaca, N.Y., 1978).
Babelon, M.E., *Catalogue des camées antiques et modernes de la Bibliothèque Nationale* (Paris 1897).
Bain, D., *Actors and Audience. A Study of Asides and Related Conventions in Greek Drama* (Oxford 1977).
———— 'Some Reflections on the Illusion in Greek Tragedy', *BICS* 34, 1987, 1–14.

207

Barner, W., 'Neuphilologische Rezeptionsforschung und die Möglichkeiten der Klassischen Philologie', *Poetica* 9, 1977, 499–521.

Bauchhenss-Thüriedl, *Der Mythos von Telephos in der antiken Bildkunst* (Würzburg 1971).

Baumeister, Th., 'Das Theater in der Sicht der Alten Kirche', in *Theaterwesen u. dramatischen Literatur. Beiträge zur Geschichte des Theaters* (Tübingen 1987) 109–25.

Beazley, J.D., 'Hydria-Fragments in Corinth', *Hesperia* 24, 1955, 305–19.

Bejor, G., 'L'edificio teatrale nell'urbanizzazione augustea', *Athenaeum* 57, 1979, 126–38.

Di Benedetto, V., 'Spazio e messa in scena nelle tragedie di Eschilo', *Dioniso* 59:2, 1989, 65–101.

Benndorf, O., *Beiträge zur Kenntnis des attischen Theaters* (Vienna 1875).

Bérard, C., 'Le corps bestial (les métamorphoses de l'homme idéal au siècle de Périclès)', in C. Reichler (ed.), *Le corps et ses fictions* (Paris 1983) 43–54.

Berczelly, L., 'The Date and Significance of the Menander Mosaics at Mytilene', *BICS* 35, 1988, 119–27.

Bernabò Brea, L., *Menandro e il teatro greco nelle terrecotte liparese* (Genoa 1981).

——— and M. Cavalier, *Meligunìs Lipára V. Scavi nella necropoli greca di Lipari* (Rome 1991).

de Bernardi Tesero, D., *Teatri classici d'Asia Minore*, i–iii (Rome 1966–70).

——— *Teatri Classici d'Asia Minore*, iv: *deduzioni e proposte* (Rome 1975).

Berthiaume, G., *Les rôles du mágeiros* (*Mnemosyne* Supplement 70, 1982).

Berti, F. and C. Gasparri (eds), *Dionysos. Mito e mistero* (Bologna 1989).

Bertino, A., 'Sulla fonte di ispirazione della scena di soggetto teatrale sui vasi a figure rosse del IV secolo a.C.', in N. Caffarello (ed.), *Archaeologica. Studi e ricerche in onore di Aldo Neppi Modona* (Arte e Archeologia, Studi e Documenti, 9, Florence 1975) 17–28.

Bieber, M., *The History of the Greek and Roman Theater* (2nd edn Princeton 1961).

Blänsdorf, J., 'Der spätantike Staat und die Schauspiele im Codex Theodosianus', in J. Blänsdorf (ed.), *Theater und Gesellschaft im Imperium Romanum* (Mainzer Forschungen zu Drama und Theater, 4, Tübingen 1990) 261–74.

Blume, H.D., *Einführung in das antike Theaterwesen* (rev. edn. Darmstadt 1984).

Bonner, S.F., *Education in Ancient Rome* (Berkeley 1977).

Bristol, M.D., *Carnival and Theater: Plebeian Culture and the Structure of Authority in Renaissance England* (London 1985).

Brock, R., 'The Emergence of Democratic Ideology', *Historia* 40, 1991, 160–9.

Brommer, F., *Satyrspiele. Bilder griechischer Vasen* (2nd edn Berlin 1959).

——— 'Satyrspielbilder', *GettyMJ* 6–7, 1978–79, 144–6.

——— 'Satyrspielvasen in Malibu', *GVGetty* 1 (Malibu 1983) 115–20.

Broneer, O., 'The Tent of Xerxes and the Greek Theater', *California Publications in Classical Archaeology* 1, 1944, 305–11.

Brown, A.L., 'Three and Scene-Painting Sophocles', *PCPS* 210, 1984, 1–17.

Brown, P.G.McC., 'Masks, Names and Characters in New Comedy', *Hermes* 115, 1987, 181–201.

——— 'Plots and Prostitutes in New Comedy', *Papers of the Leeds International Latin Seminar* 6, 1990, 241–66.

Bruno, V.J., *Hellenistic Painting Techniques. The Evidence of the Delos Fragments* (Leiden 1985).

Bulle, H., 'Von griechischen Schauspielern und Vasenmalern', in *Festschrift für James Loeb* (Munich 1930) 5–43.

Burkert, W., 'Greek Tragedy and Sacrificial Ritual', *GRBS* 7, 1966, 87–121.

——— *Greek Religion. Archaic and Classical* (London 1985).

―――― 'The Making of Homer in the Sixth Century B.C.: Rhapsodes versus Stesichorus', in *Papers on the Amasis Painter and his World*, (Colloquium ... Getty Museum, Malibu 1987) 43–62.

Burn, L., 'The Art of the State in Late Fifth-Century Athens', in M.M. MacKenzie and C. Roueché (eds), *Images of Authority. Papers Presented to Joyce Reynolds on the Occasion of her Seventieth Birthday* (*PCPS* Suppl. 16, Cambridge 1989) 62–81.

Burns, A., 'Athenian Literacy in the Fifth Century B.C.', *JHI* 42, 1981, 371–88.

Burr, D., *Terracottas from Myrina in the Museum of Fine Arts, Boston* (Vienna 1934).

Burstein, S.M., 'Menander and Politics: the Fragments of the *Halieis*', in S.M. Burstein and L.A. Okin (eds), *Panhellenica. Essays in Ancient History and Historiography in Honor of Truesdell S. Brown* (Lawrence, Kansas, 1980) 69–76.

Buschor, E., *Feldmäuse* (SB Bayer. Akademie, Munich 1937).

―――― *Satyrtänze und frühes Drama* (Munich 1943).

Butterweck, G., 'Das Dionysostheater. Neue Rekonstruktion des Grundrisses des Dionysostheaters und der theatralischen Architekturdarstellungsformen in Athen im 5. Jahrhundert v. Chr.', *Maske und Kothurn* 20, 1974, 105–47.

Cain, H.-U., 'Chronologie, Ikonographie und Bedeutung der römischen Masken-reliefs', *BJb* 188, 1988, 107–221.

Calame, C., 'Facing Otherness. The Tragic Mask in Ancient Greece', *History of Religions* 26, 1986, 125–42.

―――― *Le récit en Grèce ancienne. Enonciations et représentations de poètes* (Paris 1986).

―――― 'Quand regarder, c'est énoncer: le vase Pronomos et le masque', in *Images et société en Grèce ancienne. L'iconographie comme méthode d'analyse. Actes du Colloque international, Lausanne 8–11 février 1984* (*Cahiers d'Archéologie Romande* no. 36, Lausanne 1987) 79–88.

Calder III, W.M., 'The Alkestis Inscription from Odessos: *IGBR* I² 222', *AJA* 79, 1975, 80–3.

Capoferro Cercetti, A.M., 'Variazioni nel tempo dell' identità funzionale di un monumento. Il teatro di Pompeio', *RdA* 3, 1979, 72–85.

Capps, E., *The Introduction of Comedy into the City Dionysia: A Chronological Study in Greek Literary History* (Chicago 1904 = Decennial Publications Univ. Chicago 1:vi:11, 1903, 261–88).

Caprizzi, C., 'Gli spettacoli nella legislazione di Giustiniano', in *Spettacoli conviviali dall'antichità classica alle corti italiane del '400* (Atti del VII Convegno di Studio, Viterbo, 27–30 Maggio 1982, Centro di Studi sul Teatro Medioevale e Rinasci-mentale, Viterbo 1983) 91–118.

Cassio, A.C., 'I tempi di composizione delle commedie attiche e una parafrasi di Aristofane in Galeno (Ar.Fr. 346 K.-A.)', *RFIC* 115, 1987, 5–11.

Castle, T., *Masquerade and Civilization. The Carnivalesque in Eighteenth-Century English Culture and Fiction* (Stanford 1986).

Chapman, G.A.H., 'Some Notes on Dramatic Illusion in Aristophanes', *AJP* 104, 1983, 1–23.

Charitonides, S., L. Kahil and R. Ginouvès, *Les mosaïques de la Maison du Ménandre à Mytilène* (*AntK* Beiheft 6, Basle 1970).

Chiabò, M. and F. Doglio (eds), *Mito e realtà del potere nel teatro: dall'Antichità classica al Rinascimento. Convegno di studi, Roma 29 ottobre/1 novembre 1987* (Rome 1988).

Citti, V., 'Lo scortese e la tradizione orale dei testi tragici', *Lexis* 1989, 75–7.

Clark, M.C. and E. Csapo, 'Deconstruction, Ideology, and Goldhill's *Oresteia*', *Phoenix* 45, 1991, 95–125.

Coarelli, F., 'Il complesso Pompeiano del Campo Marzio e la sua decorazione scultorea', *RendPontAcc* 44, 1972, 99–122.

Cobin, M., 'Text, Subtext, Antitext: The Relation of Verbal and Nonverbal

Communication in the Production of Shakespeare', *Maske und Kothurn* 29, 1983, 153–60.

Cohon, R., 'An Early Augustan Throne in San Pietro in Vincoli', *Boreas* 8, 1985, 92–104.

Colli, G., 'Mimesis as Performance: A Different Approach to the Concept of Imitation', *Maske und Kothurn* 33:3, 1987, 425–31.

Collinge, N.E., 'Some Reflections on Satyr-Plays', *PCPS* ns 5, 1958–59, 28–35.

Comotti, G., 'Scenografia e spettacolo: le macchine teatrali', *Dioniso* 59, 1989, 283–95.

Connor, W.R., 'Tribes, Festivals and Processions: Civic Ceremonial and Political Manipulation in Archaic Greece', *JHS* 107, 1987, 40–50.

—— 'City Dionysia and Athenian Democracy', *Classica et Mediaevalia* 40, 1989, 7–32.

Del Corno, D., 'Spazio e messa in scena nelle commedie di Menandro', *Dioniso* 59, 1989, 201–11.

Corsini, E. (ed.), *La polis e il suo teatro*, i–ii (Padua 1986–88).

Courtois, C., *Le bâtiment de scène des théâtres d'Italie et de Sicile. Étude chronologique et typologique* (Archaeologia Transatlantica VIII, Louvain-la-Neuve – Providence R.I. 1989).

Csapo, E., 'A Note on the Würzburg Bell-Crater H 5697 ("Telephus Travestitus")', *Phoenix* 40, 1986, 379–92.

—— '*Hikesia* in the *Telephus* of Aeschylus', *QUCC* 34, 1990, 41–52.

Damen, M., 'Actors and Character in Greek Tragedy', *Theatre Journal* 41, 1989, 316–40.

Darnforth, L.M., *The Death Rituals of Rural Greece* (Princeton 1982).

Davis, N.Z., *Society and Culture in Early Modern France* (Stanford 1975).

Davison, J.A., 'Literature and Literacy in Ancient Greece', *Phoenix* 16, 1962, 141–56 and 219–33.

Dedoussi, Chr., 'Fr.246 (PSI 847): An Illustrated Fragment of Menander's *Eunouchos*', *BICS* 27, 1980, 97–102.

Denniston, J.D., 'Technical Terms in Aristophanes', *CQ* 21, 1927, 113–21.

Deonna, W., 'Notes archéologiques. I. Eros jouant avec un masque de Silène', *RevArch* 1916, 74–97.

Dessen, A.C., *Elizabethan Stage Convention and Modern Interpreters* (Cambridge 1984).

Detienne, M., *The Creation of Mythology* (Chicago 1986) (= *L'invention de la mythologie*, Paris 1981).

Dihle, A., 'Seneca und die Aufführungspraxis der römischen Tragödie', *AuA* 29, 1983, 162–71.

Dillon, M., 'Topicality in Aristophanes' Ploutos', *ClAnt* 6, 1987, 155–73.

Doehle, B., 'Beziehungen zwischen Drama und attischer Vasenmalerei in der 1. Hälfte des 5. Jhdts. v.Chr. (Zur "Achilleis" des Aischylos)', *Wiss. Zeitschrift Rostock* 16, 1967, 431–5.

Dohm, H., *Mageiros* (Zetemata 32, Munich 1964).

Donadi, F., 'Opsis e lexis: per una intepretazione aristotelica del dramma', *Quaderni del circolo filologico-linguistico padavano* 8, 1976, 3–21.

Donaldson, I., *The World Upside-Down, Comedy from Jonson to Fielding* (Oxford 1970).

Dontas, G., *Eikones kathemenon pneumatikon anthropon* (Athens 1960).

Dorandi, T., 'Den Autoren über die Schülter geschaut: Arbeitsweise und Autographie bei den antiken Schriftstellern', *ZPE* 87, 1991, 11–33.

Dorjahn, A.P., 'Some Remarks on Aeschines' Career as an Actor', *CJ* 25, 1929, 223–9.

Dover, K.J., 'Portrait-Masks in Aristophanes', in *Komoidotragemata: Studia aristophanea viri aristophanei W.J.W. Koster in honorem* (Amsterdam 1967), 16–28.

———— *Aristophanic Comedy* (London 1972).

———— 'Ancient Interpolations in Aristophanes', *Illinois Classical Studies* 2, 1977, 136–62.

Duckworth, G.E., *The Nature of Roman Comedy* (Princeton 1952).

Dwyer, E.J., 'Pompeian Oscilla Collections', *RM* 88, 1981, 247–306.

Easterling, P.E., 'Tragedy and Ritual', *Métis* 3, 1988, 87–109.

Eibl-Eibesfeldt, I., *Der vorprogrammierte Mensch. Das Ererbte als bestimmender Faktor im menschlichen Verhalten* (Kiel, rev. edn 1985).

———— *Human Ethology* (New York 1989) (trans. from *Die Biologie des menschlichen Verhaltens. Grundriss der Humanethologie* (Munich 1984)).

Eire, A. López, 'Comedia politica y utopia', *Cuadernos de Investigación filológica* 10, 1984, 137–74.

Elam, K., *The Semiotics of Theatre and Drama* (London – New York 1980).

Else, G.F., *The Origin and Early Form of Greek Tragedy* (Martin Classical Lectures, 20, Cambridge Mass. 1965).

Erbe, B., 'Theatrical Codes', *Maske und Kothurn* 29, 1983, 307–10.

Erbse, H., 'Aristoteles über Tragödie und Geschichtsschreibung', in A. Lippold and N. Himmelmann (eds), *Bonner Festgabe Johannes Straub . . . dargebracht von Kollegen und Schülern* (Bonn 1977) 127–36.

Etman, A., 'The Audience of Graeco-Roman Drama between Illusion and Reality', *Anthropologie et Théâtre antique. Cahiers du GITA* 3, 1987, 261–72.

Fantham, E., 'Quintilian on Performance: Traditional and Personal Elements in *Institutio* 11.3', *Phoenix* 36, 1982, 243–63.

———— 'Roman Experience of Menander in the Late Republic and Early Empire', *TAPA* 114, 1984, 299–310.

Fantuzzi, M., 'Oralità, scrittura, auralità. Gli studi sulle techniche della communicazione nella Grecia antica (1960–1980)', *Lingua e Stile* (Milan) 15, 1980, 593–612.

De Ficoroni, F., *Le maschere sceniche e le figure comiche d'antichi romani* (Rome 1736, repr. Sala Bolognese 1978).

Fiechter, E., *Das Dionysos-Theater in Athen* (Stuttgart 1935–1950).

Figueira, T.J. and G. Nagy (eds), *Theognis of Megara: Poetry and the Polis* (Baltimore 1985).

Flickinger, R.C., *Plutarch as a Source of Information on the Greek Theater* (Chicago 1904).

———— *The Greek Theater and its Drama* (4th edn Chicago 1936).

Flory, S., 'Who read Herodotus' Histories?', *AJP* 101, 1980, 12–28.

Forrest, W.G., 'The Stage and Politics', in M. Cropp, E. Fantham and S.E. Scully (eds), *Greek Tragedy and its Legacy. Essays Presented to D.J. Conacher* (Calgary 1986) 229–39.

Fraenkel, E., *Plautinisches im Plautus* (Berlin 1922).

———— *Elementi plautini in Plauto* (Florence 1960).

Froning, H., *Dithyrambos und Vasenmalerei in Athen* (Würzburg 1971).

Frontisi-Ducroux, F., 'Idoles, figures, images', *Revue Archéologique* 1982, 18–108.

———— 'Au miroir du masque', in C. Bérard and J.-P. Vernant (eds), *La cité des images. Religion et société en Grèce antique* (Lausanne-Paris 1984) 147–161 (= 'In the Mirror of the Mask', in *A City of Images. Iconography and Society in Ancient Greece*, Princeton 1989, 151–165).

———— 'Face et profil: les deux masques', in C. Bérard, C. Bon and A. Pomari (eds), *Images et société en Grèce ancienne. L'iconographie comme méthode d'analyse* (Actes du Colloque int., Lausanne 8–11 février 1984. Cahiers d'archéologie romande, no. 36, Lausanne 1987) 89–102.

—— 'Prosopon, le masque et le visage', in P. Ghiron-Bistagne (ed.), *Anthropologie et Théâtre antique. Cahiers du GITA* 1987, 383–92.

—— and J.-P. Vernant, 'Figures de masques en Grèce ancienne', *Journal de psychologie* 80, 1983, 53–69.

—— 'Divinités au masque dans la Grèce ancienne', in O. Aslan and D. Bablet (eds), *Le masque. Du rite au théâtre* (Paris 1985) 19–26.

Fuchs, M., *Untersuchungen zur Ausstattung römischer Theater* (Mainz 1987).

Gallo, I., *Teatro ellenistico minore* (Rome 1981).

Gallo, L., 'La capienza dei teatri e il calcolo della popolazione. Il caso di Atene', in I. Gallo (ed.), *Studi salernitani in memoria di R. Cantarella* (Salerno 1981) 271–89.

Garzya, A., 'Sulla questione delle interpolazioni degli attori nei testi tragici', *Vichiana* 9, 1980, 3–20.

—— 'Gorgia e l'apate della tragedia', in *Filologia e forme letterarie. Studi offerte a F. Della Corte*, i (Urbino 1988) 245–60.

Gebhard, E., 'The Form of the Orchestra in the Early Greek Theater', *Hesperia* 43, 1974, 428–40.

—— 'Rulers' Use of Theaters in the Greek and Roman World', *Praktika XII Diethn. Synedriou* (Athens 1988) 65–9.

Gellie, G.H., *Sophocles. A Reading* (Melbourne 1972).

Gentili, B., *Theatrical Performances in the Ancient World: Hellenistic and Early Roman Theatre* (London 1979).

—— 'Tragedia e communicazione', *Dioniso* 54, 1983, 227–40.

—— *Poetry and its Public in Ancient Greece from Homer to the Fifth Century* (Baltimore 1988).

—— and R. Pretagostini (eds), *La musica in Grecia* (Rome–Bari 1988).

George, D., 'On Ambiguity: Towards a Post-Modern Performance Theory', *Theatre Research International* 14, 1989, 71–85.

von Gerkan, A., *Das Theater von Priene* (Munich 1921).

—— and W. Müller-Wiener, *Das Theater von Epidauros* (Stuttgart 1961).

Ghiron-Bistagne, P., *Recherches sur les acteurs dans la Grèce antique* (Paris 1976).

Giannini, A., 'La figura del cuoco nella commedia greca', *Acme* 13, 1960, 135–216.

Giglioni, G. Bodei, *Menandro o la politica della convivenza. La storia attraverso i testi letterari* (Como 1984).

Gill, C., 'The Question of Character and Personality in Greek Tragedy', *Poetics Today* 7:2, 1986, 251–73.

Gluckmann, M. (ed.), *Essays on the Ritual of Social Relations* (Manchester 1962).

Goldhill, S., 'The Great Dionysia and Civic Ideology', in J.J. Winkler and F.I. Zeitlin (eds), *Nothing to Do with Dionysos? Athenian Drama in Its Social Context* (Princeton 1989) 97–129.

—— 'Reading Performance Criticism', *G&R* 36, 1989, 172–82.

Gombrich, E., *Art and Illusion* (London 1960).

—— 'The Mask and the Face. The Perception of Physiognomic Likeness in Life and in Art,' in M. Mandelbaum (ed.) *Art, Perception & Reality* (Baltimore 1972) 1–46.

Gomme, A.W. and F.H. Sandbach, *Menander. A Commentary* (Oxford 1973).

Goody, J., 'Literacy and Achievement in the Ancient World', in F. Coulmas and K. Ehlich (eds), *Writing in Focus* (Berlin–Amsterdam–New York, 1983) (Trends in Linguistics. Studies and Monographs, 24) 83–98.

—— *The Interface between the Written and the Oral* (Cambridge 1987).

—— and I. Watt, 'The Consequences of Literacy', in J. Goody (ed.), *Literacy in Traditional Societies* (Cambridge 1968) 27–68.

Gould, J., 'Greek Tragedy in Performance', *CambHistClassLit* i, (1985) 263–81.
Gredley, B., 'Greek Tragedy and the "Discovery" of the Actor', in J. Redmond (ed.), *Drama and the Actor* (Themes in Drama, 6) (Cambridge 1984) 1–14.
Green, J.R., 'Additions to *Monuments Illustrating Old and Middle Comedy*', *Bulletin of the Institute of Classical Studies* 27, 1980, 123–31.
—— 'Dedications of Masks', *RevArch* 1982, 237–48.
—— 'Drunk Again. A Study in the Iconography of the Comic Theatre', *AJA* 89, 1985, 465–72.
—— 'A Representation of the *Birds* of Aristophanes', *GVGetty* 2 (Malibu 1985) 95–118.
—— 'The Beaulieu Painter and Provincial Apulia at the End of the Fourth Century B.C.', in *Studien zur Mythologie und Veasenmalerei. Festschrift Konrad Schauenburg* (Mainz 1986) 181–6.
—— 'Greek Theatre Production, 1971–1986', *Lustrum* 31, 1989, 7–95 and 273–8.
—— 'Motif-Symbolism and Gnathia Vases', in H.-U. Cain, H. Gabelmann and D. Salzmann (eds), *Beiträge zur Ikonographie und Hermeneutik. Festschrift für N. Himmelmann-Wildschütz* (Mainz 1989) 221–6.
—— 'Carcinus and the Temple: a Lesson in the Staging of Tragedy', *GRBS* 31, 1990, 281–5.
—— 'Théâtre et société dans le monde hellénistique. Changement d'image, changement de rôles', in *Realia. Mélanges sur les réalités du théâtre antique. Cahiers du Groupe Interdisciplinaire du Théâtre Antique* 6, 1990/1991, 31–49.
—— 'On Seeing and Depicting the Theatre in Classical Athens', *GRBS* 32, 1991, 15–50.
—— 'Notes on Phlyax Vases', *NumActCl* 20, 1991, 49–56.
—— 'Theatre', *Cambridge Ancient History. Plates to Volumes V–VI* (forthcoming).
Di Gregorio, L., 'Plutarcho e la tragedia greca', *Prometheus* 2, 1976, 151–74.
—— 'Gellio e il teatro', *Aevum Antiquum* 1, 1988, 95–147.
Gregory, J., *Euripides and the Instruction of the Athenians* (Ann Arbor 1991).
Grimm, G., 'Orient und Okzident in der Kunst Alexandriens', in *Alexandrien. Kulturbegegnungen dreier Jahrtausende im Schmeltztiegel einer mediterranen Großstadt* (Mainz 1981) 13–25.
Gros, P., 'La fonction symbolique des édifices théâtraux dans le paysage urbain de la Rome augustéenne', in *L'Urbs, espace urbain et histoire. Actes du colloque ... l'École française de Rome, 8–12 mai 1985* (Coll. de l'École fr. no. 98, Rome 1987), 319–46.
—— 'Un programme augustéen. Le centre monumental de la colonie d'Arles', *JdI* 102, 1987, 339–63.
Guardi, T., 'L'attività teatrale nella Siracusa di Gerone I', *Dioniso* 51, 1980, 25–48.
Hadermann-Misguisch, L., 'L'image antique, byzantine et moderne du putto au masque', *Rayonnement Grec. Hommages à Charles Delvoye* (Brussels 1982) 513–52.
Hall, E., *Inventing the Barbarian. Greek Self-Definition through Tragedy* (Oxford 1989).
Halleran, M., *Stagecraft in Euripides* (London 1984).
Halliwell, S., *Aristotle's Poetics* (London 1986).
Hamilton, R., 'Objective Evidence for Actors' Interpolations in Greek Tragedy', *GRBS* 15, 1974, 387–402.
Handley, E.W., *The Dyskolos of Menander* (London 1965).
—— *Menander and Plautus: A Study in Comparison* (London 1968).
—— 'The Conventions of the Comic Stage and their Exploitation by Menander', in *EntrHardt* xvi, 1970, 1–42.
—— 'The Poet Inspired?', *JHS* 93, 1973, 104–8.
—— 'Plautus and his Public: Some Thoughts on New Comedy in Latin', *Dioniso* 46, 1975, 117–32.

—— 'Comedy. From Aristophanes to Menander', *CambHistClassLit* i (1985) 398–414.

—— 'A Particle of Greek Comedy', in *Studies Webster* ii, 107–10.

—— 'Aristophanes and his Theatre', in J.M. Bremer and E.W. Handley (eds), *Aristophane* (*Entr. Hardt* xxxviii, Vandœuvres–Geneva 1993) 97–123.

—— and A. Hurst (eds), *Relire Ménandre* (Geneva 1990).

Harris, W.V., *Ancient Literacy* (Cambridge, Mass., 1989).

Harvey, F.D., 'Literacy in the Athenian Democracy', *REG* 79, 1966, 585–635.

Havelock, E., 'The Oral Composition of Greek Drama', *QUCC* 35, 1980, 61–113.

—— *The Literate Revolution in Greece and its Cultural Consequences* (Princeton 1982).

Heath, M., *Political Comedy in Aristophanes* (*Hypomnemata* 87, Göttingen 1987).

—— *The Poetics of Greek Tragedy* (Stanford 1987).

—— 'Aristotelian Comedy', *CQ* 39, 1989, 344–54.

—— 'Aristophanes and his Rivals', *G&R* 37, 1990, 143–58.

Hedreen, G.M., *Silens in Attic Black-figure Vase-painting: Myth and Performance* (Ann Arbor 1992).

Heilmeyer, W.D., 'Vom modernen Mißverständnis antiker Theaterbauten', *AWelt* 18, 1987, 22–8.

Henderson, J., 'Women and the Athenian Dramatic Festivals', *TAPA* 121, 1991, 133–47.

Herrington, J., *Poetry into Drama. Early Tragedy and the Greek Poetic Tradition* (Sather Classical Lectures, 49, Berkeley 1985).

von Hesberg, H., 'Temporäre Bilder oder die Grenzen der Kunst. Zur Legitimation frühhellenistischer Königsherrschaft im Fest', *JdI* 104, 1989, 61–82.

Hill, D.K., 'Bacchic Erotes at Tarentum', *Hesperia* 16, 1947, 248–55.

Hölscher, T., *Römische Bildsprache als semantisches System* (Abh. Heidelberg 1987).

Honzl, J., 'The Hierarchy of Dramatic Devices', in L. Matejka and I.R. Titunik (eds), *Semiotics of Art. Prague School Contributions* (Cambridge, Mass., 1976) 118–27.

Hourmouziades, N., *Production and Imagination in Euripides. Form and Function of the Scenic Space* (Athens 1965).

Huddilston, J.H., *Greek Tragedy in the Light of Vase-Paintings* (London 1898).

Hughes, A., 'Acting Styles in the Ancient World', *Theatre Notebook* 45, 1991, 2–16.

Hülsemann, M., 'Theater, Kult und bürgerliche Widerstand. Die Entstehung der architektonischen Struktur des römischen Theaters in Rahmen der gesellschaftlichen Auseinandersetzungen zur Zeit der Republik', *Hephaistos* 7–8, 1985–86, 215–32.

—— *Theater, Kult und bürgerliche Widerstand im antiken Rom. Die Entstehung der architektonischen Struktur des römischen Theaters* (Frankfurt 1987).

Hundsalz, B., *Das dionysische Schmuckrelief* (Munich 1987).

Hunter, R.L., *The New Comedy of Greece and Rome* (Cambridge 1985).

Hurst, A., 'Ménandre et la tragédie', in E.W. Handley and A. Hurst (eds), *Relire Ménandre* (Geneva 1990).

Immerwahr, H.R., 'Book Rolls on Attic Vases', in *Classical, Medieval, and Renaissance Studies in Honor of B.L. Ullman*, i (*Storia e Letteratura* 93, 1964) 17–48.

—— 'More Book Rolls on Attic Vases', *AntK* 16, 1973, 143–7.

Jahn, O., 'Perseus, Herakles, Satyrn auf vasenbildern und das satyrdrama', *Philologus* 27, 1868, 1–27.

Jauss, H.R., *Towards an Aesthetic of Reception* (Minneapolis 1982).

Jenkins, I., 'Is There Life after Marriage?', *BICS* 30, 1983, 137–46.

Johne, R., 'Zur Entstehung einer "Buchkultur" in der zweiten Hälfte des 5. Jahrhunderts v.u.Z.', *Philologus* 135, 1991, 45–54.

Johnson, J.A., 'Sophocles' *Philoctetes* : Deictic Language and the Claims of Odysseus',

Eranos 86, 1988, 117–21.

Jones, C.P., *Culture and Society in Lucian* (London 1986).

―――― 'Dinner Theater', in W.J. Slater (ed.), *Dining in a Classical Context* (Ann Arbor 1991) 185–98.

Jones, F.F., *The Theater in Ancient Art* (Princeton 1951).

Jones, J., *On Aristotle and Greek Tragedy* (Oxford 1962).

Jones, L.W. and C.R. Morey, *The Miniatures of the Manuscripts of Terence* (Princeton 1931).

Jory, E.J., 'Associations of Actors in Rome', *Hermes* 98, 1970, 224–53.

―――― 'Continuity and Change in the Roman Theatre', in *Studies Webster* i, 143–52.

―――― 'Publilius Syrus and the Element of Competition in the Theatre of the Republic', in *Vir Bonus Discendi Peritus. Studies . . . O. Skutsch* (*BICS* Suppl. 51, 1988) 73–81.

Jouan, F., 'L'évocation des morts dans la tragédie grecque', *RHR* 98 (1981) 403–21.

―――― 'Réflexions sur le rôle du protagoniste tragique', in *Théâtres et spectacles dans l'antiquité. Actes du colloque de Strasburg, 5–7 novembre 1981* (Leiden 1983) 63–80.

Jouvet, L., *Témoignages sur le théâtre* (Paris 1952).

De Juliis E.M. and D. Loiacono, *Taranto. Il Museo Archeologico* (Taranto 1985).

Jürgens, H., *Pompa Diaboli. Die lateinischen Kirchenväter und das antike Theater* (Stuttgart 1972).

Kaimio, M., *Physical Contact in Greek Tragedy. A Study of Stage Conventions* (*Annales Academiæ Scientiarum Fennicæ*, Ser. B, 244, Helsinki 1988).

Katsouris, A.G., 'The Staging of Palaiai Tragodiai in Relation to Menander's Audience', *Dodone* 3, 1974, 173–204.

―――― *Tragic Patterns in Menander* (Athens 1975).

Kelly, H.A., 'Tragedy and the Performance of Tragedy in Late Roman Antiquity', *Traditio* 35, 1979, 21–44.

Kenner, H., *Das Theater und der Realismus in der griechischen Kunst* (Vienna 1954).

―――― 'Zur Archäologie des Dionysostheaters in Athen', *JhOAI* 57, 1986–87, Hauptblatt 55–91.

de Kerckhove, D., 'A Theory of Greek Tragedy', *Sub-Stance* 29, 1981, 23–36.

Kindermann, H., *Das Theaterpublikum der Antike* (Salzburg 1979).

Kitto, H.D.F., 'Aristotle and Fourth Century Tragedy', in M. Kelly (ed.), *For Service to Classical Studies. Essays in Honour of Francis Letters* (Melbourne 1966) 113–129.

Kleiner, G., *Tanagrafiguren: Untersuchungen zur hellenistischen Kunst und Geschichte* (new edn, rev. K. Parlasca, Berlin–New York, 1984).

Knox, B., *Word and Action. Essays on the Ancient Theatre* (Baltimore 1979).

―――― 'Sophocles and the Polis', in *Sophocle: Entretiens sur l'Antiquité Classique* xxix (Vandœuvres–Geneva 1983) 1–27.

Kokolakis, M., *The Dramatic Simile Of Life* (Athens 1960).

―――― *Lucian and the Tragic Performances in his Time* (Athens 1961) (= *Platon* 23/24, 67–109).

Kolb, F., 'Polis und Theater', in G.A. Seeck (ed.), *Das Griechische Drama* (Darmstadt 1979) 504–45.

―――― *Agora und Theater. Volks- und Festversammlung* (Berlin 1980).

―――― 'Theaterpublikum, Volksversammlung und Gesellschaft in der griechischen Welt', *Dioniso* 59, 1989, 345–51.

Korshak, Y., 'Frontal Faces in Attic Vase Painting of the Archaic Period', *AncW* 10, 1984, 89–105.

―――― *Frontal Faces in Attic Vase Painting of the Archaic Period* (Chicago 1987).

Kossatz-Deißmann, A., *Dramen des Aischylos auf westgriechischen Vasen* (Mainz 1978).

―――― 'Telephos travestitus', in H.A. Cahn and E. Simon (eds), *Taenia. Festschrift*

Roland Hampe (Mainz 1980) 281–90.

—— 'Satyr- und Mänadennamen auf Vasenbildern des Getty-Museums und der Sammlung Cahn (Basel) mit Addenda zu Charlotte Fränkel, *Satyr- und Bakchennamen auf Vasenbildern* (Halle 1912)', *GVGetty* 5 (Malibu 1991) 131–99.

Krauskopf, I., 'Edipo nell'arte antica', in B. Gentili and R. Pretagostini (eds), *Edipo. Il teatro greco e la cultura europea* (Atti del Convegno Internazionale, Urbino 15–19 novembre 1982, Rome 1986) 327–441.

Krien, G., 'Der Ausdruck der antiken Theatermasken nach angaben im Polluxkatalog und in der pseudoaristotelischen "Physiognomik"', *JhOAI* 42, 1955, 84–117.

Kuch, H., (ed.) *Die Griechische Tragödie in ihrer gesellschaftlichen Funktion* (Berlin 1983).

—— 'Formes de la communication dans le drame grec', *Anthropologie et Théâtre antique. Cahiers du GITA* 3, 1987, 251–60.

—— 'Towards Function and Communication of Greek Drama', *Sileno* 15, 1989, 57–67.

—— 'Funktionswandel in der greichischen Tragödie', *Philologus* 135, 1991, 105–15.

Landes, Chr., *Le goût du théâtre à Rome et en Gaule romaine* (Lattes 1989).

—— (ed.), *Spectacula II. Le théâtre antique et ses spectacles* (Lattes 1992).

Lanza, D., 'L'attore', in M. Vegetti (ed.), *Oralità scrittura spettacolo* (Turin 1983) 127–39.

—— 'Le comédien face à l'écrit', in M. Detienne (ed.), *Les savoirs de l'écriture en Grèce ancienne* (Lille 1988) 359–84.

—— 'L'attor comico sulla scena', *Dioniso* 59:2, 1989, 345–51.

—— 'Lo spazio scenico del'attor comico', in L. de Finis (ed.), *Scena e spettacolo nell'antichità. Atti del Convegno Internazionale di Studio, Trento, 28–30 marzo 1988* (Florence 1989) 179–92.

—— 'Glaubwürdigkeit auf der Bühne als gesellschaftliches Problem', *Philologus* 135, 1991, 97–104.

Lauter, H., 'Die hellenistischen Theater der Samniten und Latiner in ihrer Beziehung zur Theaterarchitektur der Griechen', in *Hellenismus in Mittelitalien* (Abh. der Akademie der Wissenschaften in Göttingen 97, 1976), 413–30.

Lefkowitz, M.R., *The Lives of the Greek Poets* (Baltimore 1981).

—— 'Aristophanes and Other Historians of the Fifth-Century Theater', *Hermes* 112, 1984, 143–53.

Leiwo, M., 'Why Velia survived through the Second Century B.C. Remarks on her Economic Connections with Delos', *Athenaeum* 63, 1985, 494–8.

Lévi-Strauss, C., *La voie des masques* (Geneva 1975) (= *Way of the Masks*, London–Seattle 1982).

De Ligt, L. and P.W. De Neeve, 'Ancient Periodic Markets: Festivals and Fairs', *Athenaeum* 66, 1988, 417–26.

Lissarrague, F., 'Pourquoi les satyres sont-ils bons à montrer?', *Anthropologie et Théâtre antique. Cahiers du GITA* 3, 1987) 93–106 (= 'Why Satyrs are Good to Represent', in J.J. Winkler and F.I. Zeitlin (eds), *Nothing to Do with Dionysis? Athenian Drama in Its Social Context* (Princeton 1989) 228–36).

Longo, O., 'Teatri e Theatra. Spazi teatrali e luoghi politici nella città greca', *Dioniso* 58, 1988, 7–33.

—— 'Atene: il teatro e la città', in M. Chiabò and F. Doglio (eds), *Mito e realtà del potere nel teatro: dall'Antichità classica al Rinascimento. Convegno di studi, Roma 20 Ottobre/1 Novembre 1987* (Rome 1988) 17–31.

—— 'La scena della città. Strutture architettoniche e spazi politici nel teatro greco', in L. de Finis (ed.), *Scena e spettacolo nell'antichità. Atti del Convegno Internationale di Studio, Trento, 28–30 marzo 1988* (Florence 1989) 23–41.

216

——— 'The Theater of the Polis', in J.J. Winkler and F.I. Zeitlin (eds), *Nothing to Do with Dionysos? Athenian Drama in Its Social Context* (Princeton 1989) 12–19.

Luppe, W., 'Ein übersehener Hinweis auf die Fünf-Zahl der Konkurrenten bei den Komiker-Agonen zur Zeit des Peloponnesischen Krieges?', *Nikephoros* 1, 1988, 185–9.

——— 'Zu den Plazierungsangaben in den Aristophanes-Didaskalien', *ZPE* 77, 1989, 18–20.

——— 'Zum Prolog der "Melanippe Sophe"', *WürzJbAltWiss* 15, 1989, 83–95.

Maaß, M., *Die Prohedrie des Dionysostheaters in Athen* (Munich 1972).

MacDowell, D.M., 'Athenian Laws about Choruses', in *Symposion 1982. Vorträge zur griechischen und hellenistischen Rechtgeschichte (Santander, 1.–4. September 1982)* (Cologne 1989) 65–77.

Maiuri, A., *La Casa del Menandro e il suo tesoro di argenteria*, i–ii (Rome 1932).

Malhadas, D., 'La rencontre d'Oreste et d'Electre. Espace et mise en scène', *Dioniso* 59, 1989, 361–3.

Manton, G.R., 'Identification of Speakers in Greek Drama', *Antichthon* 16, 1982, 1–16.

Martin, R.P., *The Language of Heroes: Speech and Performance in the Iliad* (Ithaca–London 1985).

Marzullo, B., 'Lo "spazio scenico" in Aristofane', *Dioniso* 59:2, 1989, 187–200.

Mastronarde, D.J., 'Actors on High: The Skene Roof, the Crane, and the Gods in Attic Drama', *ClAnt* 9:2, 1990, 247–94.

Meier, Chr., *Die politische Kunst der griechischen Tragödie* (Munich 1988).

——— 'Politik und Tragödie in 5. Jahrhundert', *Philologus* 135, 1991, 70–87.

Melchinger, S., *Das Theater der Tragödie. Aischylos, Sophokles, Euripides auf der Bühnen ihrer Zeit* (Munich 1975).

Melero, A., 'Origen, forma y función del drama satírico griego', in J.L. Melena (ed.), *Symbolae Ludovico Mitxelena septuagenario oblatae* (Vitoria 1985) 167–78.

Mertens, D., 'Metaponto: Il teatro-ekklesiasterion, I', *BdA* 67:16, 1982, 1–57.

Mette, H.J., *Der verlorene Aischylos* (Berlin 1963).

——— *Urkunden dramatischer Aufführungen in Griechenland* (Berlin 1977).

Metzger, H., *Les représentations dans la céramique attique du IVe siècle* (BEFAR fasc. 172, Paris 1951).

——— *Recherches sur l'imagerie athénienne* (Paris 1965).

Milbradt, J., 'Das Publikum der römischen Komödie', in J. Hermann and J. Sellnow (eds), *Die Rolle des Volksmassen in der Geschichte ver vorkapitalistischen Gesellschaftsformationen* (Berlin 1975) 287–92.

Mitchell, S., 'Festivals, Games, and Civic Life in Roman Asia Minor', *JRS* 80, 1990, 183–93.

Mitens, K., *Teatri greci e teatri ispirati all'architettura greca in Sicilia e nell'Italia meridionale, c. 350–50 a.C. Un catalogo* (*AnalRomInstDan* Suppl. 13) (Rome 1988).

Momigliano, A.D., (ed.), *The Conflict between Paganism and Christianity in the Fourth Century* (Oxford 1963).

——— *Alien Wisdom: The Limits of Hellenization* (Cambridge 1975).

Morel, J.-P., 'Céramiques d'Italie et céramiques hellénistiques (150–30 av. J.-C.)', *Hellenismus in Mittelitalien* (*Abh. der Akademie der Wissenschaften in Göttingen*, no. 97, 1976) 471–501.

——— 'Céramiques à vernis noir d'Italie trouvées à Délos', *BCH* 110, 1986, 461–93.

Moret, J.-M., *L'Ilioupersis dans la céramique italiote* (Rome 1975) (Bibl. Helvetica Rom., xiv).

——— *Oedipe, la Sphinx et les Thébains. Essai de mythologie iconographique* (Rome 1984) (Bibl.Helvetica Rom., xxiii).

Moretti, J.-Ch., 'L'Architecture des théâtres en Grèce (1980–1989)', *Topoi* 1, 1991, 7–38.

——— 'L'Architecture des théâtres en Asie Mineure (1980–1989)', *Topoi* 2, 1992, 9–32.

Moretti, L., 'Sulle didascalie del teatro attico rinvenute a Roma', *Athenaeum* 38, 1960, 263–82.

Muecke, F., 'Playing with the Play. Theatrical Self-Consciousness in Aristophanes', *Antichthon* 11, 1977, 52–67.

——— ' "I Know You by Your Rags". Costume and Disguise in Fifth Century Drama', *Antichthon* 16, 1982, 35–43.

——— 'Plautus and the Theater of Disguise', *ClAnt* 5, 1986, 216–29.

Mueller, A., *Das attische Bühnenwesen* (2nd edn, Gütersloh 1916).

Mullen, W., *Choreia: Pindar and Dance* (Princeton 1982).

Müller, C.A., *Zur Datierung des sophokleischen Oedipus* (*AbhMainz* 1984 no. 5).

Nagy, G., *Greek Mythology and Poetics* (Ithaca–London 1990).

Nellhaus, T., 'Literacy, Tyranny, and the Invention of Greek Drama', *Journal of Dramatic Theory and Criticism* 111, 1989, 53–71.

Nesselrath H.-G., *Die attische Mittlere Komödie. Ihre Stellung in der antiken Literaturkritik und Literaturgeschichte* (Berlin 1990).

Neumann, G., *Gesten und Gebärden in der griechischen Kunst* (Berlin 1965).

Newiger, H.-J., 'Zwei Bemerkungen zur Spielstätte des attischen Dramas im 5. Jh.v.Chr.', *WS* 89(10), 1976, 80–92.

——— 'Die Orestie und das Theater', *Dioniso* 48, 1977, 319–40.

——— 'Drama und Theater', in G.A. Seeck (ed.), *Das griechische Drama* (Darmstadt 1979) 434–503.

——— 'Ekkyklema e mechané nella messa in scena del dramma greco', *Dioniso* 59, 1989, 173–185 (= 'Ekkyklema und Mechané in der Inszenierung des griechischen Dramas', *WürzJbAltWiss* 16, 1990, 33–42).

Nieddu, G.F., 'Alfabetismo e diffusione sociale della scrittura nella Grecia arcaica e classica: pregiudizi recenti e realtà documentaria', *Scrittura e Civiltà* 6, 1982, 233–61.

——— 'Testo, scrittura, libro nella Grecia arcaica e classica: note e osservazioni sulla prosa scientico-filosofica', *Scrittura e Civiltà* 8, 1984, 213–61.

Novellone, A., 'Il valore contenutistico delle rappresentazioni vascolari di miti', *PdP* 26, 1971, 205–20.

O'Connor, J.B., *Chapters in the History of Actors and Acting in Ancient Greece* (Chicago 1908).

O'Donnell, J., 'The Demise of Paganism', *Traditio* 35, 1979, 45–88.

Oakley, J.H., 'Athamas, Ino, Hermes and the Infant Dionysos: a Hydria by Hermonax', *AntK* 25, 1982, 44–7.

——— 'Danae and Perseus on Seriphos', *AJA* 86, 1982, 111–15.

——— *The Phiale Painter* (Mainz 1990).

——— 'Zwei alte Vasen – zwei neue Danaebilder', *AA* 1990, 65–70.

——— ' "The Death of Hippolytus" in South Italian Vase-Painting', *NumActCl* 20, 1991, 63–83.

Ober, J. and B. Strauss, 'Political Rhetoric, and the Discourse of Athenian Democracy', in J.J. Winkler and F.I. Zeitlin (eds), *Nothing to Do with Dionysos? Athenian Drama in Its Social Context* (Princeton 1989) 237–70.

Oslon, S.D., 'Economics and Ideology in Aristophanes' *Wealth*', *HSCP* 93, 1990, 223–42.

Ong, W.J., *Orality and Literacy* (London and New York, 1982).

——— 'Writing is a Technology that Restructures Thought', in G. Baumann (ed.),

The Written Word. Literacy in Transition (Oxford 1986) 23–50.

Paganelli, L., 'Il dramma satiresco. Spazio, tematiche e messa in scena', *Dioniso* 59:2, 1989, 213–82.

Page, D.L., *Actors' Interpolations in Greek Tragedy* (Oxford 1934).

Pailler, J.-M., 'Attis, Polyphème et le thiase bacchique: quelques représentations méconnues', *MEFRA* 83, 1971, 127–39.

—— 'Les oscilla retrouvés. Du recueil des documents à une théorie d'ensemble', *MEFRA* 94, 1982, 743–822.

Parassoglou, G.M., 'Dexia cheir kai gonu. Some Thoughts on the Postures of the Greeks and Romans when Writing on Papyrus Rolls', *Scrittura e Civiltà* 3 (1979) 5–21.

—— 'A Roll upon his Knees', *YCS* 28, 1985, 273–5.

Paribeni, E., 'Il teatro e le arti figurative nel mondo ellenico del V secolo', *Prometheus* 7, 1981, 73–81.

Patzer, H., *Die Anfänge der griechischen Tragödie* (Wiesbaden 1962).

Pavis, P., *Dictionnaire du théâtre – Termes et concepts de l'analyse théâtrale* (Paris 1980).

—— *Languages of the Stage. Essays in the Semiology of the Theatre* (New York 1982).

—— *Voix et images de la scène. Essais de sémiologie théâtrale* (Lille 1982).

Pavlovskis, Z., 'The Voice of the Actor in Greek Tragedy', *CW* 71, 1977, 113–23.

Pernice, E. and F. Winter, *Der Hildesheimer Silberfund* (Berlin 1901).

Petersen, E., *Die attische Tragödie als Bild- und Bühnenkunst* (Bonn 1915).

Pfister, M., *The Theory and Analysis of Drama* (Cambridge 1988).

Philadelpheus, A., *Pelina eidolia ek Myrines* (Athens 1928).

Pickard-Cambridge, A.W., *The Theatre of Dionysus in Athens* (Oxford 1946).

—— *Dithyramb, Tragedy and Comedy* (2nd edn, rev. by T.B.L. Webster, Oxford 1962).

—— *The Dramatic Festivals of Athens* (2nd edn by J. Gould and D.M. Lewis, 1968, reissued with supplement and corrections, Oxford 1988).

Pociña, A., 'Los historiadores imperiales y el teatro latino', *Hispania Antiqua* 11–12, 1981–85, 127–81.

Podlecki, A.J., 'Could Women Attend the Theater in Ancient Athens? A Collection of Testimonia', *AncW* 21, 1990, 27–43.

Polacco, L., 'La fronte di retroscena del teatro di Epidauro', *NumAntCl* 7, 1978, 83–93.

—— 'Ancora sulle porticus eumenicae', *AttiVenezia* 137, 1978–79, 719–24.

—— 'La posizione del teatro di Siracusa nel quadro dell'architettura teatrale ...', *Aparchai Arias*, (Pisa 1982) 431–44.

—— 'Théâtre, société, organisation de l'état', in *Théâtres et spectacles dans l'antiquité. Actes du colloque de Strasbourg, 5–7 novembre 1981* (Leiden 1983) 5–15.

—— 'L'evoluzione del teatro greco comico nel IV secolo a.C.', *Dioniso* 57, 1987, 267–79.

—— 'Il teatro greco come arte della visione: scenografia e prospettiva', *Dioniso* 59, 1989, 137–71.

—— *Il teatro di Dioniso Eleutereo ad Atene* (Rome 1990).

—— and C. Anti, *Il teatro antico di Siracusa* (Rimini 1981).

Pöhlmann, E., 'Die Proedrie des Dionysostheaters im 5.Jhdt. und das Bühnenspiel der Klassik', *MusHelv* 38, 1981, 129–46.

—— 'Bühne und Handlung im Aias des Sophokles', *AuA* 32, 1986, 20–32.

—— 'Die Funktion des Chors in der Neuen Komödie', in E. Pöhlmann (ed.), *Beiträge zur antiken und neueren Musikgeschichte* (Frankfurt 1988) 41–55.

—— 'Sulla preistoria della tradizione di testi e musica per il teatro', in B. Gentili and R. Pretagostini (eds), *La musica in Grecia* (Rome–Bari 1988) 132–144 (= 'Zur

Frühgeschichte der Überlieferung griechischer Bühnendichtung und Bühnenmusik', in E Pöhlmann (ed.), *Beiträge zur antiken und neueren Musikgeschichte* (Frankfurt 1988) 55–66.

—— 'Scene di ricerca e di inseguimento nel teatro attico del quinto e quarto secolo. (La tecnica teatrale delle 'Eumenidi', dell' 'Aiace', degli 'Acarnesi' e del 'Reso')', in L. de Finis (ed.), *Scena e spettacolo nell'antichità. Atti del Convegno Internazionale di Studio, Trento, 28–30 marzo 1988* (Florence 1989) 89–109 (= 'Sucheszenen auf der attischen Bühnen des 5. und 4. Jhs. Zur Bühnentechnik der Eumenides, des Aias, der Acharner und des Rhesos', in W. Dahlheim *et al.* (eds), *Festschrift Robert Werner* (*Xenia* 22, Konstanz 1989) 41–58).

Pollit, J.J., 'The Impact of Greek Art on Rome', *TAPA* 108, 1978, 155–74.

—— *Art in the Hellenistic Age* (Cambridge 1986).

Prag, A.J.N.W., *The Oresteia: Iconographic and Narrative Tradition* (Warminster 1985).

Privitera, G.A., 'Il ditirambo come spettacolo musicale. Il ruolo di Archiloco e di Erione', in B. Gentili and R. Pretagostini (eds), *La musica in Grecia* (Rome–Bari 1988) 123–31.

—— 'Origini della tragedia e ruolo del ditirambo', *SIFC* 84, 1991, 184–95.

Rawson, E., 'Theatrical Life in Republican Rome and Italy', *BSR* 53, 1985, 97–113.

Redfield, J., 'Drama and Community: Aristophanes and Some of his Rivals', in J.J. Winkler and F.I. Zeitlin (eds), *Nothing to Do with Dionysos? Athenian Drama in Its Social Context* (Princeton 1989) 314–35.

Reggiani, A.M., 'Ipotesi di recupero del Teatro di Pompeio', in *Roma. Archeologia nel centro* 2 (Rome 1985) 369–74.

Rehm, R., *Greek Tragic Theatre* (London 1992).

Rice, E.E., *The Grand Procession of Ptolemy Philadelphus* (Oxford 1983).

Ricotti, E. Salza Prina, 'Le tende conviviali e la tenda di Tolomeo Filadelfo', in R.I. Curtis (ed.), *Studia pompeiana et classica in Honor of Wilhelmina F. Jashemski* (New Rochelle 1989) ii, 199–239.

Robert, C., *Bild und Lied. Archäologische Beiträge zur Geschichte der griechischen Heldensage* (Philologische Untersuchungen v, Berlin 1881).

—— *Die Masken der neueren attischen Komödie* (25. Hallische WPr, Halle 1911).

Rosa, F., 'Le voci dell'oratore. Oratoria e spettacolo nell'excursus quintilianeo 'De Pronuntiatione'', in L. de Finis (ed.) *Scena e spettacolo nell'antichità. Atti del Convegno Internazionale di Studio, Trento, 28–30 marzo 1988* (Florence 1989) 253–68.

Rösler, W., *Polis und Tragödie. Funktionsgeschichtliche Betracthungen zu einer antiken Literaturgattung* (Konstanz 1980).

Rossetto, P. Ciancio, 'Le maschere del teatro di Marcello', *BullComm* 88, 1982–83 [1984], 7–49.

—— 'Le maschere del teatro di Marcello a Roma', in Chr. Landes (ed.), *Spectacula II. Le théâtre antique et ses spectacles* (Lattes 1992) 187–91.

Rossi, L.E., 'Il dramma satiresco attico: forma, fortuna e funzione di un genere letterario antico', *D'Arch* 6, 1972, 248–302.

—— 'Livelli di lingua, gestualità, rapporti di spazio e situazione drammatica sulla scena attica', in L. de Finis (ed.), *Scena e spettacolo nell'antichità. Atti del Convegno Internazionale di Studio, Trento, 28–30 marzo 1988* (Florence 1989) 63–78.

Rossi, P., *La memoria del sapere. Forme di conservazione e strutture organizzative dall'antichità a oggi* (Rome–Bari 1988).

Rotroff, S.I., *The Athenian Agora xxii. Hellenistic Pottery, Athenian and Imported Moldmade Bowls* (Princeton 1982).

—— 'Silver, Glass and Clay. Evidence for the Dating of Hellenistic Luxury Tableware', *Hesperia* 51, 1982, 329–37.

Ruppel, A., *Konzeption und Ausarbeitung der Aristophanischen Komödien* (Darmstadt 1913).

Russell, D.A., *Criticism in Antiquity* (London 1981).

—— and M. Winterbottom (eds), *Ancient Literary Criticism: The Principal Texts in New Translations* (Oxford 1972).

Said, S., 'L'espace d' Euripide', *Dioniso* 59:2, 1989, 107–36.

Sallmann, K., 'Christen vor dem Theater', in J. Blänsdorf (ed.), *Theater und Gesellschaft im Imperium Romanum* (Mainzer Forschungen zu Drama und Theater, 4, Tübingen 1990) 243–59.

Saltz, D., 'How to Do Things on Stage', *Journal of Aesthetics & Art Criticism* 49, 1991, 31–45.

Salviat, F., 'Vedettes de la scène en province. Signification et date des monuments chorégiques à Thasos', *Thasiaca* (*BCH* Suppl. 5, Paris 1979) 155–67.

Sandbach, F.H., 'Menander and the Three-Actor Rule', in *Le monde grec: Hommages à Claire Préaux* (Brussels 1975) 197–204.

—— *The Comic Theatre of Greece and Rome* (London 1977).

Sarnina, A.B., 'Les associations de technitai de Dionysos dans les poleis hellénistiques', *VDI* 1987, 102–17 (Russian, with French resumé).

Scarcella, A.M., 'La tragedia greca nel contesto sociale', *Philologus* 129, 1985, 142–9.

Schechner, R., *Essays on Performance Theory* (New York 1977).

—— *Between Theater and Anthropology* (Philadelphia 1985).

—— and W. Appel, *By Means of Performance. Intercultural Studies of Theatre and Ritual* (Cambridge 1990).

—— and M. Schuman (eds), *Ritual, Play, and Performance* (New York 1976).

Schefold, K., 'Sophokles' Aias auf einer Lekythos', *AntK* 19, 1976, 71–7.

—— 'Der Andromeda des Nikias', in *Studies in Honour of A.D. Trendall* (Sydney 1979) 155–8.

Schmidt, M., 'Herakliden, Illustrationen zu Tragödien des Euripides und Sophokles', *Gestalt und Geschichte. Festschrift für Karl Schefold* (*AntK* Beih. 4, Berne 1967) 174–85.

—— 'Medea und Herakles – zwei tragische Kindermörder', in E. Böhr and W. Martini (eds), *Studien zur Mythologie und Vasenmalerei. Festschrift für Konrad Schauenburg* (Mainz 1986) 169–74.

—— 'Beziehungen zwischen Eros, dem dionysischen und dem "eleusinischen" Kreis auf apulischen Vasenbildern', in C. Bérard, C. Bon and A. Pomari (eds), *Images et société en Grèce ancienne. L'iconographie comme méthode d'analyse* (*Actes du Colloque int., Lausanne, 8–11 février 1984. Cahiers d'archéologie romande*, no. 36, Lausanne 1987) 155–67.

——, A.D. Trendall and A. Cambitoglou, *Eine Gruppe apulischer Grabvasen in Basel* (Basel 1976).

Seaford, R., 'On the Origins of Satyric Drama', *Maia* 28, 1976, 209–21.

Seale, D., *Vision and Stagecraft in Sophocles* (London 1982).

Séchan, L., *Etudes sur la tragédie grecque dans ses rapports avec la céramique* (Paris 1926, repr. 1967).

Seeberg, A., *Corinthian Komos Vases* (*BICS* Suppl. 27, London 1971).

—— 'Bronzes Referring to New Comedy', in K. Gschwantler and A. Bernhard-Walcher (eds), *Griechische und römische Statuetten und Grossbronzen* (*Akten der 9. Tagung über antike Bronzen*) (Vienna 1989) 270–4.

Segal, C., 'Visual Symbolism and Visual Effects in Sophocles', *CW* 74, 1980, 125–42.

—— 'Tragédie, oralité, écriture', *Poétique* 50, 1982, 131–54.

—— 'Greek Tragedy: Writing, Truth, and the Representation of the Self', in H.D. Evjen (ed.), *Mnemai. Classical Studies in Memory of Karl K. Hulley* (Chico,

California, 1985) 41–67.

——— *Interpreting Greek Tragedy: Myth, Poetry, Text* (Ithaca N.Y., 1986).

——— 'Vérité, tragédie et écriture', in M. Detienne (ed.), *Les savoirs de l'écriture en Grèce ancienne* (Lille 1988) 330–58.

——— 'Tragic Beginnings: Narration, Voice, and Authority in the Prologues of Greek Drama', *YCS* 29, 1992, 85–112.

Segal, E., 'The *physis* of Comedy', *HSCP* 77 (1973) 129–36.

——— *Roman Laughter. The Comedy of Plautus* (2nd edn Oxford 1987).

Seidensticker, B. (ed.), *Satyrspiel* (Wege der Forschung 579, Darmstadt 1989).

Shapiro, A., 'Kalos-Inscriptions with Patronymic', *ZPE* 68, 1987, 107–18.

Shisler, F.L., 'The Use of Stage Business to Portray Emotion in Greek Tragedy', *AJP* 66, 1945, 377–97.

Sifakis, G.M., 'High Stage and Chorus in the Hellenistic Theatre', *BICS* 10, 1963, 31–45.

——— *Studies in the History of Hellenistic Drama* (London 1967).

——— *Parabasis and Animal Choruses* (London 1971).

——— 'Aristotle E.N. IV,2, 1123a 19–24, and the Comic Chorus in the Fourth Century', *AJP* 92, 1971, 410–32.

——— 'O paradosiakos characteras tes archaias ellenikes logotechnias kai technes', *EpistEpetThess* 12, 1973, 451–70.

——— 'Boy Actors in New Comedy', in Bowersock, Burkert and Putnam (eds), *Arktouros: Hellenic Studies . . . B.M.W.Knox* (Berlin–New York 1979) 199–208.

——— 'Children in Greek Tragedy', *BICS* 26, 1979, 67–80.

——— 'The Social Function of Theater in Ancient Athens', *Archaiologia* 12, 1984, 8–10.

Simon, A.K.H., *Comicae Tabellae: die Szenenbilder zur griechischen neuen Komödie* (Emsdetten 1938).

Simon, Eckehard, *The Theatre of Medieval Europe. New Research in Early Drama* (Cambridge 1991).

Simon, Erika, *Das antike Theater* (Heidelberg 1972).

——— *Das Satyrspiel Sphinx des Aischylos* (Heidelberg 1981).

——— *The Ancient Theatre* (London 1982).

——— 'Dramen des älteren Dionysios auf italiotischen Vasen', in *Aparchai Arias* ii, 479–82.

——— 'Satyr-Plays on Vases in the Time of Aeschylus', in D. Kurtz and B.A. Sparkes (eds), *The Eye of Greece. Studies in the Art of Athens* (Cambridge 1982) 123–48 (with an up-dated German version in Seidensticker, op. cit.).

Slater, N.W., 'Vanished Players: Two Classical Reliefs and Theatre History', *GRBS* 26, 1985, 333–44.

——— 'Plays and Playwright References in Middle and New Comedy', *LCM* 10, 1985, 103–5.

——— 'Transformations of Space in New Comedy', in J. Redmond (ed.), *The Theatrical Space* (Themes in Drama, 9, Cambridge 1987) 1–10.

——— 'The Idea of the Actor', in J.J. Winkler and F.I. Zeitlin (eds), *Nothing to Do with Dionysos? Athenian Drama in Its Social Context* (Princeton 1989) 385–95.

——— 'Aristophanes' Apprenticeship Again', *GRBS* 30, 1989, 67–82.

——— *Plautus in Performance* (Princeton 1985).

de Sousa e Silva, M. de Fátima, *Crítica do teatro na comédia antiga* (Coimbra 1987).

Spawforth, A.J.S., 'Agonistic Festivals in Roman Greece', in S. Walker and A. Cameron (eds), *The Greek Renaissance in the Roman Empire* (*BICS* Suppl. 55, 1989) 193–7.

Spieser, J.M., 'La christianisation des sanctuaires païens en Grèce', in U. Jantzen (ed.), *Neue Forschungen in griechischen Heiligtümern* (Symposion Olympia 1974, Tübingen 1976) 309–20.

Spitzbarth, A., *Untersuchungen zur Spieltechnik der griechischen Tragödie* (Zurich 1946).

Stanford, W.B., *Greek Tragedy and the Emotions* (London 1983).

Stefanelli, L. Pirzio Biroli, *L'argento dei Romani. Vasellame da tavola e d'apparato* (Rome 1991).

Stelluto, S., 'La visualizzazione scenica dell' "Aiace" di Sofocle', *Civiltà Classica e Cristiana* 11, 1990, 33–64.

Stephanis, I.E., *Dionysiakoi technitai. Symboles sten prosopographia tou theatrou kai tes mousikes ton archaion ellenon* (Heraklion 1988).

Stevens, P.T., 'Euripides and the Athenians', *JHS* 76, 1956, 87–94.

Stoessl, F., 'Die Anfänge der Theatergeschichte Athens', *Grazer Beiträge* 2, 1974, 213–50.

———— 'Die Anfänge der Theatergeschichte Athens II. Die Jahre der frühesten erhaltene Texte', *Grazer Beiträge* 8, 1979, 57–73.

———— *Die Vorgeschichte des griechischen Theaters* (Darmstadt 1987).

———— 'Die Anfänge der Theatergeschichte Athens III. Die Texte vom Ende der 70er Jahre bis zum Jahr 467', *Grazer Beiträge* 16, 1989, 29–49.

Stone, L.M., *Costume in Aristophanic Comedy* (*Poetry* on title page) (New York 1981, Salem N.H. 1984).

Strauss, B.S., *Athens after the Peloponnesian War: Class, Faction and Policy 403–386 B.C.* (Ithaca, N.Y., 1986).

Strong, E., 'Three Sculptured Stelai in the Possession of Lord Newton at Lyme Park', *JHS* 23, 1903, 356–9.

Studniczka, F., *Das Symposion Ptolemaios II* (Sächs. Abh. xxx.2, Leipzig 1914).

Sturgeon, M.C., 'The Reliefs on the Theatre of Dionysos in Athens', *AJA* 81, 1977, 31–53.

Sutton, D.F., 'A Handlist of Satyr Plays', *HSCP* 78 (1974) 107–43.

———— 'A Complete Handlist to the Literary Remains of the Greek Satyr Plays', *AncW* 3, 1980, 115–30.

———— *The Greek Satyr Play* (Meisenheim/Glau 1980).

———— 'Pollux on Special Masks', *AntCl* 53, 1984, 174–83.

———— 'Scenes from Greek Satyr Plays Illustrated in Greek Vase-Paintings', *AncW* 9, 1984, 119–26.

———— 'The Theatrical Families of Athens', *AJP* 108, 1987, 9–26.

———— 'Satyr-Play', *CambHistClassLit* i, 346–54.

Szemerényi, O., 'The Origins of Roman Drama and Greek Tragedy', *Hermes* 103, 1975, 300–32.

Taglasacchi, A., 'Plutarco e la tragedia greca', *Dioniso* 34, 1960, 132–4.

Taplin, O., 'Aeschylean Silences and Silences in Aeschylus', *HSCP* 76, 1972, 57–97.

———— 'Did Greek Dramatists Write Stage Instructions?', *PCPS* 203, 1977, 121–32.

———— *The Stagecraft of Aeschylus. Observations on the Dramatic Use of Exits and Entrances* (Oxford 1977).

———— 'Sophocles in his Theatre', in *Sophocle: Entretiens sur l'Antiquité Classique* xxix (Vandœuvres–Geneva 1983) 155–74.

———— 'Fifth-Century Tragedy and Comedy: a Synkrisis', *JHS* 106, 1986, 163–74.

———— 'Phallology, Phlyakes, Iconography and Aristophanes', *PCPS* 213 (ns 33), 1987, 92–104 (somewhat revised in *Dioniso* 57, 1987, 95–109).

———— 'Spazio e messa in scena in Sofocle', *Dioniso* 59:2, 1989, 103–5.

———— *Comic Angels and Other Approaches to Greek Drama through Vase-Paintings* (Oxford 1993).

Taylor, D., *Acting and the Stage* (Greek & Roman Topics, VI, London 1978).

Thomas, R., *Oral Tradition and Written Record in Classical Athens* (Cambridge 1989).

Thompson, D.B., 'Persian Spoils in Athens', in S. Weinberg (ed.), *The Aegean and the Near East. Studies presented to Hetty Goldman* (Locust Valley, N.Y., 1956) 281–87.

Touchefeu-Meynier, O., *Le théâtre antique* (Musées Nationaux, n.d.).

Townsend, R.F., 'The Fourth-Century Skene of the Theater of Dionysos at Athens', *Hesperia* 55, 1986, 421–38.

Traversari, G., *Gli spettacoli in acqua nel teatro tardo antico* (Rome 1960).

Trendall, A.D., *Phlyax Vases* (2nd edn, *BICS* Suppl. 19, London 1967).

——— The Mourning Niobe', *RevArch* 1972, 309–16.

——— 'Adrastos on a Sicilian Calyx-Krater from Lipari', *Misc. Eugenio Manni*, vi (Rome 1980) 2101–6.

——— 'Medea at Eleusis on a Volute Krater by the Darius Painter', *Record of the Art Museum Princeton University* 43:1, 1984.

——— 'An Apulian Loutrophoros Representing the Tantalidae', *GVGetty* 2 (Malibu 1985) 129–44.

——— 'The Daughters of Anios', in E. Böhr and W. Martini (eds), *Studien zur Mythologie und Vasenmalerei. Festschrift für Konrad Schauenburg* (Mainz 1986) 166–8.

——— 'Vasi apuli raffiguranti maschere femminili con viso bianco', in *Ricerche e Studi* (Quaderni del Museo Archeologico Provinciale 'Francesco Ribezzo' di Brindisi) 12, 1980–87, 43–55.

——— *The Red-Figured Vases of Paestum* (British School at Rome, 1987).

——— 'Masks on Apulian Red-Figured Vases', in *Studies Webster* ii, 137–54.

——— *Red Figure Vases of South Italy and Sicily* (London 1989).

——— 'Farce and Tragedy in South Italian Vase-Painting', in T. Rasmussen and N. Spivey (eds), *Looking at Greek Vases* (Cambridge 1991) 151–82.

——— and T.B.L. Webster, *Illustrations of Greek Drama* (London 1970).

Treu, K., 'Griechische Tragödie und Theaterpraxis', in H. Kuch (ed.), *Die Griechische Tragödie in ihrer gesellschaftlichen Funktion* (Berlin 1983) 141–51.

——— 'Menanders Menschen als Polisbürger', *Philologus* 125, 1981, 211–14.

Trillmich, W. and P. Zanker (eds), *Stadtbild und Ideologie. Die Monumentalisierung hispanischer Städte zwischen Republik und Kaiserzeit. Kolloquium in Madrid vom 19. bis 23. Oktober 1987* (*AbhMünchen* NF 103, 1990).

Turner, E.G., *Athenian Books in the Fifth and Fourth Centuries B.C.* (London 1951, 2nd edn 1971).

——— 'Dramatic Representations in Graeco-Roman Egypt: How Long do They Continue?', *AntClass* 32, 1963, 120–8.

Turner, V., *The Ritual Process. Structure and Anti-Structure* (Chicago–London 1969).

——— *From Ritual to Theatre. The Human Seriousness of Play* (New York 1982).

——— 'Dramatic Ritual/Ritual Drama: Performative and Reflexive Anthropology', in J. Ruby (ed.), *A Crack in the Mirror: Reflexive Perspectives in Anthropology* (Philadelphia 1982) 83–97.

——— 'Liminality and the Performative Genres', in J.J. MacAloon (ed.), *Rite, Drama, Festival, Spectacle* (Philadelphia 1984).

Valenti, G. Prosperi, 'Attori-bambini del mondo romano attraverso le testimonianze epigrafiche', *Epigraphica* 47, 1985, 71–82.

Vansina, J., *Oral Tradition as History* (Madison, Wisconsin, 1985).

Vegetti, M. (ed.), *Oralità scrittura spettacolo* (Turin 1983).

Ventrone, P., 'On the Use of Figurative Art as a Source for the Study of Medieval Spectacles', *Comparative Drama* 25, 1991, 4–16.

Vermeule, E., 'More Sleeping Furies', in G. Kopcke and M.B. Moore (eds), *Studies in Classical Art and Archaeology ... P.H. von Blanckenhagen* (Locust Valley, N.Y., 1979) 185–8.

Vernant, J.-P. and P. Vidal-Nacquet, *Mythe et tragédie en Grèce ancienne* (Paris 1972).

Verzár-Bass, M., 'I teatri nell'Italia settentrionale', in *La città nell'Italia settentrionale. Morfologie, strutture e funzianamento dei centri urbani delle Regiones X e XI. Atti del convegno . . . Trieste e Roma, 13–15 marzo 1987, Trieste–Rome 1990* (Coll. École fr. de Rome no. 130), 411–40.

Veyne, P., 'Diaskeuai. Le théâtre grec sous l'Empire (Dion de Pruse, XXXII, 94)', *REG* 102, 1989, 339–45.

Vickers, B., *Towards Greek Tragedy: Drama, Myth, Society* (London 1979).

Vogel, J., *Scenen euripideischer tragödien in griechischen vasengemälden. Archäologische beiträge zur geschichte des griechischen dramas* (Leipzig 1886).

Wachter, R., 'The Inscriptions on the François Vase', *MusHelv* 48, 1991, 86–113.

Walcot, P., *Greek Drama in its Theatrical and Social Context* (Cardiff 1976).

——— 'Aristophanic and Other Audiences', *G&R* 18, 1971, 35–50.

Walton, J.M., *Greek Theater Practice* (Westport 1980).

——— *The Greek Sense of Theatre. Tragedy Reviewed* (London 1984).

Webster, T.B.L., 'Fourth-Century Tragedy and the *Poetics*', *Hermes* 82, 1954, 294–308.

——— *Griechische Bühnenaltertümer* (Göttingen 1963).

——— 'The Poet and the Mask', in M.J. Anderson (ed.), *Classical Drama and its Influence: Studies . . . Kitto* (London 1965) 5–13.

——— *Hellenistic Art* (London 1966).

——— 'Classical Antiquity. The Theatre and the Artist', *Apollo*, August 1967, 94–101.

——— *Monuments Illustrating Tragedy and Satyr Play* (2nd edn, *BICS* Suppl. 20, London 1967).

——— *The Greek Chorus* (London 1970).

——— *Greek Theatre Production* (2nd edn, London 1970).

——— *Studies in Later Greek Comedy* (2nd edn, Manchester 1970).

——— 'Scenic Notes II', in R. Hanslik, A. Lesky and H. Schwabl (eds), *Antidosis. Festschrift für Walter Kraus* (Vienna 1972) 454–7.

——— *An Introduction to Menander* (Manchester 1974).

——— *Monuments Illustrating Old and Middle Comedy* (3rd edn, rev. and enl. by J.R. Green, *BICS* Suppl. 39, London 1978).

Weismann, W., *Kirche und Schauspiele. Die Schauspiele im Urteil der lateinischen Kirchenväter unter besonderer Berücksichtigung von Augustin* (Cassiciacum XXVII, Würzburg 1972).

Weitzmann, K., *Illustrations in Roll and Codex* (Princeton 1970).

Werner, G., 'Wie gefährlich ist das Theater? Platon und Aristoteles zur Spezifik theatralischer Kommunikation', *Philologus* 135, 1991, 258–63.

West, M.L., 'The Early Chronology of Attic Tragedy', *CQ* 39, 1989, 251–4.

West, S., *The Image of the Actor. Verbal and Visual Representation in the Age of Garrick and Kemble* (New York 1991).

Wieseler, F., *Theatergebäude und Denkmäler des Bühnenwesens* (Göttingen 1851).

Wiles, D., 'Reading Greek Performance', *G&R* 34, 1987, 136–51.

——— *The Masks of Menander. Sign and Meaning in Greek and Roman Performances* (Cambridge 1991).

Wilson, A.M., 'Breach of Dramatic Illusion in the Old Comic Fragments', *Euphrosyne* 9, 1978–79, 145–50.

Winkler, J.J., 'The Ephebes' Song: Tragoidia and Polis', in J.J. Winkler and F.I. Zeitlin (eds), *Nothing to Do with Dionysos? Athenian Drama in Its Social Context* (Princeton 1989) 20–62.

——— and F.I. Zeitlin (eds), *Nothing to Do with Dionysos? Athenian Drama in its Social*

Context (Princeton 1989).

Winter, F.E., 'The Stage of New Comedy', *Phoenix* 37, 1983, 38–47.

—— 'The Symposium-Tent of Ptolemy II: A New Proposal', *EMC/CV* 29, 1985, 289–308.

Wolters, P., 'Zu griechischen Agonen', *30. Programm d. Kunstgeschichtl. Museums Univ. Würzburg* (1901) 5–9.

—— 'Faden und Knoten als Amulett' (Suppl. *ArchivRelWiss* 8, Leipzig 1905).

Woodbury, L., 'Aristophanes' Frogs and Athenian Literacy', *TAPA* 106, 1976, 349–57.

—— 'The Judgment of Dionysos: Books, Taste and Teaching in the *Frogs*', in M. Cropp, E. Fantham and S.E. Scully (eds), *Greek Tragedy and its Legacy. Essays Presented to D.J. Conacher* (Calgary 1986) 241–57.

Wörrle, M., *Stadt und Fest in kaiserzeitliche Kleinasien. Studien zu einer agonistischen Stiftung aus Oenoanda* (Vestigia xxxix, Munich 1988).

Wurster, W.W., 'Die neuen Untersuchungen am Dionysostheater in Athen', *Architectura* 9, 1979, 58–76.

Xanthakis-Karamanos, G., *Studies in Fourth-Century Tragedy* (Athens 1980).

Yalouris, N., 'Die Anfänge der griechischen Porträtkunst und der Physiognomon Zopyros', *AntK* 29, 1986, 5–7.

Yates, F.A., *The Art of Memory* (London 1966).

Zumthor, P., 'Pour une poétique de la voix', *Poétique* 40, 1979, 514–24.

GENERAL INDEX

INDEX OF
PRINCIPAL OBJECTS
DISCUSSED

This is a select list and does not include all the parallels mentioned in the footnotes. Pages on which items are illustrated are given in italics.